PATHS OF JUSTICE

T0345375

PATHS
OF
JUSTICE

Johannes M. M. Chan

HKU PRESS
香港大學出版社

Hong Kong University Press
The University of Hong Kong
Pokfulam Road
Hong Kong
https://hkupress.hku.hk

ISBN 978-988-8455-93-5 (*Hardback*)
ISBN 978-988-8455-94-2 (*Paperback*)

British Library Cataloguing-in-Publication Data
A catalogue record for this book is available from the British Library.

10 9 8 7 6 5 4 3

Printed and bound in Hong Kong, China

To

Priscilla and Andreana

Contents

Preface

What is justice? Can justice be done? Jurists and philosophers have been asking these questions for centuries. While there is a huge body of learned work on these questions, no theory can tell what justice is or whether justice has been done in any particular case. At the end of the day, justice perhaps just lies in the hearts of ordinary people. Like the concept of the reasonable man, justice may not be something that can be formulated in abstraction but by and large is something that we recognize when we see it in practice.

I have long wanted to write a book to explore these themes through real cases. As an academic lawyer, I have the privilege of being involved in the two related but in fact quite separate worlds of academia and legal practice. I was particularly inspired by Geoffrey Robertson's book *The Justice Game*, in which he shared his own experience and insights as to whether justice has been achieved through the cases he has been involved with. While there is no doubt that justice is the fundamental value sought by our legal system, it is unjustifiably romantic if not self-deceiving to believe that justice is or will always be achieved in real life. There are times when our legal system will simply fail us, and admitting its failure is the first step towards improving it.

I was also inspired by the two books by Patrick Shuk-siu Yu, *The Seventh Child in the Law* and *No. 9 Ice House Street*, in which he recounted many of his own cases and explained how our legal system works (and fails to work). I have tremendous respect for Patrick, who is a legendary figure in the legal field and a man of great principles. He had retired when I started practice, and I am glad that our paths have crossed. I was particularly honoured when Patrick came to my admission to the Inner Bar, as he had seldom made public appearances and held strong views about the institution of Senior/Queen's Counsel. The stories that Patrick recounted in his books are fascinating, but they reinforce my impression that, while Hong Kong may be a relatively affluent society, there is a shocking level of ignorance about the law among the general public. Thus, I hope I have written a book on our legal system that lay members of the community will find approachable and interesting, without losing some of the sophistication in the arguments through which we can explore together the meaning of justice.

This book is not intended to be comprehensive, nor is it meant to be a scholarly thesis. The cases serve to provide a snapshot rather than a full picture. They were selected in the hope that they could offer some insights into some of the most frequently asked questions in law: How does a lawyer defend someone who is guilty (Chapters 9, 11, 12, and 13)? The 'guilty' defendants went free in Chapter 13, whereas the 'innocent' defendants in Chapter 11 were convicted. The defendants in both Chapters 9 and 12 were prepared to accept their responsibility, but one was acquitted and one was convicted. Had justice been done in those cases? Does the law favour the rich and the resourceful (Chapters 9 and 10)? Could access to justice ever be restricted (Chapters 18 and 19)? Is there a duty to obey the law in all circumstances (Chapter 27)?

Freedom is not free. There is always a price to be paid, and the real issue is how much we are prepared to pay for these rights and freedoms. Few would dispute that we should protect the environment, but are we prepared to pay the price of a much costlier bridge after a full environmental impact assessment, or the price of development in order to protect a pristine harbour (Chapters 4 and 5)? Or, have we adopted a double standard of fairness in the treatment of foreign domestic helpers (Chapter 7)? Again, few would argue against the requirement of fairness in administrative proceedings, but are we prepared to impose a requirement that a decision maker must always give reasons for his or her decisions, and if not, why not (Chapter 17)? The right to legal representation is important, but what if it impedes the efficiency of disciplinary or administrative proceedings (Chapters 15 and 16)? How do we reconcile fairness with administrative efficacy (Chapters 15, 16, and 17)? Few people would dispute the sanctity of human rights in the cool and calm atmosphere of a university classroom, but the choice may be very different in real life when there are competing interests, when we are caught up in moral controversy, or when we find ourselves in emotionally charged scenarios. A commitment to fundamental rights is put to a strenuous test when protection of human rights requires giving up some vested interests, such as extending the right of abode to a group perceived to be competing 'undeservedly' for social welfare and employment opportunities with local people (Chapters 6 and 7). Time and again it has been said that human rights are not absolute, but to what extent and how do we weigh the two sides of the scale when human rights are measured against other competing interests such as national security or prevention of crime (Chapter 8)? The justification of national security is easy to make, but with all its wrappings in secrecy and confidentiality, should it still be subject to judicial scrutiny? Is the excuse the beginning of a question rather than an answer (Chapters 14, 20, 24, 25, and 26)? Is the occurrence of an abuse of freedom a justification for denying it (Chapters 19, 20, and 21)?

Fundamental values may well be in conflict with one another: It is noble to protect the right to life, but is it fair to force a mother to give birth to a child with severe disabilities and to put the burden of taking care of this child for the rest of her life on the reluctant parents, who may not have the resources or the support to enable them to cope (Chapter 29)? This is not just about the price to be paid but who is paying the price. What is just in such circumstances, and justice for whom?

There are also a few chapters that deal with the legal profession and professional-ism (Chapters 1, 2, 3, and 28). The legal profession is honourable only because lawyers, by and large, do live up to a high ethical standard and are committed to the values of justice and fairness. There are times when a lawyer will have to defend an unpopular cause (Chapters 3, 4, 6, and 7). It is reassuring that, when the time comes, there are always lawyers who are prepared to rise to the occasion (Chapter 3). On the other hand, a fair trial does not guarantee substantive justice (Chapter 23). A few chapters recount some personal experience with jurisdictions that do not have high regard for human rights (Chapters 22, 23, and 26).

Law involves a value choice. We may not always agree with the choice that is made, and there may be more than one plausible and rational choice (Chapters 29 and 30). Sometimes we may be thankful to be the advocate and not the judge, so that the choice is not in our hands. Sometimes the value choice may not be explicit and can only be discovered by reading between the lines of the learned judgments. This book tries to unfold some of these value choices (Chapters 4, 5, 6, 7, 20, 21, 29, and 30). These cases span a period of 30 years. Some are well-known cases; others involve ordinary people. They are not law reports but human stories. Justice is done in some of these cases, while in some others, our system has failed to deliver justice. Sometimes there may be more than one version of justice. And when justice is done, it is not always rosy; sometimes it is achieved only at a great human cost (Chapter 4). Sometimes it just fails us. Some of these cases also illustrate how our government works and what transparency and accountability mean in reality (Chapters 4, 15, 17, 22, and 23). Through the descrip-tion of real action in the court, this book will give readers a better understanding of our legal system and how it works in practice. This book will achieve its purpose if it can provoke further thought about the institution of the law and lawyers and the meaning of justice and the rule of law.

The book was conceived some time ago. I then put it aside for a while, until my good friends Professor Douglas Kerr and Professor Elaine Ho encouraged me to put my thoughts on paper after the turbulent year of 2015. I would particularly like to thank Douglas and Elaine for their inspiration and friendship, and Douglas for agree-ing to go through every story in this book and for suggesting the title of this book. Any mistake, of course, remains mine. I would also like to thank my colleagues and friends Vivian Wong, Dr Marco Wan, Cora Chan, Eddie Leung, Alan Tsang, Anthony Neoh SC, Dr Margaret Ng, Winston Chu, Jeff Tse, Herman Tang, Simon Fung, and Dr Sarah Lau for their continuous support, inspiring discussions, and helpful comments and assistance on different chapters of the book, as well as the helpful comments of the anonymous reviewers of this book. I was personally involved in some of the cases and would like to thank my clients and solicitors for consenting to my publishing their stories. I have relied on publicly available information as much as possible. I would also like to thank the Society for Protection of the Harbour Ltd. and Winston Chu for their permission to reproduce the photos and plans in this book. Let me also thank Susie Han Jia of Hong Kong University Press, who readily supported this project when

I first approached her, and Clara Ho of Hong Kong University Press for her patience, accommodation, and valuable assistance throughout the editing process. Finally, I have used gender neutral terms as far as possible. On those few occasions when such usage may affect the flow of reading, the use of gender specific term means no disrespect for gender equality, and the use of male gender will include female gender and vice versa, unless the context otherwise suggests.

The last two years have been both eventful and challenging to me and my family. I am grateful for the unfailing support of Priscilla, my wife, and Andreana, my daughter, who are always by my side. They have kept me going with this project, put up patiently with the writing process, and provided me with inspiration as well as invaluable comments and suggestions on various draft chapters. To them this book is dedicated.

Johannes Chan
The University of Hong Kong
December 2017

I

Joining the Legal Profession

1

Town and gown

Early life

Like many of my contemporaries in the 1970s, I grew up in a public housing estate. Both of my parents were migrants from the Mainland who came to Hong Kong in the late 1950s. Indeed, my maternal grandfather was well educated and spoke fluent English. He was a small landowner and suffered badly during the Cultural Revolution. Not only were his land and property confiscated, but he was mock-executed three times in front of his family. My parents came to Hong Kong to seek refuge from the internal turmoil in the Mainland, and given their background, they understandably took the Communist Party with great distrust.

Life in the 1960s and 1970s in Hong Kong was rather simple. There was no computer, no internet, and no mobile phone. Listening to the radio was the common pastime; a tape recorder was very fashionable, and a television set was a luxury. Free television broadcast was only available in the early 1970s. As a young boy, I used to enjoy an evening radio programme called 'Diary of the Great Husband' (大丈夫日記), which was a very popular programme that was broadcast at around 8:30 p.m. every weekday. It was about the daily life of a couple. The husband was played by an actor called Lam Bun (林彬), who was killed during the riot in 1967 for his outspoken criticism against the rioters. That was the first time I encountered life and death.

While many parents these days want their children to study law, it was not a popular choice in the late 1970s, partly because, thanks to colonial education, very few secondary students knew what law was about, and partly because the generation of my parents generally considered law inseparable from politics, and politics was bad and dirty. Thirty years later, this division between law and politics is still deeply entrenched in the minds of many well-educated people, though now law is regarded as respectable, at least in financial term, whereas politics is still something to keep a distance from. One of the best-known remarks was made by my dear friend Ronny Tong SC, when he said, on the eve of his assumption of chairmanship of the Bar Association, that the Bar should only comment on law and not on politics. A few months later, he was one of the most vociferous critics against the interpretation made by the Standing Committee of the National People's Congress, which effectively reversed the judgment of the Court of Final Appeal in the popularly known 'right of abode case' and later an elected member of the Legislative Council.[1] After all, politics is about the business of the public and is neither good nor bad in itself; it is the people who take part in it that determine its nature. As long as there are people, there is politics. It is not something to be afraid of; nor can we run away from it. Who can really say that there is no politics at work, at home, at the sacred church of God, or in the intellectual temple of academia? Just like many other things in life, we just have to face it and deal with it.

I first came across law where I met, in a voluntary service programme, some young-sters in a detention centre. They came from a deprived family background; the education system failed them, and in those days, doing well in public examinations was the only avenue for upward social mobility. For them, the future, if there was one at all, was bleak. Some of them told me that they hated to go to school; they didn't want to stay at their overcrowded home either. They wandered around at public playgrounds, came across some gangsters, attracted by the freedom and excitement on the streets, and some of them started committing petty crimes. They were arrested and convicted. Some were abandoned by their families, who felt ashamed of them. They did not stay long in a detention or a training centre. When they were released, they were sent back to exactly the same environment. Nothing was changed, save that they were now labelled as convicted—an untouchable group. It was a pretty gloomy experience that had shackled my dream of becoming a social worker. It seemed to me, at least at that moment, that there was so little that a social worker could do. At the same time, I became curious about how law works. In fact, I entered law school out of curiosity rather than due to any aspiration to becoming a lawyer, a profession which, honestly, I had very little idea about at that time.

Law turned out to be a highly intellectual and rewarding discipline that provides excellent training of the mind. I enjoyed the study of law as a discipline but had no idea whether I would enjoy the legal profession. I worked in two law firms and one chambers as a summer student during my undergraduate years. The two law firms were very different; one offered a very cordial environment with some very nice people, and the other gave me the first taste of what criminal law practice was about. I was attracted to the life at the Bar, but I was not sure if I would be sufficiently competent to be a barrister. After four years of study, I felt I was still not ready to commit myself to the legal profession. Why should I bind myself to a legal career merely because I had made a choice to study law at the age of 19? I decided to see more of the world and went to do a master's degree at the London School of Economics and Political Science (LSE).

I decided to choose some subjects that were not available in Hong Kong and that might be of some relevance to the future of Hong Kong. At that time, the Sino-British negotiation on the future of Hong Kong had just begun. The future of Hong Kong was filled with uncertainty. So, I chose to focus on human rights. I recalled when I was interviewed for scholarship I was repeatedly asked why I wanted to do impractical

---

1. *Ng Ka Ling v Director of Immigration* (1999) 2 HKCFAR 4. See also Chapter 3 on the clarification.

subjects like human rights and not something more practical like intellectual property. It was to some extent true that human rights was then not a practical subject in Hong Kong (and indeed not even a subject on offer). But who could foresee that it would suddenly become an area of great practical importance when the government decided to introduce the Bill of Rights Ordinance in 1991, as one of the measures to restore the confidence of the people of Hong Kong, shattered by what many had witnessed to have taken place at Tiananmen Square on 4 June 1989? I always tell my students that they should choose electives according to their interest. There is no such thing as 'practical', as much depends on what comes your way in future. In a rapidly changing world, the half-life of knowledge is increasingly shortened. What really counts are intellectual capability, analytical power, problem-solving skills, and the ability to communicate.

London

I had a fruitful and rewarding year in London. LSE was well known for producing non-conformists, and it had attracted many world-renowned scholars who were critical of the establishment. At LSE, I met a number of very inspiring teachers, such as my supervisor, Professor Rosalyn Higgins QC, who later became the president of the International Court of Justice, and the late Professor Peter Duffy QC, who was then the president of Amnesty International. Rosalyn has a particular influence on me. She is inspiring, extremely knowledgeable, highly focused, frank and direct, kind and patient but would not stand nonsense. She taught, wrote, and practised at the Bar, being one of the practising academic silks. Peter introduced me to the work of the European Court of Human Rights. We became good friends and later worked together on the *European Reports of Human Rights*, of which he was the editor, and various missions of Amnesty International. The LSE master curriculum required us to do four subjects, and I audited another four. I also did a non-law subject in social planning, which taught me something about planning the national health system, the building of Terminal 3 of Heathrow Airport, and human resources planning. I met Professor Howard Glennester, another inspiring and non-conforming professor. One of my classmates in social planning was Rosanna Wong, who was then doing her second master's degree. Rosanna has subsequently had a distinguished career in the public life of Hong Kong. I did attend a class in intellectual property once. The only reason was that it was taught by Professor Bill Cornish, a leading world figure on intellectual property. Professor Cornish was a tall and slim gentleman who spoke in a rather gentle but monotonous tone. He reminded me of Professor Peter Wesley-Smith, one of my teachers and later a colleague at the University of Hong Kong, who was a learned scholar and a kind mentor to junior academics like me. Professor Cornish was a great scholar, but the subject did not strike a chord in me, no doubt due to my own inadequacies!

London was a fascinating city with a lot to offer. The year broadened my horizons in many aspects of life. Living on a tight scholarship budget was another great experience. I had to plan carefully my weekly spending, limiting myself to not more than £25 a week. If I wanted to have a better meal one day, or to buy an expensive book, I would have to fast for a few days to save up the money. Fortunately, there were plenty of free museums, exhibitions, and cultural events, and of course the lovely parks, in London. Musicals were expensive, but if you were willing to spend a few hours queuing for specially discounted returned tickets, it was quite possible to be able to enjoy world-class performances at a very reasonable price. I managed to watch the great musical *Cats* and hear Elaine Page singing *Memory* for just £1!

The year in London was also a year of fruitful reflection. I kept asking myself what I wanted to do in future. I had practically decided that I would not be a solicitor. The Bar was still an attractive option. I knew I would like to look for a people-oriented job. Law, and particularly barristers, is not really a profession with a lot of human interaction. Teachers and social workers fall within this category. I also found that I enjoyed research. Hong Kong adopted the English legal system. The transplantation of an English legal system, rooted in the English language and culture, to a Chinese community is itself a fascinating subject for research, as is the likely interaction between the Hong Kong and the Mainland Chinese legal system in the years to come. We followed English law in many areas, sometimes too slavishly, without sufficient consideration of local circumstances. There are also many areas of local significance that have not been researched at all. I read as much as I could in London and followed closely the Sino-British negotiations on the future of Hong Kong. London offered one the peace of mind that allowed one to focus and concentrate, something which strangely (and sadly) was absent in Hong Kong. Finally, I thought there was a need for local teachers in legal education in Hong Kong. With the ongoing uncertainty of the future of Hong Kong, the rule of law would be of critical importance to Hong Kong in the days to come, and the best way to strengthen the rule of law would be to nurture young minds through legal education. At that time, Albert Chen, who later became a professor, was the only Chinese lecturer in the only law school in Hong Kong.[2] Albert was a solid but also relatively shy scholar. I believed education is to be achieved not just in the classrooms but more effectively through interaction with students and by what the teacher has done and stands for outside the classroom. For these reasons, I decided to join academia, but I think I had to acquire sufficient life experience before I had anything valuable to offer to my students. On my return to London, I joined the Bar, and indeed, since then, I have never left the Bar.

---

2. The Department of Law of the University of Hong Kong was initially set up as a department in the Faculty of Social Sciences in 1969. It became a School of Law in 1978, and subsequently a Faculty of Law with two departments in 1984. The term 'law school' in this book is used to refer generically to the Faculty of Law at the University of Hong Kong at different stages of its development. It remains the only law school in Hong Kong until City University set up the second law school in 1987. Likewise, the term 'the University' refers to The University of Hong Kong, unless the context suggests otherwise.

The legal profession

Let me digress and say something about the legal profession. The Bar is a very challenging and demanding profession. It is a profession with a long history and comes with fascinating tradition and a set of firmly entrenched values. It has its share of eccentricity as well. In Chinese, the word 'barrister' (大律師) is literally translated as 'big lawyer', which gives barristers a sense of superiority and solicitors a sense of grievance, as solicitors are sometimes asked when they will be promoted to 'big lawyers'. This is a misunderstanding, as solicitors and barristers are just two different branches of the profession without one branch being more senior than the other, though admittedly some barristers do think that they are the more superior branch. This is unwarranted, as there are many very bright as well as not-so-bright members in both branches. Barristers work primarily on referral from solicitors and focus exclusively on litigation. The work of a barrister includes mainly advocacy (appearance at all levels of courts), drafting of pleadings (litigation-related documents), and written advice (known as opinion). Barristers are easily distinguishable from solicitors in courts. A barrister wears a horsetail wig and dresses in a different gown from that of a solicitor in open court. All barristers practise as sole practitioners. Some of them may join together to form a set of chambers, but that simply means they share some common expenses. In a set of chambers, each barrister works independently and is not subject to the order or authority of another barrister. Hence, it is quite possible for a barrister to act for one side of a case and another barrister in the same chambers to act for the other side of the case.

Solicitors are the first port of call for anyone who needs legal service. They provide all kinds of legal services and advice, ranging from commercial, listing, intellectual property, shipping, matrimonial, litigation, property, and so on. In that sense, solicitors may be regarded as general practitioners though this is not entirely accurate, as many solicitors do practise in highly specialized areas. Solicitors may also appear in court (known as the right of audience), but they are restricted to District Court or below, unless they have acquired the status of solicitor-advocates by passing a statutory assessment. The right of audience at the higher court has been a matter of controversy between the two branches of the profession for many years, and the system of solicitor-advocates is a compromise to allow eligible solicitors to acquire a higher right of audience, which until 2010 was a monopoly of the Bar. My colleague at the University, Eric Cheung, who is also the director of our Clinical Legal Education Programme, is among the first batch of solicitors to have acquired a higher right of audience in criminal practice.

Admission to the Bar is a court process that is commenced by filing a motion in court. Barristers are listed according to seniority, and the action number determines the seniority of barristers who are admitted in the same hearing. The admission is also known as 'call to the Bar', the bar being literally a wooden barrier in an old common law courtroom that separated the inner precincts of the court from the public gallery. Only a barrister was allowed to come up to the bar to address the court. The more distinguished members of the Bar are appointed as Senior Counsel, or Queen's Counsel before 1997. In the old days, upon their appointment, Queen's Counsel is allowed to cross the bar to address the court, and hence their admission is also known as 'call to the Inner Bar'. Any barrister who is not a Senior Counsel is known as a 'junior', no matter how many years of experience he or she may have. So there are senior-juniors and junior-juniors but still 'juniors'. Junior barristers wear a cotton gown in court, whereas Senior Counsel wears a silk gown. Hence, Senior Counsel is also known as silk, and admission as Senior Counsel is known as 'taking silk'. It usually takes at least 15 years before one considers applying for silk, and some never do. The first Queen's Counsel was Sir Francis Bacon in the late sixteenth century, and nowadays about 10 per cent of the barristers are Senior Counsel. Appointments used to be made by the monarch upon recommendation, but they are now made more systematically by the Chief Justice in consultation with senior judges and chairpersons of the professional bodies upon application, which application is open in December each year. The Chairperson of the Bar consults all Senior Counsel on the applications. Of course, not all applications are successful. An old tradition is that any junior barrister who applies for silk has to write to all junior barristers who are senior to him or her, informing them as a matter of courtesy and affording them an opportunity to object (as he or she will overtake their seniority upon appointment as Senior Counsel). I think this is a good tradition, but sadly it is not always adhered to nowadays. Senior Counsel are the leaders of the Bar and have the responsibility of upholding the rule of law, the values of the legal profession, and the transmission of knowledge and experience to the next generation. Many Senior Counsel are also prominent community leaders who render valuable and voluntary service to the community.

The Bar still retains many interesting traditions. At the Ceremonial Opening of the Legal Year, which takes place annually in January, Senior Counsel join the judiciary in a procession and are dressed in full-bottomed wigs, buckle shoes with knee breeches, a silk gown, a dress coat, and a tricorn (for carrying); that is, dresses that were fashionable at the time of Mozart. Some people criticized this dress as anachronistic; others believe that it symbolizes the solemnity of justice. In a General Meeting of the Bar held shortly before the change of sovereignty, members voted by an overwhelming majority to retain the wig and gown. Barristers do not shake hands with one another and address one another in court as 'my learned friend'. Some barristers still carry their wig and gown in a drawstring bag of cotton damask (a cotton-silk mixture) embroidered with their initials, and put their wig in an oval or round shaped travel tin, also with personal engraving. A junior barrister carries a blue bag and a senior counsel a red bag though it is also traditional for a Senior Counsel to give a red bag to a junior and the right to use it when the junior has rendered outstanding assistance on a case.

In other respects, the Bar will probably have to catch up with times. It is a fairly small profession, slightly over 1,000 members in 2017 (compared with over 8,000 solicitors). The Bar still adopts an apprentice system. A young member serves a year of pupillage with one or more pupil masters, who have to have at least 5 years of experience. Pupillage is unpaid (which is anachronistic and unjustifiable in modern days), and once it is completed, the young barristers are expected to set up their own chambers (or join an existing set of chambers), with considerable outgoings and expenses. This has deterred some talented young people from joining the Bar in recent years, especially when they are offered an attractive package with a systematic and overseas training opportunity by leading law firms. Reputation at the Bar is to be established by word of mouth. Publicity or marketing is strictly regulated by the Bar and the restriction is generally even more restrictive than that in the UK. Many good practices in the modern business world seem irrelevant to the Bar although it has tried hard in recent years to keep up with modern development. In contrast, law firms are much better organized and have posed great challenges to the Bar in the recruitment of talented new members.

Joining the University

I was lucky to have a very good start at the Bar, and it was tempting to stay at the Bar, the work of which I enjoyed, but I knew I wanted to join academia. It was not an easy decision, as everyone around me, including my pupil master, asked me to rethink about it. We have to make choices all the time, and the decision to choose one thing in life is always a decision to give up something else. At that time, there was a clear division between town and gown, and in this regard, between lawyers in private practice and lawyers in academia. Practising lawyers considered academic lawyers too theoretical and focused on issues that were mostly irrelevant to the real world, while academic lawyers believed that legal practice was not sufficiently intellectual. There seems to be a lot of misunderstanding between the two branches of lawyer, and such misinformed distinction still persists, for example, between more valued academic research and less valued practice research, as research is research and there are only good research and bad research rather than academic research versus practice research. From what I have observed in London, and particularly from people like Rosalyn and Peter, both academic silks, there should be a healthier relationship between the two branches, and maybe through my continuing practice at the Bar, I will be able to help facilitate the interaction. I joined the University but maintained a part-time practice so that I would not be out of touch with the practical side of the law. The practice enriches my research and allows me to provide a practical dimension in my teaching and writings. It also provides me with a rare and exciting opportunity, particularly in my later years of practice, to test in courts what I advocate in class and in my research as to what ought to be the law or how the law should develop. Sadly, the approach of the University, even up to the present day, towards professional practice is unduly restrictive.

In the early 1980s, Albert Chen and I were the only two local academics at the law school. Apart from a huge difference in remuneration between university appointment and legal practice in town, we were offered an appointment on local terms, following the then general practice at the civil service. The main difference between local term appointment and expatriate term appointment included housing benefits and passage. Appointees on expatriate terms would be entitled to university housing, usually an apartment of over 2,000 square feet overlooking the harbour, and an annual passage subsidy for returning to their home place. In contrast, as a local who lived with my parents in Sha Tin at that time, all I was entitled was a transport subsidy of $300 per month, barely enough to pay for crossing the harbour tunnel, even though I was at the same grade and doing exactly the same job as an expatriate appointee. Not everyone from overseas would be entitled to appointment on expatriate terms. Any appointee who was born in Hong Kong, the Mainland, Macau and Taiwan, that is, in short, Chinese, irrespective of how long one had lived overseas, would be offered local terms only. Such discriminatory treatment was only abolished in the early 1990s, with the support of many of my expatriate colleagues.

As one of the only two legal academics who could speak and write Chinese at that time, and due to the large number of legal and constitutional issues in the mid-1980s, notably arising from the drafting of the Basic Law, I was privileged to be presented with numerous opportunities to do very interesting work and contribute to the community. Albert and I were the two most-often consulted local legal scholars on many legal and constitutional issues (probably because of our ability to communicate in the local language more than our legal knowledge!). While we were only one year apart in joining the law school, we were, or at least perceived to be, a world apart on many constitutional issues. Albert was a distinguished scholar who preferred harmony and non-confrontation. His view was often closer to that of the Mainland government, and he was labelled, somewhat unfairly, I think, as 'pro-China', whereas I was perceived as one of those who were 'contaminated' by the Western liberal tradition. The media loved to portray us as representing two different spectra of views on many constitutional debates. Shortly before 1997, I was on the Central Policy Unit advising the outgoing British Hong Kong government, whereas after 1997, Albert was appointed to the Basic Law Committee advising the incoming master on various matters under the Basic Law. I have great respect for Albert even though we disagree on many issues. We always invited our students to hear the views of each other so that they could have the benefit of arguments on both sides and make up their own minds. Both of us have taught in the Faculty of Law for more than 30 years, and I think it is always a sign of the strengths of an institution when it could simultaneously accommodate diverse if not diametrically opposing views—a phenomenon that is gradually disappearing in our society.

A constant dilemma that both Albert and I have to face is how much we should write for academic journals and how much we should write in popular media. At a time of great constitutional and historical moment when changes in constitutionalism were taking place at an unprecedented scale and pace, views expressed in the media would make immediate impact and might influence the course of constitutional development, whereas the same views expressed in academic journals would be read by no more than a handful of academics and well after the event. We tried to strike a balance, and with limited time, this was easier said than done. Both of us have published widely in academic journals and in the media in both English and Chinese, the latter of which has played the role of both promulgating legal education and promoting the use of Chinese in law. It was a novel challenge to write about law in Chinese, as until as late as in 1989, all laws in Hong Kong were drafted in English only, and all judicial proceedings were conducted in English. It was a mockery that everyone was presumed to know the law and that ignorance of the law was no defence, when the law was written and promulgated in a language that was foreign to 90 per cent of the population and when legal literature in Chinese was practically non-existent. We had to start practically from nothing, as publications of law in Chinese at that time existed only in Taiwan, which was a civil law jurisdiction, and the Chinese expressions as used in Taiwan, or, for that purpose, in the Mainland as well, could be quite different from the daily usage of Chinese in Hong Kong. I was once tasked by the International Committee of the Red Cross to chair a working group to work on an official Chinese version of an explanation of the four Geneva Conventions on the law of wars that would be acceptable to both Taiwan and the Mainland. I had one expert from each side on the working party. It took us many months to go through each and every sentence, and it was fascinating to see how the same words or expressions could be understood completely differently in the two regions that have had roots in the same language and culture for thousands of years!

Language can be a very sensitive issue. The common law is embedded in the English language and culture. Judges and lawyers have their legal training in English, and they think and work in the English language. A bilingual legal system would require not only proficiency in language skills but also a change of attitude. I was on the Working Party on the Use of Chinese in Court, chaired by Sir T. L. Yang, in the mid-1980s. In the course of our deliberation, some magistrates expressed their anxiety to us that the respect for the law might be diminished once the judge began to communicate with the defendants in the Chinese language! The English language is to maintain decorum if not also the mystification of the law. While such concern might be misplaced, it was telling as to the difficulties of introducing a bilingual legal system. And it is not just in the legal profession. When I first introduced a Chinese version of my congratulatory speech at the formal Graduation Ceremony of the Faculty in the mid-2000s so that I could directly address many parents who may not be fluent in the English language on this very special occasion, I could see a massive change in the atmosphere. I remember that Kenneth Kwok SC, then president of the Law Alumni Association and a mentor and good friend of mine, told me after the ceremony that he had been waiting for this occasion for 30 years!

Legal writings in Chinese could be sensitive in academia as well. The absence of a Chinese legal lexicon and the paucity of legal literature in Chinese presented one of the major challenges to the introduction of a bilingual legal system. Albert and I considered that it was our duty as local legal academics proficient in the two languages not only to fill this gap but also to raise the quality of Chinese legal writings. Yet we were told, on more than one occasion, that our writings in Chinese would not be counted for the purpose of career development. The polite explanation was that there was no qualified assessor to evaluate the quality of these writings. It did not bother me, as I published these works because they were the right thing to do and not for institutional recognition or career advancement. Yet this kind of anachronistic attitude continues to the present day, albeit in a slightly different form. Academics were required to produce annually a number of academic articles, and the worth of an academic was measured entirely by how many so-called 'three-star' or 'four-star' articles he or she could produce, as if this was the sole purpose of universities. I fully accept that an important role of academics is to generate knowledge through research, but it would be a failing of a university's mission if all it cares about is the single and myopic task of producing three-star and four-star academic articles to the exclusion of everything else. It reminds me of the book *Federalist Papers*,[3] which was essentially a collection of newspaper articles on various aspects of the constitution that were published at the time of drafting the US Constitution. This book has stood the test of time and has since become a classic work on the US Constitution and political philosophy. Yet it would probably have been considered to be of nil value if it were to be done under the present research assessment climate at our tertiary institutions. Likewise, if we just focus on factors like 'impact factors' or journal ranking (which may be influenced by language bias or cultural and regional arrogance) rather than the worth of the publications themselves, or membership in distinguished academies, people like Kazuo Ishiguro or Tu Youyou would never have been awarded Nobel prize. University is about education and research, and meaningful research does extend beyond the production of three-star or four-star academic articles in academic journals. Sadly, the myopic pursuit of 'stars' seems to be where our tertiary institutions in Hong Kong are heading.

London to Strasbourg

In 1988, I decided to pursue my doctoral study under the supervision of Professor Rosalyn Higgins. Unfortunately, shortly before I arrived in London, she became seriously ill, and it delayed the start of my doctoral study for almost six months. As part of my field work, I spent a couple of months working at the European Commission of Human Rights at Strasbourg. The European Commission of Human Rights was set up under the European Convention of Human Rights, under which an individual may bring a claim against her own country for a violation of her human rights. The claim would first be considered by the European Commission, which would make a report on whether a violation was established. If the report was not accepted by the parties, they could bring the matter to the European Court of Human Rights, whose judgment was final and binding on the State concerned.[4]

The Commission and the Court were situated next to one another in the same building and right opposite the European Parliament. The Secretariat of the

---

3. A. Hamilton, J. Madison, and J. Jay, *The Federalist Papers* (New York: New American Library, 1961).
4. The Commission was merged with the Court two decades later.

Commission was a truly international office, the lawyers and scholars coming from many different jurisdictions. English and French were the working languages, and virtually everyone was at least bilingual. The Commission was divided into three language sections. I worked in the English language section with a Dutch lady, who became a very good friend of mine and later a prosecutor and then a judge in the Netherlands. Also in our office was a French lady who spoke hardly any English. We were supervised by Michael O'Boyle, an English lawyer who subsequently published a learned volume on the European Convention of Human Rights. I was privileged to have met many nice colleagues there. Apart from preparing reports, which was essentially judgments of the Commission reached after considering the submissions of the parties, the Commission was an independent party before the European Court if the case went to the court. One of the cases that I was involved was the *Spycatcher* case. It involved a memoir written by a former MI6 member who detailed some of the activities of the secret agency. The book was first published in the United States, and when the *Sunday Times* tried to publish a series of extracts in the United Kingdom, the British government applied for an injunction and started worldwide litigation to prevent the book from being published. Litigation was started in Australia, New Zealand, and Hong Kong. I was one of the junior counsels representing the *South China Morning Post* in opposing an application for injunction restraining the *Post* from publishing extracts of the book in Hong Kong. By the late 1980s, the *Sunday Times* case had reached Strasbourg, as the *Sunday Times* argued that the injunction order was a violation of the guarantee of freedom of expression under the European Convention.

Strasbourg is a beautiful and peaceful town in the Alsace-Loraine region of France. It is less than an hour from Fribourg, the famous old German town which is the gate to the Black Forest, and about an hour from Basel in Switzerland. The town of Strasbourg was shaped by the French, German, and Swiss culture. It was a very enjoyable stay, but the town was so serene and tranquil that it could make you forget about the real world, if not for the occasional demonstrations outside the European Parliament. The experience was wonderful, but it also made me think about what I was pursuing in my doctoral study.

I returned to London in late 1988, by which time Professor Higgins had recovered from her illness. I worked on the change of nationality upon territorial change. While the topic had some bearing on the situation in Hong Kong, it was also a major issue in Europe, especially after the Second World War when the map of Europe was essentially redrawn, and the interaction between different nationality regimes had resulted in numerous cases of multiple nationalities or statelessness, which in turn led to many international conflicts. It was an interesting topic, and I had published a few articles on that subject and a Chinese book in the first year of my study. Yet as I went deeper into the subject, the project became increasingly unreal. This topic was remote from the situation in Hong Kong, especially after June 1989, when fear for the future became a real issue. Many people lost confidence in the future of the territory. Those who could afford to leave had made arrangement to emigrate. In 1990 alone, 60,000 families left, primarily professionals and well-educated people. There was no sign that the haemorrhage of talents would slow down. As part of the confidence-saving measures, the government decided to build a new airport, to speed up the pace of introducing democratic elections to the Legislative Council, and to introduce a Bill of Rights Ordinance. It was a challenging time for Hong Kong, and I felt helpless in London not being able to contribute to the process. By mid-1990, I decided to return to Hong Kong. Had I decided to stay in London, it would probably have taken me another 10 months to complete the doctoral thesis. I asked myself why I wanted to do it. Unlike other disciplines, a doctoral degree was never required in law. Many established legal scholars did not have a doctoral degree, and I would not need the degree for my career development. The research experience is of course by itself valuable, but a doctoral degree is not the only way to acquire such experience. To me, the successful completion of it simply means that I could claim that I know a lot about a tiny subject that is by and large irrelevant to the world (and remain ignorant of many other things). Instead of spending another year working on a thesis that would have little impact other than satisfying my own pride, I thought I could make more useful contributions to Hong Kong by working on the more burning issues there. Of course, at that time, I could not have foreseen that this decision was going to haunt me 25 years later.

Returning to Hong Kong

I returned to the Faculty of Law at the end of 1990. By then Professor Yash Ghai, a very eminent human rights scholar and our first Sir Y. K. Pao Chair in Public Law, and Professor Andrew Byrnes, now chair professor at the University of New South Wales, had just joined the Faculty. Both of them became my lifelong friends. Together we established a master's programme in human rights with a focus in Asia. Andrew and I worked on numerous training programmes and workshops on the newly enacted Bill of Rights Ordinance for the judiciary, civil servants, and the civil societies. We set up a new set of private law reports, the *Hong Kong Public Law Reports*, which documented all the judicial decisions on the Bill of Rights and provided a historical record of the early phase of the implementation of the Bill of Rights. The series has earned quite a positive reputation and was subsequently taken over by a commercial publisher. We also worked on a *Bill of Rights Bulletin* that provided our commentaries on recent judgments and legal developments. Yash, Andrew, and I also gradually assembled volumes of literature on human rights in Hong Kong. We brought in international experts on human rights and recruited the next generation of scholars. Within a few years' time, we had established a strong international reputation in public law and built up a strong public law team within the Faculty, the expertise and experience of which has continued to benefit the Hong Kong community. Not only did we enhance the much-needed knowledge and expertise on human rights among members of the civil society in Hong Kong, but we also provided training to students from many Asian countries, producing a number of fine graduates who continued to serve the cause of human rights in their own countries upon graduation. The master's programme in human rights, introduced in 1999, has been one of the most internationalized academic programmes even up to today, covering most of the countries that are now included in the 'One Belt, One Road' strategy, save that we did it 15 years in advance!

Professor Yash Ghai is a remarkable academic who has made immense contributions to constitutional developments in Hong Kong. He is inspiring, perceptive, critical, outspoken, and highly respected. His book *Hong Kong New Constitutional Order*, the first edition published in 1997, is the classic work on this subject. I recalled Yash came to my office one day when I was the head of the department of law. 'Johannes,' Yash said, 'I would like to apply for 12 months' leave. I have just received a phone call from the president of Kenya. The country is at the brink of civil war. He is setting up a constitutional commission, which is tasked to bring different factions together by drawing up a new constitution for the country. The president wants me to chair this commission. I don't think I can say "no".' 'I don't think I can say "no" either,' I replied with a smile. 'How often do our colleagues receive a phone call from the president of their country? I doubt if you can finish the work in 12 months. Why don't I give you initially 18 months and review the situation after that? And keep me posted on your work.' In the following two years, Yash managed to bring different factions to the negotiation table and avoid a civil war, and the new constitution eventually went through parliament many years later. He returned, and later upon his retirement, he was appointed by the UN Secretary-General as the Special Rapporteur of Human Rights in Cambodia.

We would not have been able to bring Yash to Hong Kong had it not been due to the generous support of Dr Helmut Sohmen, one of the most successful entrepreneurs in Hong Kong and the region, who later became a good friend. In the mid-1980s, he was a member of the Legislative Council. Apparently none of his colleagues knew what he was talking about when he referred to the Austrian Constitution, which was also known as the Basic Law. Helmut was disappointed and felt that something had to be done to promote knowledge of public law within the community. Hence the Sir Y. K. Pao Chair was established. Since then Helmut has remained a staunch supporter of the Faculty and a good friend of mine. The endowment for the Sir Y. K. Pao Chair ran out at some point in the late 1990s, and one of the first things I did when I took over the deanship in 2002 was to promise Helmut that the chair would be absorbed as a structural chair and would continue perpetually. Helmut has also done a lot to support the master's programme in human rights, and generations of students, apart from being beneficiaries of his generous scholarships, have also enjoyed sumptuous dinners and hospitality at his home. The last time I met Helmut was at the public lecture of Chris Patten, the last governor of Hong Kong, in 2016. Helmut was still in good shape, although his years of hard work seemed to have taken a toll on his health. As an Austrian who has spent most of his life in Hong Kong, Helmut has done a lot for Hong Kong, and I wish him well.

China

I always see the law school as something more than an institution to teach law. Britain has left a legacy of the rule of law and a well-established legal system in Hong Kong. The model of 'One Country, Two Systems' presents us with an unprecedented challenge. On one side of the border, there is a well-established system that is founded on respect for individual freedoms, diversity, and checks and balances of public powers. On the other side of the border, there is a rising power that has just emerged from a state of complete lawlessness, with an ideology that rejects the doctrine of separation of powers and no tradition of exercising constraints on public powers. Will the model work? Many people have doubts, but for those who have decided to stay in Hong Kong, there is no choice but to try our best to make it work. The law school is in the forefront of training the younger minds for this challenge, and we are in a particularly privileged position to contribute to the maintenance of the rule of law in both Hong Kong and China.

As we moved towards the transition, we modified the curriculum at the law school to prepare our students for the changes. For instance, we have introduced a compulsory course on Introduction to Chinese Law, a course on Use of Chinese in Law, and introduced a complete master of laws programme in Chinese Law. We also saw that we could bridge the gap between the two systems by exposing Mainland students and lawyers to the common law system. Our master of common law programme was introduced with that in mind in 1997, when Albert Chen was the dean, and I was in charge of its implementation and further development when I took up the headship of the department of law in 1999. The students came from three main sources: government officials, judges, and fresh graduates. A year of study of common law is too short, but our aim is not to impart to the students detailed, technical knowledge of the common law but rather to expose them to the thinking behind our system, to understand the application of the common law, and to appreciate the values underpinning and shaping the system. With great support of the Department of Justice and the Judiciary, we supplement the academic programme by a period of attachment with various government departments and the Judiciary, so that the students can better understand how our system works in practice. In the early days, the number of students was kept small, about ten of them being government officials, another ten being judges, and the rest fresh graduates from leading Mainland law schools. Apart from adequate proficiency in English, we have set an age limit of 42. The rationale is that if the student is under 42 years of age (which is regarded as youthful in public office career in the Mainland), and is proficient in a foreign language, he or she is likely to be a high flyer at an energetic stage of life and is likely to move into a position of influence in the years to come. We were proved right. In 2009 we hosted a celebration dinner in Beijing to mark the fortieth anniversary of the Faculty. Many alumni, who had been promoted to considerably senior levels, came to join the dinner from all parts of the country. It was a most touching and enjoyable event. Professor Cheng Kai Ming, who was then a pro-vice-chancellor of the University of Hong Kong, later told me that he was very moved when I addressed our alumni, as he could see that we were working on the future of the country.

On one occasion when I visited our alumni at the Shenzhen People's Court, I asked them how their study in Hong Kong had had an impact on their work. There are over 100 judges at the Shenzhen People's Court who are our alumni. A number of them have occupied positions as division heads, and they have implemented many procedural reforms, many of which are modelled after or inspired by the Hong Kong system. Of course, they admitted frankly that some systemic issues are beyond their control or ability to tackle. Yet in their day-to-day operation, they are more ready to challenge written evidence presented by the State and are more willing to listen to the arguments of both sides. They tend to write longer judgments to address the arguments put forward by both sides and to give their reasons for the arguments that they have rejected. Some graduates working in regulatory institutions decided to publish their internal decisions so as to make the decision-making process more transparent. These changes mark the beginning of rationality in the system, and rationality is the first step towards a fair system. They told me that these changes were inspired by their study in Hong Kong.

Throughout my tenure of deanship I have maintained a close collaboration with all the major law schools in the Mainland. In the early days, I hoped we were able to raise their academic standards through our collaboration and to help expose them to the international academic community. At the same time, through these collaborations we are able to learn more about the Mainland system. We had annual conferences with Peking University; we organized regular conferences to bring together scholars and academics from the Mainland, Taiwan, Macau, and Hong Kong to enhance better understanding of legal development on both sides of the Straits. At the same time, I continued to work with the Mainland judiciary with a view to providing training programmes to the judges. I believe judges are the key players in upholding the rule of law, and we hope we can contribute to the enhancement of judicial quality in the Mainland through our experience of judicial training in the Western legal system. Of course the interflow is two-way. We introduced summer study and internship programmes in the Mainland for our own students. I have also worked on an idea of teaching our compulsory course on Introduction to Chinese Law in the Mainland, so that we can enhance our students' understanding of how the Mainland legal system works in practice. I am glad that the first of such courses took place in 2016. As most practitioners who have worked in the Mainland will appreciate, any collaborative work there requires the highest level of patience. There were occasions when we thought we had reached an agreement, but that the agreement was brushed aside at the last minute, and negotiations had to start all over again for no reason but a change of personnel. Programmes could be delayed and suspended without any prior notice, simply because a new head had been appointed. I have had my own share of experience and frustration with the worst aspects of bureaucracy and politics but was at the same time most encouraged by the liberal and enthusiastic partners and friends that I have collaborated with in the Mainland.

In or around 2011, together with my good friend Professor Dame Hazel Genn, then the dean of law of University College London, we launched a rule of law programme in the Mainland, first with Renmin University and then with Peking University. Essentially, we held a mock trial in the Mainland on a case that was modelled on a real case in the Mainland and then presented a trial and full arguments of that case before a common law judge. We managed to invite some of the best judges from the United Kingdom and our Court of Final Appeal to preside over the trial, with advocates from the common law system arguing for both sides. The trial was observed by Mainland judges, academics, policymakers, and students. After the trial, we had very fruitful and interesting discussions on the differences in treating the same case—why certain things were done in a certain way under our system, and how that very same case would be tried under the Mainland system. The programme was a great success in bringing two major legal jurisdictions into fruitful dialogues.

In around 2014, I had come to almost the last stage of discussion with the National Judicial College of an ambitious programme for judicial training of judges in the Mainland. Unfortunately, all discussions were halted after my stepping down from the deanship and the outbreak of Occupy Central in the autumn of 2014.

The twenty-first century: A turbulent time

I became dean of the Faculty of Law in 2002 and remained in that position for 12 years. I am glad to see how the Faculty has over that period emerged from a local teaching law school to become one of the leading international law schools in the world. Very few academics have joined the university with a view to eventually becoming a university administrator. Indeed, when one gets such an administrative position, most colleagues would commiserate rather than congratulate you. Most colleagues did it out of a sense of duty, and I was no exception. It is a very onerous (and thankless) job with an extremely broad portfolio that requires very different skills and mindset from being an academic. A dean these days has to handle human resources planning, financial planning, budgeting, institutional advancement, international development, public relations, fundraising, alumni networking, crisis management, in addition to teaching and research. Worst of all, a dean has to manage people with extremely high egos in an environment that rests on respect, consultation, and persuasion, with power and authority that can hardly be relied upon. I have learned a lot on the job, and the best part of the job has been to be able to meet and work with many wonderful people during my tenure. Yet deans, or any senior administrators, are given virtually no training when they are appointed to the job. Most universities are still working on the archaic assumption that an accomplished academic means that he or she can also take up management jobs in the university, without giving sufficient emphasis on practical management experience. The hitherto assumption that a good academic would be a good administrator is proved more often than not by refute! Research accomplishment, which is a necessary but insufficient requirement by itself, and administrative leadership or competence can be as far apart as two different planets.

I stepped down from the deanship in July 2014 and took my sabbatical leave in the following nine months. I taught a constitutional law course at the University of Pennsylvania Law School, an Ivy League university where I had a wonderful time and met wonderful colleagues and students, and then spent some most fruitful time for research at the University of Cambridge as a visiting fellow. The autumn of 2014 witnessed the outbreak of Occupy Central, or the Umbrella Movement, as it was subsequently known, in Hong Kong, where protestors occupied the financial district for 79 days in protest of the highly controlled model of the nomination of the Chief Executive and the lack of progress of democracy in Hong Kong. Despite my physical absence from Hong Kong at that time, I was unexpectedly drawn into a turbulent political storm in relation to the movement. I was then recommended for appointment to a vice-president position at the University. When I was first approached for the position, I was hesitant, as it would be a difficult decision whether to continue in administration, which I might be able to make some contribution to with my experience, or to return to research and teaching, which I longed to resume after serving many years in administration. Eventually I decided to take up the challenge of a leadership position, hoping to bring some needed changes to the institution and without knowing what was awaiting me. Apparently some quarters of the community considered it undesirable, in the aftermath of Occupy Central in Hong Kong, for a liberal academic to take up an important leadership position of a university which was perceived to be the cradle of the liberal ideas of the student protestors. For over 12 months, I was continuously bombarded with scathing and frivolous personal attacks, including accusing me of supporting the Occupy Central movement in Hong Kong, which I was not involved in at all, or for not stopping my colleague who was one of the instigators of Occupy Central to carry out his ideas. But what power did I have over my colleague on his political activities outside the campus, and why should I interfere with his beliefs and activities as long as he has satisfactorily discharged his academic duties? A handful of these critics also somehow portrayed me as a dean interested only in politicking at the expense of our academic standards, whereas international rankings, like Quacquarelli Symonds (QS) and, more recently, Times Higher Education (THES), have since 2012 consistently ranked the Faculty within the top 20 law schools in the world, based on criteria including teaching, research, and citation.

It was a turbulent time. The process was most unpleasant, and the public attacks have taken a toll on me and my family, but it is reassuring that there are many, many supporting friends around, both from Hong Kong and overseas. I could easily have withdrawn from the appointment process to spare myself from the vicious attacks, had it not been that the withdrawal would have been perceived to be a surrender of the principle of academic freedom. I have been telling my students that our commitment to fundamental values would only be tested when such commitment requires some kind of sacrifice, and it appears that I am to be tested by my own belief. I adhered to my principles and conscience, though not without a price. It took almost 18 months for the storm to die down. I am pleased to regain my peace of mind since the dust has settled. A very senior and well respected professor at the University once asked me if I was angry at the University. Not at all; probably sadness rather than anger. I don't have any feeling of animosity towards anyone who was involved in the process; such feeling would not have changed anything. Life is too short to be spent on grief, anger, regret and lament. Perhaps I prefer to see things from the positive side. The experience makes my life more interesting. I have at least been given time to reflect on my own inadequacies and to consider how blessed I am with the friendship and support that I have received. I would in particular like to thank Professor Peter Mathieson, the then President of the University, who has to face tremendous political pressure in support-ing my appointment.[5] There is no point in looking back at those days, as life has had to move on. It is indeed a blessing in disguise as I can resume what I have always intended to do when I joined academia—teaching and research.

I started my academic career partly with the hope to bridge the gap between town and gown. The relation between town and gown has become a lot healthier than, say, it was 30 years ago. The Court of Final Appeal under the great leadership of Chief Justice Andrew Li has been very receptive to academic work. Indeed, Hong Kong is fortunate and privileged to have our Court of Final Appeal led by enlightened and liberal judicial leaders like the successive Chief Justices Andrew Li, who taught me modesty and per-severance, and Geoffrey Ma, who is always warm and pleasant, Justice Kemy Bokhary, a personal friend with whom I have the privilege of collaborating on a number of aca-demic works, Justice Bob Ribeiro who was once my teacher at the University, Justice Patrick Chan, our first alumnus on the Court of Final Appeal, Sir Anthony Mason, who is a strong believer in close collaboration between town and gown, and who has made immense contributions to legal scholarship, and many, many others who, for space constraints, could not be named here. It is increasingly accepted that a strong tie among academia, the judiciary, and the practitioners would benefit and strengthen our legal system. Scholarship and practice are not mutually exclusive. In fact, interaction and understanding will complement and enrich one another's work. In this regard, I am particularly honoured when Chief Justice Andrew Li conferred on me the title of Honorary Senior Counsel, also known as 'academic silk'. The title itself is the best testimony that town and gown should work together to serve our legal system and our community.

---

5. See 'A Turbulent Tenure: HKU Vice-Chancellor Reflects on His Time at the Helm of Hong Kong's Oldest University', *South China Morning Post*, 8 January 2018 (http://www.scmp.com/news/hong-kong/politics/article/2127163/turbulent-tenure-hku-vice-chancellor-reflects-his-time-helm). For more details of the incident, see Johannes Chan and Douglas Kerr, 'Academic Freedom, Political Interference and Public Accountability', (2016) 7 *Journal of Academic Freedom* 1–21.

II

Professionalism and Professional Privilege

2

In memory of Mr Justice Charles Ching

One of the best advocates of our times

It was 1994, in the heyday of Hong Kong's property market. The price of real property kept soaring from one height to another, and there was no sign of its reaching the peak. On 26 May 1994, a land auction took place at City Hall, which was, as usual, packed with all the major developers and reporters. As the bidding went on, messages were apparently passed among various developers. The following day, many newspapers carried a story that major developers had joined hands to keep down the price of the land sold. In most newspapers, the participants were identified by name and photograph. Some newspapers described the developers involved as a 'cartel', 'an unholy alliance', and their actions as 'blatantly rigging', and even a 'ganging-up of the big boys'. Some magazines recited every detail of the incident, including who was talking to whom and what the various messages were. The extensive coverage of this event led to a review of the auction process in due course.

About two months later, the Independent Commission Against Corruption (ICAC), upon receipt of a complaint, began to investigate the matter. On 2 August 1994, as part of the investigation, two ICAC investigators went to the headquarters of *Ming Pao*. They were apparently too early: most senior members of the newspaper industry don't go to the office until late afternoon. So, they left a message with the secretary of the editor-in-chief that they were 'investigating the conduct of the land auction' in question and wished to interview the reporters who had been assigned by *Ming Pao* to cover the story of the auction on the material day. There was no mention of any offence or any suspect.

The following day, *Ming Pao* carried an article, the relevant part of which reads: 'The ICAC took steps to meet reporters in its investigation in relation to the developers' joint bidding (for) land' and '[t]he ICAC is investigating whether anyone infringed any Ordinance in a land auction held on 26 May this year in which over 10 developers combined to bid for land.' The article went on to explain that, in order to collect information, ICAC investigators had approached media organizations with a view to meeting reporters and others who had attended the bidding process. It then added: 'The target of this ICAC investigation has not yet been ascertained.'

As a result of this article, *Ming Pao* and its three most senior chief editors were charged with the offence of unlawful disclosure of the details of an ICAC investigation, contrary to section 30 of the Prevention of Bribery Ordinance. Section 30(1) provides that 'any person who, without lawful authority or reasonable excuse, discloses to any person who is the subject of an investigation in respect of an offence alleged or suspected to have been committed by him under this Ordinance the fact that he is subject to such an investigation or any details of such investigation . . . shall be guilty of an offence'.

The prosecution

I was briefed to act for *Ming Pao* and its three chief editors as a junior to the late Charles Ching QC. It was one of his last cases in practice at the Bar, as rumour had it (subsequently confirmed) that he would soon join the Bench. As soon as I got my coffee in his conference room, Charles flipped through the ordinance and fired a series of questions at me: 'Section 30 says "an offence alleged or suspected". "Alleged" by whom? "Suspected" by whom? What were the "details" of an investigation that have been disclosed?' As usual, Charles had already done a thorough analysis of the case and had a detailed picture in mind of how he wanted to conduct the defence and was merely testing how well prepared the junior was! We had a good hour of discussion, and I didn't even have a chance to sip my coffee. Eventually Charles seemed satisfied and was prepared to conclude the conference when I brought up the Bill of Rights defence. Charles raised his eyebrows slightly. 'Johannes, we have a good case. I think it would be a sign of weakness if we need to rely on the Bill of Rights,' he said. 'Not necessarily,' I feebly began my mission impossible to convince Charles that there was a respectable case under the Bill of Rights as well. I had worked with Charles before and knew his view on the Bill of Rights (or Bill of Wrongs, as he called it). Nonetheless, Charles was exceptionally patient, and after half an hour or so, he thought for a while and said, 'Very well; you will prepare this part of the submission.'

The prosecution took place at Eastern Magistrates' Court. I offered to pick up Charles from his chambers on my way to the court. A lover of racing cars, Charles kept telling me that my car lock was absolutely useless, as it would take only three seconds to unlock it, and he kept saying the same whenever he saw my car. His persistence certainly wasn't limited to law and the courts.

The courtroom was packed with reporters, members of the public, and even some members of the Bar who wished to see Charles's cross-examination, which was rightly considered to be the 'Jewel in the Crown' of the legal profession.

In front of the formidable Charles, the ICAC officer appeared to be rather timid and nervous.

'Mr Officer, I have great respect for the ICAC. So please relax. I have just a few questions to ask you about two letters. Do take your time to think before you answer. The prosecution may object to some of my questions. You may wish to answer after the prosecution has not indicated any objection.' Charles began his cross-examination in a gentle manner.

Q: Is it true that these two letters were received from members of the public concerning this public land auction?

A: Yes.

Q: One to the Attorney General?

A: Yes.

Q: The other to the ICAC Commissioner?

A: Yes.

Q: Neither of the letters asserted any facts?

A: Correct.

Q: They merely complained about what had happened at the Land Auction?

A: Yes.

Q: And suggested that there might have been one or other offence?

A: Yes.

Q: Neither writer said that the writer had been at that auction?

A: Agreed.

[After referring to various newspaper reports on the land auction, Charles continued.]

Q: So it was quite clear that allegations were being made that named property developers had rigged the auction to buy the two properties at less than estimated value?

A: Yes.

Q: Articles to the same effect appeared in the Chinese language newspapers?

A: Yes.

Q: So you would expect developers to know of these allegations?

A: Yes.

Charles finished his cross-examination in about half an hour and got everything he wanted. There were no tears, no bloodshed. The final outcome of this case was determined by the above opening questions!

What people had seen was a master advocate at work for half an hour; what most people did not see was the many hours of preparation behind it. I once asked Charles what drove him to work so hard. 'Trust,' he said. 'When your client places their trust in you, you just have to do your best. This is professionalism. There is of course the pride as well—the pride to be at your best in every case, and the pride to surpass your best performance in every case.'

The hearing lasted for three days. At the end of the prosecution case, we submitted that there was no case to answer. Our main argument was that the offence was not made out, that there was no allegation or suspicion of any offence by any person, that no details were disclosed, that the disclosure had caused no prejudice to the investigation, and that section 30 of the Prevention of Bribery Ordinance was inconsistent with the Bill of Rights. The Magistrate adjourned the hearing for ruling, and we had a good lunch at which Charles enjoyed all the unhealthy food.

It took the Magistrate a month to deliver the ruling. In a carefully reasoned decision, the learned Magistrate rejected all our arguments on the interpretation of the offence but held that section 30 of the Prevention of Bribery Ordinance was inconsistent with the Bill of Rights and was therefore repealed to the extent of inconsistency.[1] The charge was accordingly dismissed. A great victory, though on the only point that Charles had initially been reluctant to take. Not surprisingly, the Attorney General appealed by way of case stated, and the appeal, which was confined to the constitutionality of the repealed part of section 30, was reserved to the Court of Appeal.

The appeal

By this time Charles's appointment to the Bench was announced. He was distinguished as only the second member of the Bar to be appointed directly to the Court of Appeal. Not surprisingly, on 1 July 1997, he was made one of the three Permanent Judges of the Court of Final Appeal and continued to make his mark on the legal development in Hong Kong.

The Bar held a special Bar Mess in honour of Charles's appointment. Charles was in a jubilant mood that evening. He started his speech by talking about the meaning of 'barrister'. 'I looked in the *Oxford Dictionary* and found that "barrister" lies between "bankruptcy" and "bastard"', he said, and so he went on.

Gladys Li QC led me on the appeal. In her eloquent English with a royal accent, Gladys opened her case by launching a full-scale attack on the extremely wide reach of section 30 and the chilling effect it had had on freedom of expression. Section 30 prohibited disclosure of the details of the investigation of an offence under the Prevention of Bribery Ordinance. What if the investigation turned out not to relate to the Prevention of Bribery Ordinance at all but, for instance, to the Corrupt and Illegal Practices Ordinance? This was something within the peculiar knowledge of the ICAC, which would never confirm what offence it was investigating. Since there was no way of knowing what offence the ICAC was investigating, section 30 could be held in terror over the heads of newspaper editors, and the safest course was not to report on anything about the ICAC, not even any abuse of power by the ICAC itself.

---

1. *R v Ming Pao Newspapers Ltd* (1994) 4 HKPLR 621.

The arguments were completed in the early afternoon. The Court of Appeal adjourned for about 20 minutes and gave judgment at 3:30 p.m.[2] The appeal was allowed, and the court ordered that the case be remitted back to the Magistrates' Court for trial. The judgment was given by Litton VP (as he then was). The court found that the primary purpose of section 30 was to protect the reputation of persons under suspicion and to protect the integrity of investigations into offences alleged or suspected under the ordinance. Since it pursued a legitimate objective, it was consistent with the Bill of Rights. This is a classic example of the court failing to consider proportionality at all. The mere fact that the offence pursued a legitimate objective did not by itself justify the offence, if the scope of the offence was disproportionate to the objective to be pursued. This is perhaps the danger of an *ex tempore* judgment. In consolation, Litton VP held that, if the purpose of disclosure was to reveal an abuse of power by the ICAC officer, this would be covered by the defence of 'reasonable excuse'.

Section 30 has long been criticized for being a press gagging law. As a matter of principle, *Ming Pao* decided to further appeal to the Privy Council. Special leave to appeal to the Privy Council was required, as such an appeal was not as of right. Surprisingly, the Crown decided to oppose the leave application, so we had to start another battle in London.

Further appeal to London

It was a cold winter morning when my instructing solicitor and I arrived in London for the leave application. We arrived at Heathrow before 5 a.m. and reached the hotel at Westminster around 6 a.m. I thought I might take a short rest before the conference with Anthony Lester QC (subsequently Lord Lester QC), my leader, and then realized that I had forgotten to collect at the airport a piece of luggage which I had agreed to bring to a friend in London. It was still on the luggage belt when I returned to Heathrow (so much for London's efficiency!).

The Privy Council, or more accurately the Judicial Committee of the Privy Council, is the court of final appeal of the British Empire (except Britain). At the heyday of the British Empire, this court served as the court of final appeal of almost half of the globe. It was situated at Downing Street until its relocation to its present home at Middlesex Guildhall Building (which also houses the UK Supreme Court) in 2009. The prime minister's residence next door is of course a well-known tourist spot. The entrance to Downing Street is blocked with a barricade and guarded by a police officer. Tourists can only get a glimpse of Downing Street from behind the barricade. Yet if you told the police officer that you were going to the Privy Council (when it was in session), he would let you through!

The then court of final appeal of the British Empire was housed in a rather dull Georgian building. Counsel waited outside the courtroom to be called. The judges are

---

2. *Attorney General v Ming Pao Newspapers Ltd* (1995) 5 HKPLR 13.

not robed. Counsel table, which was a very narrow and uncomfortable wooden panel, lay perpendicular to the Bench, and to address the court, counsel had to walk to the middle of the courtroom before a standing lectern in a rather exposed position without assistance from his junior or instructing solicitor. We had a good hour of argument, and leave was granted.

It was the early spring of 1996 when I was back in London for the substantive hearing. The morning breeze at Heathrow was as always refreshing and welcoming. This time I had collected all of my luggage and managed to have a substantial English breakfast at a sidewalk cafeteria near Lincoln's Inn before the conference with my leader, who had since our last conference been made a peer.

Chambers in London are not much different from chambers in Hong Kong, except perhaps that their fittings are more classic. Anthony Lester QC, or Lord Lester of Hernie Hill QC, is a leading human rights counsel as well as a visiting professor in public law at University College London. I first met Anthony in the late 1980s when I was his junior in the *Spycatcher* case in Hong Kong. He brought with him another junior, David Pannick, later to become Lord Pannick QC and one of the most eminent London silks, who was to appear regularly in Hong Kong many years later. Anthony used to complain that since David, as a London junior at that time, did not manage to get admitted to Hong Kong in that case, David spent his time at the swimming pool of the luxurious Mandarin Hotel when Anthony was working hard in court, and when David eventually took silk, said Anthony jokingly, he also took away most of Anthony's Hong Kong cases! David is an affable and learned gentleman. Our paths have since crossed on a number of occasions, when I have both acted with him and against him.

Back to the *Ming Pao* appeal, I arrived at Anthony's chambers shortly before 9 a.m. This was only my second visit to his chambers. We were greeted by his clerk, an old gentleman in a dark pinstriped jacket with a pair of gold-rimmed spectacles. As is typical of many leading counsel, Anthony's papers were scattered all over the place, and I was delighted to see the red ribbon tying his briefs and even the seal at the top of his paper, a tradition which has long since disappeared in Hong Kong. We went through the respective cases of both the appellant and the respondent and gave a final touch to our submissions. We were all set for the final stage of the hearing.

In contrast to the half-day hearing before the Court of Appeal, the hearing before the Privy Council lasted for two days. It took no time for the Bench to engage with counsel. The law lords were well versed with the case, and one question after another was fired at counsel before counsel could even develop his argument. The questions also went well beyond our submission, and counsel and the Bench freely engaged in detailed arguments on cases that were not cited at all. Judgment was reserved.

At the end of the case, Anthony took us to the lovely terrace at the House of Lords for coffee. There was a private path which could take you from the Privy Council to Parliament—so much for the separation of powers! The terrace overlooked the Thames. It was very enjoyable, particularly after a full day in court, to be able to relax under the sun on the grassy terrace and be greeted by the refreshing breeze from the Thames. No wonder there were rumours that some of the law lords strongly opposed the relocation of the House of Lords to another venue, so that the highest court in England and Wales would no longer be part of Parliament—another anomaly in English constitutional law about separation of powers.

Judgment, or more accurately, the Opinion of the Judicial Committee was handed down on 20 May 1996.[3] Their Lordships reaffirmed certain fundamental principles on freedom of expression, and after conducting a balancing exercise between the evil of corruption and the scope of section 30 and giving due regard to the margin of appreciation, decided that section 30 was a proportionate restriction on freedom of expression. In so doing the Privy Council also limited the scope of section 30. Among other things, it held that section 30 could only apply when there was a suspect or an allegation of a bribery ordinance offence against a specified person. As there was no evidence that at the date of publication of the newspaper article anything other than a general investigation was being carried on by the ICAC with no suspect in view, no offence could have been committed. Thus, in a finely balanced judgment, their Lordships laid down sufficient general principles on freedom of expression that were of great importance to Hong Kong, confirmed the acquittal of the respondents by restricting the scope of section 30, and yet left sufficient room to protect the integrity of ICAC investigations. After two years of legal battle, everyone got something from the judgment.

Although the point that section 30 could only operate with an identified suspect was not taken at first instance, it was Charles's cross-examination that had laid the factual basis for such a finding by the Privy Council. I wrote to Charles, who was a judge on the Court of Appeal by then, about the judgment, and he sent me a nice handwritten reply saying, 'it proves how wrong I was at first instance.' I was so touched. It was a great privilege to be able to work with three of the best leading counsel in one case. They have different styles, different approaches, and yet they share something in common—an unshakeable belief in justice and a determination to pursue it rigorously with powerful advocacy and yet at the same time a fine and almost paradoxical combination of humility and nobility. In the Great Hall of Justice, we play only a humble part, but it is precisely such humility that enshrines the nobility of the Great Hall. In the few words of Charles's letter, I again see the great virtue of modesty, a virtue which seems to have paled with many other fine traditions in our community.

---

3. *Ming Pao Newspapers Ltd v Attorney General of Hong Kong* (1996) 6 HKPLR 103; [1996] 2 HKLR 239.

3

A clarification that did not clarify anything

It was 25 February 1999. I still vividly remember that it was a Thursday evening, as the Bar Council had its biweekly meeting at 5 p.m. I had to be in the Legislative Council to attend, on behalf of the Bar, a meeting of the Legal Services and Administration Panel at that time. By the time I arrived at the Bar Council it was already 7 p.m. and the meeting was about to finish.

I had barely taken a seat at the meeting when Ronny Tong SC, the chairman, said to me: 'Johannes, I have one piece of good news and one piece of bad news for you. Which one do you want to know first?'

'Give me the bad news first,' I replied.

'The bad news is that you will appear on behalf of the Bar in the Court of Final Appeal tomorrow.' The Court of Final Appeal had delivered a very controversial judgment in *Ng Ka Ling v Director of Immigration* on 29 January 1999, under which the court held that it had jurisdiction to strike down a decision of the Standing Committee of the National People's Congress for being inconsistent with the Basic Law.[1] This had provoked strong criticism from the Mainland. As a result of immense political pressure, the Director of Immigration decided to make an unprecedented application to the Court of Final Appeal for a clarification of its judgment, whatever that meant, so as 'to allay the worries of some quarters of the community who may not have full understanding of the common law'. The trouble was that the application was made long after the judgment had been delivered. How could the court reopen its judgment after it had been delivered? The Bar decided to intervene in the proceedings to oppose

---

1. *Ng Ka Ling v Director of Immigration* [1999] 1 HKLR 315. In this case, the issue was whether children born in the Mainland to parents who were Hong Kong Permanent Residents could claim a right of abode in Hong Kong after 1 July 1997. In order to stop the arrival of a large number of such claimants, the Provisional Legislative Council amended the Immigration Ordinance on 10 July 1997 to require any such claimant to produce a certificate of entitlement. It was argued that this requirement of a certificate of entitlement was inconsistent with the Basic Law, which had not prescribed such a requirement. An alternative argument was that this additional requirement was introduced by the Provisional Legislative Council, which was not provided for in the Basic Law. It was set up pursuant to a resolution of the Standing Committee of the National People's Congress, and it was argued that this resolution was inconsistent with the Basic Law. This gave rise to the question whether the Hong Kong court could query the legality or constitutionality of a decision of the Standing Committee of the National People's Congress.

the application. Yes, this was a very noble cause, but how many times would one be told to appear before the highest court of the land on less than 15 hours' notice?

'And the good news?' I asked.

'The good news is that you will be led by Clive Grossman SC, and you will have the services of half of the members of the Bar Council tonight!' Clive is one of the most experienced senior counsel specializing in criminal law in Hong Kong. He is an affable and kind gentleman. We had served on the Bar Council together for some time, though our paths had not crossed professionally in court.

The meeting was over with this 'good' news. A few members of the Bar Council kindly stayed behind to help. They included Ambrose Ho (who took silk a year later and was the chairman of the Communications Authority years later) and Godfrey Lam, another very competent junior counsel (who also took silk later and is now Mr Justice Lam of the High Court). One could not have expected more; this was a dream team. We had also arranged to have a solicitor at short notice. Dorothy Siron, a charming lady solicitor who was a year junior to me in the university, kindly turned up at Clive's chambers to help out. Clive had already ordered some fried noodles, and after a few mouthfuls, we rolled up our sleeves and started to work.

We had to divide up the work. Someone would have to look up the law on the substantive issues of when a court could revisit its own judgment after judgment had been delivered (and the court therefore became *functus*). Another team would have to look at the procedural issues, such as whether the Bar had standing to intervene. A further team would have to work with the solicitor to prepare the necessary documentation to be filed in court early the following morning, as well as to give notice to the court and the parties of our intended intervention. We also had a word with Denis Chang SC, who represented Ng Ka Ling at the Court of Final Appeal. Denis thought that this was such an important constitutional issue that it was only right that the Bar should intervene. It was also better that way because, as a party to the proceedings, he had to protect the interest of his client, and this might prevent him from saying much about the government's application for clarification.

By 10 p.m. we had more or less completed our research and had worked out our arguments. By midnight, the skeleton argument was in shape, and bundles of authorities and other necessary papers were prepared. Clive suggested that we should call it a day; it had indeed been a long day for everyone. Even so, without our knowing, he continued to prepare for the case, as all great advocates would do, until he felt he was completely on top of it.

We arrived at the Court of Final Appeal at 9 a.m. the following day. Given the short notice of intervention, there were a lot of procedural matters that had to be attended to by the solicitor. The court was situated at the end of Battery Path, a lovely cobblestone path leading up to the top of a small hill where the court stood next to the formidable St John's Cathedral, only to be overlooked by the dull and grey Central Government Building (now known as Justice Place). The court was housed in a red-brick Victorian building, which used to be a chapel of the French missionaries. Sitting at the top of Battery Path, the court itself overlooked the Central District, the heart of this financial metropolis. At the bottom of the hill, on each of the two sides of the court, stood the Hong Kong Bank and the old Bank of China, representing respectively the British empire of yesterday and the rising master of today. The two banks were separated by a short Banking Street, at the end of which was the then Legislative Council (which was to become the Court of Final Appeal in 2015) and Statue Square, where Queen Victoria's statue once stood, a reminiscence of the colonial era. It was a remarkable thoroughfare, linking the executive, the judiciary, the financial powers, the sovereign, and the legislature all in a straight line, intermingled with the history of over two centuries.

By 9:30 a.m. the court was already packed with eager journalists, concerned lawyers, and curious members of the public. Many lawyers were in the courtroom; many more were outside. The oval-shaped courtroom, though intimate, was originally a chapel and not really designed as a courtroom. The acoustics were horrible, and the courtroom was too small to befit the character of a Court of Final Appeal. Some people managed to squeeze in and grabbed whatever standing room there was in the courtroom. Others squeezed into the public gallery, which was indeed a small side chapel, to watch the proceedings on a television screen. Many more could not get into the courtroom at all and just waited anxiously for the outcome outside.

The hearing began at 10 a.m. after Chief Justice Li, Henry Litton PJ, Charles Ching PJ, Kemal Bokhary PJ, and Anthony Mason NPJ took their seats. Clive Grossman SC rose to make an application for intervention. Soon after he started his submission, he was interrupted by Litton PJ. 'If the Bar has the standing to intervene, so must the Law Society, and there may well be other busybodies too, so where will this end?' asked Litton PJ. It was not in dispute that the Law Society would have the same standing as the Bar, but it remained a fact that neither the Law Society, nor indeed any other body, had applied to intervene in the proceedings. After all, when it came to the rule of law and the jurisdiction of the court, who else other than the Bar (and for that matter, the Law Society) would be best placed and would have better standing and interest to intervene? Clive rose graciously to the challenge and put our case as forcefully and as courteously as he could. After the completion of our submission, the court adjourned for a short while. When it resumed, it declared that the application to intervene was refused and proceeded to hear the government's application for clarification.

The government was represented by Geoffrey Ma SC, a great lawyer who subsequently became the Chief Justice. Geoffrey made a very fair submission in the best tradition of the Bar. He set out his case succinctly without overdoing it. Then it was Denis Chang SC's turn. He stood up and began by saying, 'My Lords, my client has already won the case, and it is my anxious wish that nothing happens today would in any way prejudice the interest of my client. And yet the government's application for clarification raises a most important constitutional issue that goes to the very heart of the independence of the judiciary and the separation of powers.' With this opening, Denis then made a most eloquent and passionate submission why it was wrong for the court to entertain this application. The principle was clear: Once the court had delivered a final judgment, it had no power to reopen or add to or modify the judgment. It was a principle of constitutional importance. So the submission went on. Denis had said everything we wanted to say if our application for intervention had been allowed, and it came out just naturally from him! This was a classic moment of a great lawyer who found himself at the right moment of history, and he rose to the challenge and did what justice and history required of him.

The entire courtroom fell into dead silence after Denis had completed his powerful submission. After a few seconds of silence, the Chief Justice announced that the hearing would be adjourned to the afternoon.

Upon resumption, the court read out a short judgment, which became the well-known Clarification that did not clarify anything.[2] What the government hoped for was that the court would admit that it had no power to question a decision of the National People's Congress or its Standing Committee. The court's reply was a qualified 'yes'. In a short judgment, the court repeated four times that it could not question and its judgment did not question the authority of the National People's Congress or the Standing Committee—but authority to do what? To do 'anything that is in accordance with the Basic Law'! This was almost like stating the obvious: The court would not and did not question their decision so long as it was consistent with the Basic Law. The court just stopped short of saying that it would not question their act or decision if such act or decision were *not* in accordance with the Basic Law! Despite this ambivalence, the clarification moderated, for a short time, the pressure from across the border, as the very act of clarification was taken to mean that the court admitted that it had no jurisdiction to strike down any decision or act of the sovereign. The peace was, however, short-lived, and four months later, the Standing Committee of the National People's Congress adopted an interpretation of the Basic Law that had the effect of reversing the judgment of the Court of Final Appeal in *Ng Ka Ling*.[3]

Nonetheless, although we had lost our case, the feeling could not have been better when we walked out of the Court of Final Appeal that afternoon. At the very least, we had done our best to answer the calling of our profession: to defend the rule of law, a fundamental and honourable duty that falls on any member of the legal profession.

In accordance with Article 158 of the Basic Law, the clarification does not 'affect judgments previously rendered'. The meaning of this phrase led to another round of litigation, as there were over 5,000 children in positions similar to that of the applicants in *Ng Ka Ling*, which comprised only four representative cases that had been chosen as test cases for litigation. The second round of litigation resulted in another leading judgment of the Court of Final Appeal on substantive legitimate expectation.[4] Of the four test cases in *Ng Ka Ling*, one of the applicants was Tam Nga Yin, who was

---

2. *Ng Ka Ling v Director of Immigration (No 2)* (1999) 2 HKCFAR 141.
3. The Interpretation was reproduced in J. M. M. Chan, H. L Fu, and Y. Ghai (eds.), *Hong Kong's Constitutional Debate: Conflict over Interpretation* (Hong Kong: Hong Kong University Press, 2000), 478.
4. *Ng Siu Tung v Director of Immigration* (2002) 5 HKCFAR 1.

later admitted to the Faculty of Law of the University of Hong Kong. I do not know what has happened to the other three applicants, but the last time I met Tam Nga Yin was at our congregation ceremony when I read out her name for the conferral of the law degree.

III

Public Interest: Whose Interests?

4

David v Goliath

Reclamation of Victoria Harbour

This is a story about the workings of the law and the government in Hong Kong, about what is at stake in big infrastructure projects where multimillion-dollar interests are involved and—in the end—about how much can nonetheless be achieved by a stubborn individual determined to protect the environment that we all treasure.

> He [Dunross, the protagonist] stared out of the window at the gardens and at the vast northern panorama of city and seascape below. Ships and junks and sampans dotted the azure sea. There was a fine sky above and no promise of rain weather, the summer monsoon steady from the southwest and he wondered absently what the clippers had looked like as they sailed before the wind or beat up against the winds in his ancestors' time. (James Clavell, *Noble House*, 156)

This was how we started our written submission before the Court of First Instance in the remarkable harbour case. It all began on the day I got a call from Winston Chu, a successful solicitor and a long-time friend for whom I have great respect. He asked if I could help with a cause that would probably be unpopular and be counsel in a case that, as he described it, would be a 'David v Goliath attempt'. While his firm would be the instructing solicitors, he would technically be a client this time, acting in his capacity as chairman of the Society for Protection of the Harbour.

When I was a young student in Hong Kong, we learned that Victoria Harbour was known as a 'deep and wide harbour' (水深港闊) that provided a safe haven for generations of ocean-going vessels. Beyond that, the harbour was just a stretch of waters between Hong Kong Island and the Kowloon Peninsula. For those of us who lived most of our early lives on the Kowloon Peninsula, crossing the harbour was an exciting event (as exciting as taking the coal-fuelled train to Sha Tin for a school picnic)! Before the construction of the Cross-Harbour Tunnel, the Star Ferry was the major mode of transport across the harbour, and when the ferry ceased service after midnight, small dinghies called 'wala-wala' were available but at a far higher fare. To the government, for more than a century Victoria Harbour served as a convenient source of land supply. It may be difficult for younger readers to imagine, but Cheung Sha Wan, Hung Hom, To Kwa Wan, Causeway Bay, Tsuen Wan Bay, the old Kai Tak Airport, Gin Drinkers Bay, and Kwun Tong were all once part of Victoria Harbour, and they emerged from the sea between 1946 and 1967. The original coastline of Hong Kong Island was

Wan Chai and Victoria Harbour in 1920. Courtesy of the Society for Protection of the Harbour Ltd. and Winston Chu.

along Queen's Road and Hennessy Road. The Kowloon Peninsula has doubled in size through reclamation, and nearly all the islands in the harbour were reclaimed when the coastline on both sides extended into the waters. By 1984, almost half of the original Victoria Harbour had gone, though largely unnoticed, without any public debate or consultation.

The very name and *raison d'être* of Hong Kong is its harbour. Victoria Harbour has been celebrated in the literature of many nations since the nineteenth century. As a gift of nature, the harbour guarded the origin of the settlement of the fishing community in the nineteenth century, and it is now the heart of a world financial centre. It has witnessed the transformation of Hong Kong from a 'barren rock' to a thriving and prosperous metropolis over the last 160 years. Whether at times of turmoil and great uncertainty or at times of economic prosperity and stability, the harbour has always been associated with Hong Kong which, literally translated, means 'fragrant' (香) 'harbour' (港).

In 1994, the Town Planning Board put forward a plan for extensive reclamation. According to this paper, 661 hectares of the harbour area were in the process of reclamation or committed to reclamation, and a further 636 hectares were planned for reclamation.[1] Under these proposals, areas in West Kowloon, Green Island, Hung Hom Bay, Central, Wan Chai, and Aldrich Bay were to be reclaimed. Indeed, the channel between Green Island and Aberdeen, which is one of the busiest channels in the region and the main waterway to Macau and many outlying islands, was to be filled up to build a new residential estate. The whole of the harbour to the west of the Star Ferry

---

1. One hectare is equivalent to 10,000 square metres or about 107,000 square feet.

The narrowest part of the harbour is only about 800 metres: The 'Victoria River', as described by Kate Winslet. Courtesy of the Society for Protection of the Harbour Ltd. and Winston Chu.

in Kowloon was to be reclaimed so that the whole of Ocean Terminal would become inland. To the east of Star Ferry, a straight line was drawn to Lei Yue Mun, so that Tsim Sha Tsui East, Hung Hom Bay, and all of Kowloon Bay up to the end of Kai Tak Airport runway would be filled up. On Hong Kong Island, the whole of the coastline between Hong Kong and Macau Ferry and North Point would be pushed into the harbour by 300 metres, and everything, including the Tamar Naval Basin and the Causeway Bay Typhoon Shelter, would be reclaimed. The end result would be that the width of the entire Victoria Harbour would be reduced by half to become a channel of about 800 metres and 1,000 metres. Victoria Harbour would become Victoria River, as Kate Winslet, the famous Hollywood star, called it (mistakenly but well intended) on her visit to Hong Kong! The idea of Hong Kong as a deep and wide harbour would forever be consigned to history.

Winston, who was on the Town Planning Board, was shocked when he came across this Town Planning Board paper. Together with the Hon. Christine Loh, then the director of Civic Exchange, a private think tank, they formed the Society for Protection of the Harbour, a non-governmental organization with the objective of protecting the harbour from further excessive reclamation. After Christine was appointed to the Legislative Council by the last governor, Chris Patten, she managed to get through the Protection of the Harbour Ordinance as a private member's bill in 1996, in order to protect not the harbour but what was left of the harbour. The ordinance came into effect on 30 June 1997. Shortly after the changeover, the government attempted unsuccessfully to suspend the ordinance. Section 3 of the ordinance provides for a presumption against reclamation in Victoria Harbour.

One day when Winston was taking his mother on the Star Ferry and told her about the government's massive reclamation plan, she said to him, 'You must do something about this.' Without her knowing it, her wish sparked a series of litigations between Winston and the government about the harbour, spanning the following two decades.

Central–Wan Chai Bypass

The opportunity arose when the Town Planning Board published the draft Wan Chai North Outline Zoning Plan (Wan Chai North OZP) in April 2002. The government had long been considering constructing a Central–Wan Chai Bypass to ease traffic congestion in the Central and Wan Chai areas. The bypass would allow direct east–west traffic without having to go into the heart of Central or Wan Chai. It would start from around Rumsey Street in Central, then go underground along the harbour via the then Star Ferry, the Convention Centre, and then come up above ground in Wan Chai North to link to the Eastern Corridor. The project fell within two planning zones: Central and Wan Chai North, the Convention Centre as the dividing point. The part from Central to the western side of the Convention Centre fell within the Central Outline Zoning Plan (Central OZP). The Draft Wan Chai North OZP, which covered the Wan Chai section of the bypass and ran from the eastern part of the Convention Centre to Causeway Bay Typhoon Shelter, proposed to reclaim about 26 hectares of land from the harbour along the Wan Chai Harbour front. The design could be further divided into two major zones: the Convention and Exhibition Zone and the Causeway Bay Waterfront Zone. In the Causeway Bay Waterfront Zone, it was proposed to reclaim 52 per cent of the existing Causeway Bay Typhoon Shelter. An area outside the existing breakwater would also be reclaimed for a harbour park of 2.8 hectares. As a result of the loss of mooring areas within the shelter due to reclamation, it was also proposed that a new breakwater be built, to create a new mooring area to replace the existing Causeway Bay Typhoon Shelter.

In the Convention and Exhibition Zone, the reclaimed land to the north of the World Trade Centre was to be zoned as 'Commercial' for hotel use. A site located to the north of Harbour Road and west of Wan Chai Sports Ground was zoned as Comprehensive Development Areas. Other areas of the proposed reclamation were zoned for various uses, including Open Space (O), Government Institution or Community (GIC), Comprehensive Development Area (CDA), and Other Specified Uses (OU). An exhibition hall and a harbour museum were envisaged.

The manner of adoption of the Wan Chai North OZP was most interesting and gave a valuable insight into how public decisions were made in Hong Kong. A first draft was published for consultation. As the bypass would create a significant amount of land, various organizations put forward suggestions for its use. Among them, the Convention Centre proposed to extend the Convention Centre, claiming that exhibition business was of crucial importance to the economic development of Hong Kong and that there was a scarcity of exhibition venues in the urban area. This was accepted

Proposed reclamation as set out in Plan Ref No. S/H25/1. Source: Legislative Council Archives of Hong Kong Special Administrative Region, Panel on Planning, Lands and Works, LC Paper CB1/1570/01-02: Wan Chai North Outline Zoning Plan No S/H25/1. Courtesy of the Society for Protection of the Harbour Ltd. and Winston Chu.

by the Town Planning Board, and a massive structure appeared in the amended OZP. Various objections were then lodged against the height of the proposed extension, notably by major land developers who owned skyscrapers with unabated sea views along the harbour front. In order to meet these objections without reducing the floor areas of the proposed extension of the Convention Centre, the only solution was to protrude the reclamation further into the harbour. A promenade was proposed to allow pedestrians to stroll along the harbour front. Some people then suggested that it would be nice to have shops along the promenade (as Hong Kong people enjoy shopping), and in order to accommodate these commercial activities, the promenade would have to be widened into the harbour. What started as an exercise to provide land to meet a public need for a road system to alleviate the choking traffic of Hong Kong Island North had been turned into an exercise to supply artificial amenities and development along the waterfront under the pretext of 'optimal land use'.

The proposal for the Harbour Park was even more interesting. It was inserted at the insistence of the chairman of the Town Planning Board with a view to bringing people to the harbour, though ironically with highly restricted access, since this tiny harbour park was to be built on reclaimed land around the existing breakwater of the Causeway Bay Typhoon Shelter. Visitors would have to cross two busy highways to get to Harbour Park; and in cases of emergency, fire engines and ambulances might have difficulty getting to the park. Neither the Hong Kong Tourist Association nor the Wan Chai District Council found the idea attractive. Yet Harbour Park was inserted, probably as a precedent, in the OZP without any feasibility study or environmental impact assessment.

Winston decided that the excessive reclamation in the OZP would provide a good test case to establish the principles underlying the case for the protection of the harbour. He soon lined up a formidable legal team. Anthony Neoh SC (who later became chairman of the Securities and Futures Commission) was instructed to lead the team. An able junior barrister, Jin Pao, joined us later. Winston also enlisted the assistance of Professor Malcolm Grant QC, a prominent London silk who later became president of University College London and then the chair of the National Health Service of the United Kingdom. Malcolm was later appointed to our University Grants Committee. In 2016, he chaired a review panel on the governance of the University of Hong Kong, and his report, which was known to be fairly critical of the university governance structure, was effectively shelved. Our instructing solicitors, including Jeff Tse and Toby Lo, two very able partners, and Dennis Li, an assistant solicitor of Winston's firm, were most impressive. Jeff, the leader of the solicitors' team, was a few years senior to me in law school. I worked closely with his wife, who is also a solicitor, in my early days of practice on many heartbreaking immigration cases. The solicitor team worked extremely hard and made a most valuable contribution to the preparation of the case, but it was their dedication, professionalism, and enthusiasm that impressed me most. As the case involved a fair amount of geotechnical knowledge, an engineering consultant was also engaged.

The legal battle

At the outset, we made a few decisions to define the boundary of the litigation. First, while the bypass was to run through both the Central OZP and the Wan Chai North OZP and both plans were approved by the same Town Planning Board, we decided to concentrate on the Wan Chai section first in order to keep the litigation within a manageable scale, especially in costs. Any legal principles that we managed to establish would apply equally to the Central section. Secondly, our objection was not to the bypass; we accepted that there was a strong public interest to justify reclamation for this purpose. Instead, our concern was the excessive amount of reclamation that was not necessary for the construction of the bypass. Harbour Park was the most vulnerable part of the Wan Chai North OZP and would be a convenient and easy target to establish our case. Thirdly, the Protection of the Harbour Ordinance created a rebuttable presumption against reclamation; that is to say, it established that there should in general be no reclamation of the harbour, unless a sufficiently strong case was made to override this presumption against reclamation. Given the importance and the value of the harbour, we would argue that the presumption against reclamation could only be rebutted by compelling public interest, and the extent of reclamation would have to be proportionate to the achievement of such public interest. In running this argument, we had to overcome two hurdles. The first was to establish the value of the harbour. Tony decided that the best way to achieve this was to present the harbour and successive reclamation of the harbour over the years in a series of video slides. He was involved in producing an animated film and would be able to make use of the expertise in that project. The Judiciary had just set up a Technology Court at that time, and we distinguished ourselves by being the first team to make use of it.

The second hurdle was more technical. There was no reference in the ordinance on how the presumption against reclamation could be rebutted. We tried to introduce the concept of proportionality, but this concept was mainly developed in human rights law. I was responsible for this part of the submission and tried to marry international law on sustainability with human rights law on proportionality. I had done a few drafts, but none was satisfactory. On a Sunday afternoon, I decided to walk around the harbour to get some inspiration. The part of the harbour along Hung Hing Road had long been used for loading and unloading goods. We were probably the only city in the world in which the most scenic part of the harbour was used for cargo loading! Further east, the rock on which the Yacht Club stood was the only remaining natural shoreline. The Typhoon Shelter was full of luxurious private yachts. I had never tried the seafood in the shelter, as it appears to me that the idea of dining on waters was more attractive than the food. The Noon Day Gun, a lonely cannon on the edge of the shelter, looked rather out of place. Further east towards Electricity Road, the waters were murky and filthy, partly because it was a dead-water corner with little current. To be honest, while I enjoyed the presence of the harbour, I did not feel a strong affinity to it. There were some seagulls around, and with the light of the setting sun shimmering on the waters, it created a rather odd but picturesque setting. There was some quiet tidal movement, which meant it did not have to be a dead-water corner. Indeed, given the opportunity, nature was perfectly capable of rejuvenating itself. It struck me at that point that this was just what sustainability was about.

The walk that afternoon turned out to be quite inspiring after all. It changed my perception of the harbour. I completed the submission that evening.

The first instance hearing

The hearing took place before Madam Justice Carlye Chu, a most courteous and able judge who was later appointed to the Court of Appeal.[2] Tony, with his usual eloquence, made a most impressive submission. The video slides, starting with a nostalgic view of the harbour in the late nineteenth century, conveyed powerfully just how the harbour had been treated as a convenient source of land supply and what the landscape would look like once the draft Wan Chai North OZP had been implemented. Robert Tang SC (a most able counsel who later became a judge of the Court of Final Appeal) presented a convincing case for the government. The ordinance created a rebuttable presumption, not a prohibition, against reclamation. All public officers need to take this presumption into account, and this had been done. However, the presumption could be rebutted if there were competing public interests. The weight of competing factors was a matter for the government; the court should not intervene unless the decision of the government was one that no reasonable officer would have reached. As long as the reclamation was to serve some important public needs, the court, it was argued, should not descend into details and inquire into the needs of each component of the project. Our reply was that this classic principle of review over administrative action had no application here. The legislature had conferred a special status on the harbour, describing it as a special asset and a natural heritage of the people of Hong Kong. Thus, any attempt to rebut the presumption against reclamation had to be commensurate with this special status. It could only be overridden by a compelling public need which was present and urgent and which could not be met by any reasonable alternative means. The reclamation had to be restricted to the minimum that was necessary to achieve the overriding need, and each part of the reclamation would have to be individually justified. The court agreed with our submission and found in our favour.

Alongside the legal battle inside the courtroom, an equally vigorous campaign to protect the harbour had been launched, thanks to the efforts of Christine Loh. Various successful rallies were organized, and the harbour gradually caught the attention of the public. A yellow ribbon campaign was launched. Supporters of the protection of the harbour were urged to tie a yellow ribbon along the harbour front, and within weeks, a line of yellow ribbons ran from Wan Chai to Central. The harbour was not just a stretch of waters. It embraced the history of Hong Kong and was perhaps the single

---

2. *Society for Protection of the Harbour Ltd v Town Planning Board* [2003] 2 HKLRD 787.

most prominent symbol of the territory. This tarnished jewel had finally become bright and alive again and re-established its special status and significance among the people of Hong Kong.

Legal costs in public interest litigation

A notable feature of civil litigation is the rule that costs follow event. This means that the losing party is responsible for the legal costs of the winning party. Legal costs refer to the expenses incurred by the party in preparing for the litigation, including the legal fees paid to lawyers and expert consultants. This rule presents a major stumbling block to public interest litigation. While an individual or organization might be able to retain lawyers to provide free legal services for a worthwhile cause of great public importance, they would still face the risk of being liable for a substantial bill for the legal fees of the other side if the case was lost. At the same time, even if the case is won, the winner won't be able to recover all of the costs. Legal costs are awarded under different scales. This means that in general the winning party can only recover about 60–70 per cent of the costs incurred, unless the court is prepared to award costs on a more generous scale.

In this case we had stacks (over a foot high) of engineering consultant reports from the government. We had to rely on our own engineering consultant to help us to plough through the technical data and to prepare our own expert report in reply. Winston had to finance the litigation by himself. After judgment was delivered, we decided to ask the court to award legal costs on the most generous basis, given that the litigation was taken out to advance a matter of considerable public interest with no private gain. Our application was successful. The court laid down important principles on the circumstances under which it would be prepared to order full indemnity costs. These principles, which were subsequently endorsed by the Court of Final Appeal, set up a milestone for the development of public interest litigation.

Leapfrog procedure

With our triumph against the Wan Chai North OZP, we thought the government would cease and reconsider the scale of reclamation in the Central section between the Star Ferry and the western side of the Convention Centre. Quite to the contrary, while the litigation on the Wan Chai section was ongoing, reclamation work on the Central section was expedited. After the judgment of Madam Justice Chu was delivered, the government decided to appeal. As a major public project would now be considerably delayed (at least for the Wan Chai section), both sides agreed to invoke the 'leapfrog procedure' to appeal directly to the Court of Final Appeal, bypassing the Court of Appeal. The leapfrog procedure is a special procedure which may be invoked under certain circumstances, and one of the requirements is that both sides have to agree to it. Both sides considered that this was a sensible approach, and this case became the first and, as far as I am aware, the only case so far that has successfully invoked this procedure, as the government has since consistently refused to give consent to its use.

Caught between the devil and the deep blue sea

The government was gravely concerned about the delay in the completion of the bypass. As soon as leave to apply for judicial review was granted in relation to the Wan Chai section, the government was determined to expedite the reclamation process, so that by the time the judgment was delivered, the reclamation would have gone too far to be reversed and the judgment would only be a paper victory. Instead of holding up reclamation on the Central section, the government expedited it. The tendering process for public works was completed within a remarkably short time, and dredging work commenced within weeks of the completion of tender. Such efficiency was almost unheard of! Unfortunately, in acting like this the government had failed to comply with certain fairness requirements in the tendering process as stipulated by the World Trade Organization (WTO), to which Hong Kong is an independent member. The WTO has a dispute settlement procedure among members. A tendering party that was not awarded a contract decided to complain to a WTO panel, and the panel eventually adjudicated in favour of that party. That put the government in an awkward position. A normal remedy would have been to set aside the tendering process and to start all over again, but this would defeat the purpose of expediting the tendering process in the first place. The other remedy was to buy off the losing party, which not surprisingly saw fit to demand a ransom as compensation. Rumour had it that the government chose to settle with a very handsome compensation, the amount of which remains confidential.

The Court of Final Appeal and the Harbourfront Authority

The hearing before the Court of Final Appeal was basically a re-run of the arguments at the court below.[3] Robert Tang SC accepted that the presumption against reclamation in section 3 of the ordinance was a material, weighty, and compulsory consideration in any resumption, and that any public officer must perform a weighing exercise to balance the public needs for reclamation and the presumption. He also accepted that there must exist a substantial reason in favour of reclamation but argued that whether the reason was weighty enough to override the presumption was a matter for the executive government alone to decide. The Court of Final Appeal rejected this argument as a matter of statutory intention. Its description of the harbour, which set the tone of the judgment, is worth quoting in full:

---

3.   *Town Planning Board v Society for Protection of the Harbour* (2004) 7 HKCFAR 1.

33. As was observed at the outset, the harbour is undoubtedly a central part of Hong Kong's identity. It is at the heart of the metropolis both physically and metaphorically. The statute characterizes this in the most distinctive terms. It is recognized not merely as a public asset but as a 'special' one. It is something extraordinary. The recognition does not stop there. It is further acknowledged to be a natural heritage. 'Natural' in that it was not created artificially by man but is part of nature. A 'heritage' in that it is inherited as a legacy from previous generations and is to be transmitted from generation to generation. The harbour as a special public asset and natural heritage is declared to belong to Hong Kong people. This reinforces its character as a 'public' asset. It is a community asset and as such, is to be enjoyed by the people of Hong Kong. By representing the harbour in such special terms in the statute, the legislature was giving legal recognition to its unique character.

34. It is because of its unique character that the harbour must be protected and preserved. The meaning of these words in the statutory principle is plain. There must be protection, that is, it must be kept from harm, defended and guarded. And there must be not merely protection. There must also be preservation. Preservation connotes maintenance and conservation in its present state. What must be emphasized is that under the principle, what is to be protected and preserved is the harbour as a special public asset and a natural heritage of Hong Kong people.

On the basis of the statutory recognition of the unique character of the harbour, the court developed a number of principles governing reclamation of the harbour. The presumption against reclamation could only be rebutted when there was an overriding public need for reclamation. The public need would be overriding only when it was a present and compelling need. Such need went beyond what was desirable, preferable, or beneficial and must arise within a definite and reasonable time frame. An overriding need would not be made out if there were reasonable alternatives. The burden of proof rests on those who tried to rebut the presumption, and the burden would only be discharged by producing cogent and persuasive evidence. Mere incantation that there was an overriding need for reclamation without substantiating the claim by evidence would not be sufficient.

This landmark judgment, which represented a major triumph in the protection of the harbour, has effectively halted the reclamation in the Wan Chai section. The government was forced to go back to the drawing board to reconsider the extent of reclamation. By now the community was far more conscious of the need to protect and preserve the harbour. The extent of reclamation was significantly reduced. A Harbourfront Enhancement Committee, which was later turned into a statutory body, was appointed to provide better planning for the harbour front. New standards and guidelines were promulgated. A number of earlier proposals for harbour reclamation were shelved or abandoned, and since then the government has practically given up any attempt to do further reclamation within Victoria Harbour (but not outside Victoria Harbour). As foreshadowed in the Good Book, David has won the battle.

All that sounds well and good, but how about the Central section of the bypass?

The Central reclamation

It will be recalled that, instead of ceasing the reclamation work in Central after the judgment of Madam Justice Chu was delivered, the government indeed expedited the reclamation work. An application for an interim injunction failed, as the government successfully argued that what it was doing was only the early phase of a reclamation that could still be reversed and that it would have to pay a heavy daily penalty to the construction company if the reclamation work were suspended. But as time passed, the reclamation became far from reversible. Thus, Winston was forced to start another legal battle.

The effect of the judgment of Madam Justice Chu was that the Town Planning Board had applied the wrong test in approving the reclamation. She held that the draft Wan Chai North OZP should be remitted to the Town Planning Board for reconsideration. While her judgment was directed at the Wan Chai section of the bypass, it must apply equally to the Central section, as it was the same bypass. The decision of the Town Planning Board should likewise be tainted by the error.

The Central OZP had already been approved by the Chief Executive in Council. Instead of remitting the OZP to the Town Planning Board for reconsideration, the Chief Executive in Council took it upon itself to reconsider the OZP in light of the judgment of Madam Justice Chu. It also engaged an academic consultant to advise the government. The conclusion was that, notwithstanding the mistaken test adopted by the Town Planning Board, the Central OZP could still be supported by applying the correct test as propounded by the judgment of Madam Justice Chu. So, upon reconsideration, the Chief Executive in Council decided that no change to the Central OZP was required and the reclamation work could proceed.

This so-called reconsideration by the Chief Executive in Council looked artificial and was far from convincing. Yet, as a result of these manoeuvres, this part of the litigation took a very different turn. Instead of determining whether the government had applied the correct test in approving reclamation, the issue now became whether there was sufficient reason to challenge the decision of the Chief Executive in Council, which had applied the correct test, in refusing to remit the Central OZP to the Town Planning Board for reconsideration. This was a far more difficult challenge. The hearing took place shortly after the Court of Final Appeal had rendered its judgment in relation to the Wan Chai section, and the challenge was rejected by Mr Justice Hartmann.[4]

An embarrassing moment

The Wan Chai Harbour case was important in many ways. It was the first case to use the Technology Court. It was the first case to lay down important principles for the protection of the harbour. It was the first case to invoke the leapfrog procedure on

---

4. *Society for Protection of the Harbour Ltd v Chief Executive in Council* [2004] 2 HKLRD 902.

appeal to the Court of Final Appeal, and it was the first case to lay down far-reaching principles on the award of indemnity cost in public interest litigation. It was also a case of specific significance to me personally.

On the last day of the hearing before Madam Justice Chu, the Chief Justice announced the appointment of new silks. I was among them and became the first Honorary Senior Counsel in Hong Kong. The appointment came as a surprise. One day I received an unexpected phone call from the Chief Justice, who told me that he was considering conferring on me the title of Honorary Senior Counsel and asked if I would accept it. How could one possibly decline? It is a great honour, and in the great tradition of the Bar, it also comes with a great responsibility to uphold and defend the rule of law.

Then came the Central reclamation case. As our team was then focusing on the litigation on the Wan Chai section, Winston had instructed Mok Yeuk Chi as counsel, with me as his junior counsel, to take charge of this part of the litigation. Mo Chi, as he is generally known, is a cheerful and a most competent counsel, who was among the first batch of graduates from the law school. Both Mo Chi and his wife, Lucy Yen, are my good friends. I have worked closely with Lucy, a charming solicitor, who was once the chair of the HKU Law Alumni Association, succeeding Kenneth Kwok SC, who is a chamber mate of Mo Chi. I learned a lot from Mo Chi from his meticulous preparation for the case. However, when the case came up for hearing before Mr Justice Hartmann, I had just taken silk. Traditionally the silk should be the leader, but it would have been very awkward for me to lead Mo Chi when he had all along been the leader. To save me from embarrassment, Mo Chi quietly assumed the role of leader in addressing the court.[5] He made a most eloquent opening that I do not think I could have matched. But then, even more embarrassingly, Mr Justice Hartmann, in his judgment, kindly referred to me as the leading counsel!

The Tamar Base

The reclamation work in Central ran through the former Tamar Naval Base. This former British base was delivered to the People's Liberation Army under the Joint Declaration. Apparently, it was agreed between the People's Liberation Army and the Hong Kong government that the Tamar Pier would be retained for use by the army. This would mean that the portion of the reclaimed harbour around the Tamar Pier would not be accessible to the public. This agreement was not reflected in the Central OZP. The Society for Protection of the Harbour objected to the provision for the army, arguing that there were alternatives available which would allow public access to an unbroken harbour front and still let the army retain the use of the Pier whenever it

---

5. Under the Bar's Code of Conduct, a Senior Counsel may, within a year of taking silk, continue to act as a junior in a civil suit where he was instructed as a junior before he took silk: Annex 6, para 8(b)(ii), becoming para 6.23(b)(ii) after 20 July 2017.

was necessary. But the parties failed to settle their disagreement, and in 2015, Winston found that he had to assume the role of David again and took the government to court.

Epilogue

In early 2017, on a social occasion Winston told me that the judicial review relating to the Tamar base was ongoing. It has been almost 20 years since Winston first engaged in litigation to protect the harbour. It is due to his persistence and relentless efforts that the harbour was finally preserved. As a result, in the years to come, the people of Hong Kong will continue to be able to enjoy this pristine harbour. I used to jog along the harbour promenade from Siu Sai Wan to North Point in the early morning. It always occurs to me how nice it would be if we could stroll along the harbour from east to west. This would no doubt be the dream of Winston. To the government, Winston is branded as a troublemaker (which is probably an honour!). He has done all he could to protect the harbour and in so doing may well have disturbed the vested interests of the powerful and the dubious. He has even received threats to his personal safety from unknown people. Yet he has stood firm on his principles all these years and has devoted himself selflessly to an important public cause. According to the old Good Book, David has won the battle against Goliath. What the old Good Book does not say is that the battle lasted for more than 20 years, and the stubborn David won it only at great personal cost. To Winston, my dear old friend, I take my hat off!

5

The most misunderstood case

The Zhuhai Bridge case

Few cases have been so badly misunderstood as the one known as the 'Zhuhai Bridge case'.[1] This case has been criticized as an abuse of judicial process and was blamed for being a major factor contributing to the substantially increased construction cost of the bridge. In his blistering public lecture on abuse of judicial process delivered in the winter of 2015, Professor Henry Litton, a former judge of the Court of Final Appeal, characterized the case as a non-starter and expressed his amazement at how the case could even have reached the Court of Appeal!

When Henry retired from the Court of Final Appeal, I invited him to join the Faculty of Law at the University of Hong Kong as an honorary professor, so that he could share his wealth of legal knowledge and experience with our students. It is a great good fortune for our students to be able to learn from such an eminent jurist. His office was just next to mine, and we spent quite a few afternoons discussing this case over coffee before his public lecture. Henry is a strong believer in brevity and clarity. He even set up an annual Bluebell Prize in the Faculty: an award for students who could rewrite a selected judgment in clear, concise, and comprehensible language. As I understand it, part of his misgivings about this case concerned the pages and pages of consideration of technical information in the judgment, making it almost incomprehensible so that, as a result, it missed the real issue. 'How could anyone even start to understand a judgment like that? How could anyone challenge an environmental impact assessment in 2031? There are so many variables in the future. We don't even know what the technology will be like by then, and technological changes are sure to affect the reliability of the environmental impact assessment,' Henry explained in his lecture. 'These are not matters for the court. How could the court even entertain such a challenge? This is a clear case of an abuse of judicial process.'

'But Henry, wait a minute, the applicant won at first instance!'

'And that lost me completely!'

I tried to offer my explanation of the case as best I could, but, not surprisingly, Henry was not convinced. Finally, he challenged me to explain that judgment in simple terms. So let me try here.

---

1. *Chu Yee Wah v Director of Environmental Protection* [2011] HKEC 555 (CFI); [2011] 5 HKLRD 469 (CA).

As its name implies, the bridge is a major project that links Hong Kong, Macau, and Zhuhai. The bridge runs through some environmentally sensitive areas in Hong Kong, and over the years it has caused a lot of concern among environmentalists. The applicant was a resident in the area where the Hong Kong section of the bridge was constructed. She argued, among other things, that the government had failed to carry out properly the environmental impact assessment of the project.

The government had chosen the year 2031 as the relevant year for assessment, as it was projected that by then the volume of traffic on the bridge would be at its peak. The government conducted an environmental impact assessment by estimating the number of air pollutants at that time and found that the level of air pollutants was within an acceptable level. This finding was not challenged.

As Justice Fok pointed out, the court was not concerned with the wisdom of the decision to construct the bridge. Nor was this a case about the adequacy of the air quality objectives that were in force in Hong Kong. It was not the function of the court to determine government policy. The role of the court was to ensure that government policies were formulated in accordance with the law and carried out within a proper legal framework.

Likewise, the case was not about whether the choice of the year 2031 or the adoption of the particular air pollution indicators in the study was appropriate, or whether the assessment of air pollution in 2031 was reliable. These were matters for the executive government. The court should not intervene unless the decision was one that no reasonable government could reasonably have reached in the circumstances—the so-called *Wednesbury* unreasonable threshold. The applicant was nowhere near establishing *Wednesbury* unreasonableness regarding these issues.

Unfortunately, the judgment was far too often criticized for what it was not about.

The only substantive issue in this case was about the standard of duty of the government in minimizing adverse environmental impact. Would the government have discharged its duty so long as the pollution level of the bridge did not exceed the prescribed limit, or whether it has to further ensure that the pollution was kept to the minimum? The applicant argued for the latter. In order to consider whether the government had discharged its duty to minimize adverse environmental impact, the applicant argued that it was necessary to consider the situation in which there was no bridge—the so-called stand-alone assessment. Only when you knew of the starting point could you then compare and consider if the adverse environmental impact of constructing a bridge had been kept to the minimum. The mere fact that the end product did not exceed the acceptable level of environmental pollution was not sufficient to show *minimum* adverse environmental impact. The environment was not to be treated as a bucket of pollutants and waste, which could be filled up to a given level. It was argued that the requirement of a stand-alone assessment was indeed set out in the relevant planning documents that guided the conduct of any environmental impact assessment (namely the Technical Memorandum, which applied generally, and the Environmental Impact Assessment Study Brief, which applied to the specific project concerned).

The government disagreed and argued that there was no duty in law or in the relevant planning documents to do a stand-alone assessment. It further argued that environmental impact assessment was about a process, not about a particular philosophy or approach to protecting the environment. In any event, it was argued that the government could discharge its duty to minimize adverse environmental impact without a stand-alone assessment.

It was not in dispute that the government has a duty to comply with the relevant planning documents, in particular the Technical Memorandum which set out the principles, procedures, and requirements for the project. One of the requirements of these documents was that the project proponent was obliged to ensure that measures would be taken to reduce pollution to a minimum.

Once it was established that there was a duty to reduce pollution to a minimum, which was agreed by both the Court of First Instance and the Court of Appeal, the remaining question was whether this duty could be discharged without conducting a stand-alone assessment. The legislation was silent on this question, so its answer would be dependent on what the planning documents required. The Court of First Instance and the Court of Appeal differed in their interpretation of what these voluminous documents required, and that explained the two different outcomes. Mr Justice Fok, the trial judge who later became a judge of our Court of Final Appeal, found that, on a proper construction, the documents did require a stand-alone environmental impact assessment, and since this had not been done, the government had failed to discharge its duty and the project could not proceed until this requirement had been complied with. The government appealed and asked for an expedited hearing. Four months later, the Court of Appeal reversed his decision.

Stripped of the analysis of all the technical documents, this is essentially what this case was about. The short question before the court was whether the government has a duty, under the law or the planning documents which were accepted to be binding on the government, to carry out a stand-alone assessment in order to discharge its duty to ensure that the construction of the bridge would minimize environmental pollution. It is a legitimate question, the resolution of which would depend on the construction of the relevant documents. It is difficult to understand the view that there was an abuse of process, when the applicant had successfully convinced the Court of First Instance that the government was under such a duty and had failed to discharge this duty. It is true that the result took a toll on the general revenue, as the construction cost had (allegedly) been increased substantially beyond the original budget. The critics said that the litigation, which was eventually dismissed, had cost the taxpayers HK$8 billion. Yet it is not clear that the increase in construction cost could be wholly or substantially attributed to the litigation. The construction work was halted only after the government had lost the case before the Court of First Instance. The appeal proceeded with great expedition. The Court of Appeal reversed the decision within four months and the project was resumed. It is difficult to see how the construction cost could be increased by HK$8 billion within a short period of four months (or a loss of HK$67 million per day). The more likely explanation is that the litigation was merely taken as the convenient scapegoat and excuse for a poorly managed project that has resulted in substantially inflated construction costs. And yet, unfortunately, rumours repeated a hundred times may well become the truth.

Dennis Kwok, the junior counsel representing the applicant in this case, was a member of the Civic Party. Dennis was later elected to the Legislative Council as the representative of the legal functional constituency. As a result of Dennis's political affiliation, some people said that the Civic Party was behind the case and that it was all about political manoeuvring! Although Dennis explained that he was simply the counsel for the applicant and the case had nothing to do with the Civic Party, the allegation continued to spin. The critics could not understand that an advocate does not have to identify himself with the cause of his client in order to represent that client. Otherwise, nobody charged with a criminal offence would be able to get any legal representation!

6

Defending an unpopular cause

The social welfare case

Do you know what we call opinion in the absence of evidence? We call it prejudice.
—Michael Crichton, *State of Fear* (2004)

It is difficult to change personal prejudice; it is next to impossible to change social prejudice, for whatever form of prejudice it is, it exists beyond reason and rationality.

Madam Kong was a Mainland resident. She was married to Mr Chan Wing, a Hong Kong permanent resident, in October 2003. In November 2005, she was granted a one-way permit to join her husband and settle in Hong Kong. She arrived in Hong Kong on 21 December 2005, a few days before Christmas, and was given seven years of stay by the Immigration Department, which gave her the status of a non-permanent Hong Kong resident. Yet the festive atmosphere in Hong Kong did not bring her any joy. Her husband passed away the day after her arrival. Not having been registered as a spouse at her late husband's public housing unit, she was not allowed to stay in the unit, which was immediately repossessed by the Hong Kong Housing Authority. Her husband left her with a mere $982.37. She was without family or friends in Hong Kong and had to spend her first Christmas in the city as a homeless person. A charitable shelter for street sleepers later offered her temporary accommodation, and she survived on some financial help in the form of one-off payments from certain charities. Not willing to succumb to destiny, she tried hard to find employment, which was not easy for a woman at the age of 56. She attended some government training courses and managed to find sporadic casual jobs as a dishwasher at a restaurant (at $175 per day) and later as a substitute security guard (at $200 per 12-hour shift). The shelter home was closed at midnight when she came off work as a dishwasher and didn't open until 5:30 a.m., so that she had to sleep in a park. She applied for Comprehensive Social Security Assistance (CSSA) to meet her housing needs 'in order to get some rest before she could find stable gainful employment'. Her application was rejected on the sole ground that she did not satisfy the seven years' residence requirement. Before 2004, the residence requirement for CSSA was one year, but it was raised to seven years with effect from 1 January 2004. Her request to the Director of Social Welfare to waive the residence requirement was turned down, and her appeal to the Social Security Appeal Board was also rejected. Under the guidelines set down by the director, the discretion to waive the residence requirement would only be exercised in exceptional circumstances, and financial hardship alone did not qualify as 'exceptional'. The board found that the death of her husband did not amount to a 'substantial and unexpected change in circumstances beyond her control', as she should have realized that she could not depend financially on her late husband, who was himself an aged CSSA recipient suffering from chronic illness. Given that she had no relatives or friends in Hong Kong, the board concluded that 'it would be a better alternative for Madam Kong to return to her native place'.

With the assistance of legal aid, she mounted a challenge against the decision of the Director of Social Welfare. Madam Kong's case was not an isolated incident. Many applications for CSSA from persons in a similar situation were denied on the ground of failure to satisfy the seven years' residence requirement. However, when the decision of the director was challenged on the ground that it was unreasonable (in the public law sense) not to waive the requirement in the particular circumstances of those cases, they were invariably settled. Hence, it was decided in Madam Kong's case that the focus of the challenge should not be on the refusal to waive the residential requirement, on which she would likely be successful and would be offered a settlement, but on the residential requirement itself, which would be a challenge to the system.

She was represented by Hectar Pun, who took silk later, before the Court of First Instance. It was argued that the seven years' residence requirement was an unconstitutional restriction on her right to equality and her right to social welfare respectively, under Articles 25 and 36 of the Basic Law. Her application was refused and an appeal was filed.

I led Hectar on the appeal. I first met Madam Kong at our conference, and she impressed me as a resolute and resilient person. While she was not highly educated, she had a strong sense of right and wrong. She felt strongly that the denial of her CSSA application was a result of prejudice against new arrivals from the Mainland and was determined to take the matter all the way to the Court of Final Appeal. I told her that it was not an easy case and that she had to be psychologically prepared for a lengthy litigation process. It was also not a popular social cause. The case had attracted a lot of adverse publicity, the social pressure of which would only add to the psychological pressure that she had to bear. My concern was subsequently proved right. The case generated an outpouring of derogatory criticism, mostly uninformed and the result of prejudice, in the following days and years. It also met with a series of delays for one reason or another, so that by the time we reached the Court of Final Appeal, she had already fulfilled the seven years' residence requirement. She told me at that conference that even if she were successful in the judicial review, she would not apply for CSSA. She would rather earn her own living than rely on social welfare, but it was a matter of principle that she should be treated fairly.

The evolution of the residence requirement

Social welfare, initially in the form of provision of cooked food, was first introduced in Hong Kong shortly after the Second World War, to alleviate the plight of the large number of refugees from the Mainland who came to Hong Kong to avoid the civil war. The residential criterion was established in 1948 at ten years, which was reduced to five years in 1959, a year after the establishment of the Social Welfare Department. The thinking behind the residential qualification was that public assistance should not be made freely available, so as to avoid attracting a mass influx of new immigrants from China. In 1970, as a result of a comprehensive review of the system, it was concluded that 'the stage of development now reached by Hong Kong justifies a more liberal policy, and one which more closely meets the needs of the indigent'.[1] The residential requirement was reduced to one year. A new system was put in place, which was developed into the present CSSA scheme in July 1993. The one-year residence requirement had been in place for over three decades, until it was raised to seven years on 1 January 2004.

The curtain rises

The Director of Social Welfare was represented by Lord Pannick QC, leading Abraham Chan, who also took silk later. I first met David Pannick in the early 1980s, when we were both junior counsel to Lord Lester QC in representing the *South China Morning Post* to resist an application for injunction by the government to restrain the *Post* from publishing a serial extract of the book *Spycatcher*, a memoir by a former MI5 officer. Since then David has had a most distinguished career at the Bar and is one of the best advocates in London. He has appeared in Hong Kong courts so often that I once teased him that he should pay a full membership fee to the Hong Kong Bar Association!

When I arrived at the court building, I was greeted by two groups of protesters, one group supporting Madam Kong and another, larger, group opposing her claim. The size of these groups grew bigger when the case reached the Court of Final Appeal. Some of the protesters displayed banners with remarks that were quite derogatory of the new arrivals. While I have full respect for the right to demonstration, I have always thought that the court, or more precisely the square outside the court building, is not a proper place for holding demonstrations. The demonstrations would not have any influence on either the judges or the advocates. The court stands for rationality, independence, and justice. None of these values can be enhanced by the chanting of emotional, and sometimes discriminatory, slogans.

Before the Court of Appeal and later the Court of Final Appeal, I decided that we should focus just on the social welfare right. It was also a strategic decision, as it was easier to establish an unjustifiable restriction of a fundamental right than to compare

---

1. Memorandum of the Executive Council in March 1970, cited by the Court of Final Appeal in *Kong Yunming v Director of Social Welfare* (2013) 16 HKCFAR 950, at [14].

her case with some comparators, which would not be easy to identify, in order to demonstrate unequal treatment. We argued that the increase in residence requirement from one year to seven years constituted an unjustifiable restriction of the right to social welfare, as the lengthened residence requirement could not satisfy the constitutional tests of rationality and proportionality under Article 36 of the Basic Law. This article provides that 'Hong Kong residents shall have the right to social welfare in accordance with law'. Article 145 further provides that 'on the basis of the previous social welfare system, the Government of the Hong Kong Special Administrative Region shall, on its own, formulate policies on the development and improvement of this system in the light of the economic conditions and social needs'. Lord Pannick argued that Article 36 did not confer any form or level of social welfare benefits. The right to receive social welfare was subject to the policies and economic constraints in Article 145 and carried within itself eligibility criteria. It was a matter for the government to determine these eligibility criteria, which would have to be adjusted from time to time in discharge of its duty under Article 145. The relationship between these two articles formed the main focus of the legal arguments.

What does the right to social welfare mean?

An immediate obstacle that we faced was the meaning of the right to social welfare. There was a wide range and variety of social welfare benefits. Different kinds of welfare benefits carried different eligibility criteria and different levels of benefits. Justice Stock, the vice-president of the Court of Appeal for whom I have great respect, pressed me for a definition of the right to social welfare. What exactly did the right entail? Would I be arguing that a Hong Kong resident had a right to all kinds of social welfare, irrespective of eligibility requirements? If not, why single out CSSA? Our reply was that Article 36 provided a constitutional framework for a right to social welfare. The precise level of benefits and eligibility were to be prescribed by local law. It was undesirable to adopt a rigid definition of social welfare under Article 36, but whatever definition one were to adopt, it would be an inescapable conclusion that CSSA must fall within the meaning of social welfare. That is why Article 36 referred to a right to social welfare 'in accordance with law'. The right was a right to social welfare, subject to such restrictions as provided by law, that had to be formulated with sufficient precision as the occasion required and to be accessible to the public.

The Court of Appeal was not convinced. Our argument would have to presuppose that a Hong Kong resident was entitled to all forms of social welfare. We could not just single out CSSA, which was just one facet of social welfare. There were also other forms of public expenditure that the government had to take into consideration. Article 36 had to be read in conjunction with Article 145. These provisions envisaged the continuous formulation and promulgation of policy in the realm of social welfare for the benefit of Hong Kong residents in the light of the prevailing economic and social conditions, which were bound to change from time to time. The right to social welfare did not guarantee all or any particular form of welfare. Therefore, so found Justice Stock, to ensure sustainability of the system for both the present and future generations, the right to social welfare carried with it qualifying conditions. These eligibility conditions form part of the right and should not be regarded as a restriction of the right. As long as the conditions were not discriminatory, there would be no violation of the right to social welfare. The right did not carry any specific level of benefits.

There were two problems with this reasoning. The first was that the right to social welfare would be practically meaningless. It did not guarantee any benefit at all. On the court's formulation, the eligibility conditions form part of the right and would therefore not be subject to any constitutional restraints, save that they should not be discriminatory. As a result, and this led to the second problem, the right to social welfare was nothing more than a right not to be discriminated against in receiving social welfare, if any. We decided to take the case further to the Court of Final Appeal.

The Court of Final Appeal

The hearing was presided over by Chief Justice Geoffrey Ma, Justice Ribeiro, Justice Robert Tang, Justice Bokhary, and Lord Phillips of Worth Matravers, the overseas judge. Lord Pannick QC continued to represent the government. The court was packed with journalists and interested members of the public. By this time there were heated, and sometimes emotional, discussions in the community on the new arrivals' claim for social welfare benefits, and the public was eager to know the decision of the Court of Final Appeal. I opened my case, and not unusually at this final appellate level, I was soon bombarded with questions from all directions. It was always intellectually challenging before the Court of Final Appeal. The Bench had been very kind to me, but this did not prevent them from raising some extremely difficult questions. Lord Pannick was, as usual, most eloquent and concise at his submission. The hearing lasted for two days, and at the end of it, both Lord Pannick and I thought that I was going to lose the case. I believed I had persuaded Justice Bokhary and, perhaps, Lord Phillips, and might probably lose with a dissenting judgment.

On the meaning of the right to social welfare, we had refined our argument before the Court of Final Appeal. There had to be some meaning for the right to social welfare, and Article 36 had to be considered in the context of the changeover. To be meaningful, there must be a minimum content of the right to social welfare to provide a safety net for essential survival of those who do not have the means to cover even the basis needs. This was exactly what the CSSA was for. At the same time, an overriding theme of the Basic Law was to preserve the previous system, including the previous social welfare system. Article 143 referred to the previous welfare system. It also referred to development and improvement 'on the basis of the previous social welfare system'. One can only measure 'development' and 'improvement' when there is a starting point for comparison, and this starting point had to be the level of social welfare benefits as existing on 1 July 1997. Therefore, when Article 36 referred to the right to 'social welfare', it was not intended to refer to a mere abstract concept. Instead, it referred to the social welfare benefits that existed on 1 July 1997, together with the eligibility conditions. We accepted that the right to social welfare carried eligibility conditions. Therefore, it was the level of benefits, together with the then eligibility conditions, that constituted the body of social welfare rights. Those were the benefits that Hong Kong residents were entitled to and were preserved and protected by the Basic Law. We also accepted that these conditions could be changed in light of changing social and economic conditions.[2] However, any retrogressive change would be subject to constitutional restraints. That is, the form and level of benefits could be improved or restricted, but any restriction would have to satisfy the constitutional requirement that it was rationally justifiable for the goals to be attained and that it was a proportionate response. In this sense, the right to social welfare had a substantive content, and it was more than a right not to be discriminated against.

The Court of Final Appeal agreed that the right to social welfare had to mean more than a right not to be discriminated against. The leading judgment was delivered by Justice Ribeiro, who was once my teacher at law school and one of the most respected judges in Hong Kong. As Justice Ribeiro pointed out, the Court of Appeal's formulation 'focuses on the Administration's role in formulating social welfare policies, regarding it as free to define the eligibility and other conditions for any particular benefit, provided only that such conditions are not discriminatory. But that allows the equality rights entirely to eclipse the welfare right' and would leave Article 36 with no meaning.[3]

Article 36 was intended to operate as a framework provision. Once an administrative scheme such as the CSSA scheme had crystallized a set of accessible and predictable eligibility rules, those rules would be regarded as embodying a right, which would qualify for protection by Article 36. Thus, the relevant right given constitutional protection by Article 36 was 'the right defined by the eligibility rules for CSSA derived from the previous system of social welfare and in existence as at 1 July 1997'.[4] This was an important decision, as it gave substantive content to the right to social welfare by constitutionalizing the level of benefits on 1 July 1997. In the present case, it meant that the one-year residence requirement formed part of the right. Any further restriction of this residence requirement would have to be justified. This also explained why the court subsequently found that the right would still be subject to the one-year residence requirement when it held that the seven years' residence requirement was unconstitutional. The one year's residence requirement was very much part of the 'right'.

---

2. The court was not quite correct to suggest that I argued that social welfare could only be developed and improved but not be restricted and reduced: see [37]. My argument was that any retrogressive change would have to be made by law and to satisfy the constitutional tests of rationality and proportionality.
3. At [32].
4. At [35].

In accordance with law

Another interesting issue is the meaning of 'law'. As Article 36 provided for a right to social welfare 'in accordance with law', our position was that the restriction, the seven years' residence requirement, was only an administrative rule with no force of law and therefore failed to comply with Article 36. Indeed, the entire CSSA scheme was an administrative scheme without any legal backing. It meant that the government could easily change the scheme or the eligibility conditions. This was more than a technicality. The reason why a restriction of a fundamental right had to be 'in accordance with law' was that this allowed the legislature to scrutinize the restriction. A constitutional right was of such a fundamental character that any restriction had to have the blessing of the legislature and should not lie at the whim of the administration. That went to the rule of law. The requirement of 'law' ensured that a government decision would not be made arbitrarily or discriminatorily, and its formal law-making process reinforces the transparency of the decision process and fosters legitimacy and public acceptance of the restriction. We accepted that there could be a liberal interpretation of what constituted 'law', but, however we defined it, the administrative scheme could not be 'law'. It was devised within the four walls of the government building and was implemented without having to go through any legislative process. Lord Pannick replied by saying that Article 145 would provide the legal basis for the restriction. We countered that would be a circular argument and would defeat the purpose of 'law'. If the Basic Law provided a right and then constituted the legal source of restriction, the phrase 'in accordance with law' would have no meaning. We asked rhetorically, where was the 'law'?

Admittedly there was one problem with this argument. In Hong Kong, social welfare had always been administered by the executive government. Unlike other jurisdictions, we did not have any social welfare legislation. No doubt the reason for this was administrative convenience. We were able to point to schemes similar to CSSA in the social welfare legislation in the United Kingdom, Canada, and Australia. The eligibility conditions were set out in the legislation, together with an appeal system. So, technically, there was no difficulty in turning the CSSA scheme into a legislative scheme. However, our argument might also mean that, on 1 July 1997, all social welfare schemes would become unconstitutional, as they were not set up 'in accordance with law'.[5] To address this problem, our response was that bulk of social welfare rights as existed on 30 June 1997 formed the core of the right to social welfare, and the Basic Law did not prohibit the government from continuing to provide social welfare administratively. What it tried to do was to protect such right so that any restriction, or retrogressive development, had to be made in accordance with law. Therefore, as long as there was no change or there was improvement to the social welfare scheme as it existed on 1 July 1997, they would not be affected. The requirement of 'law' only bit

---

5. It was on this reason that Justice Ribeiro said that this argument would not help Madam Kong: at [26].

when the government tried to reduce the level of benefit. It was also on such an occasion that legislative scrutiny was most important.

Neither the Court of Appeal nor the Court of Final Appeal was convinced. The Court of Appeal's response was first, that qualifying conditions were not restrictions so that they did not have to satisfy the requirement of 'law', and secondly, that these conditions could be described as 'law', as they were made pursuant to Article 145—they were widely accessible; they established rules of general application and did not permit arbitrary or random decision-making.[6] Likewise, the Court of Final Appeal held that 'the administrative system—consisting of rules that are accessible, systematically applied and subject to a process of administrative appeal—is to be treated as a system providing "social welfare in accordance with law" within the meaning of Article 36'.[7] With respect, this reasoning blurred the distinction between an administrative scheme and law. 'Law' envisages a formal process, besides checks and balance against administrative action by an elected legislature. Accessibility, systematic application, and the availability of an appeal were necessary conditions but not sufficient elements of 'law'; they did not by themselves turn something that was not law into 'law'. Many scientific rules were accessible and systematically applied, and many internal regulations of schools and institutions provided for an appeal, but these rules and regulations were not regarded as 'law'. The CSSA Scheme did not have to go through any formal legal process. Theoretically it could be changed overnight without any legislative sanction. As Justice Andrew Cheung at first instance noted, 'What constitutes development and improvement of the pre-existing social welfare system is best judged by the government, subject to the scrutiny of the Legislative Council.' But how could there be legislative scrutiny if the CSSA system is made up entirely of administrative rules? On the one hand, the court justified its deference to the government because social welfare involved distribution of resources, which was normally outside the expertise of the court and which was better monitored by the legislature. Yet on the other hand, its decision to extend the meaning of 'law' to include an administrative scheme would defeat any legislative scrutiny. It is true that the introduction of the seven years' residence requirement was discussed extensively in the Finance Committee of the Legislative Council, but technically the government did not have to do so, as it would not require any legislative approval for a *reduction* of expenditure, which was what the seven years' residence requirement was said to achieve. In any event, the Finance Committee did not discuss policy and had no power to amend or change the new condition of eligibility. However, since the Court of Final Appeal has pronounced, further clarification of what constituted 'law' would have to be left to a future occasion.

---

6. Judgment of the Court of Appeal, CACV 185 and 153 of 2009, at [73]–[74].
7. At [25].

The main battlefield

Once we succeeded in arguing that the seven years' residence requirement constituted a restriction on the right to social welfare, which was previously subject to only a one-year residence requirement, the government had to justify the introduction of the seven years' residence requirement as a rational and proportionate response. Extensive materials were put before the courts. There were arguments as to whether the restriction had to be justified by a proportionality test, or whether it could be upheld so long as it was not manifestly without reasonable foundation, which suggested a lower or a more tolerant threshold of scrutiny. The Court of Final Appeal held that the right to social welfare was not a fundamental right but a right which intrinsically involved the government setting rules determining eligibility and benefit levels. Therefore, the court should acknowledge a wide margin of discretion for the government and would only intervene if the restriction was not rationally connected to a legitimate societal concern or if it was manifestly without reasonable foundation.[8] Having said that, the level of scrutiny that was eventually adopted by the court was as extensive as any proportionality test although the court seemed to lean more heavily on the limb of rational connection than on proportionate response in its conclusion.

We made two points at the outset. First, the period of seven years was adopted readily without consideration of any other length of residence requirement. Seven years was chosen because it was the period required to acquire permanent residence. We argued that the introduction of 'seven years' residence requirement' was no coincidence but a response that was targeted at new arrivals from the Mainland. If the concern were financial sustainability, one would have expected that different periods of residence requirement would have been considered. Secondly, contrary to widespread social beliefs that the new arrivals from the Mainland were responsible for the escalating expenses in social welfare, the evidence showed that new arrivals consistently made up only 12–15 per cent of the total number of CSSA recipients. The sharp increase in CSSA expenditure was not due to the new arrivals.

The government's arguments were primarily that the lengthened residence requirement was necessary to ensure the long-term sustainability of the CSSA Scheme. It relied on three main factors: (1) the policy of accepting immigrants from the Mainland under the One-Way Permit Scheme (OWP) which resulted in a continuing flow of OWP holders with a concomitant absence of control of immigration intake from that direction; (2) Hong Kong's aging population and low fertility rate; and (3) the rise in expenditure on CSSA and expected fiscal deficit.

---

8. At [42]–[43]. When the court said that the right to social welfare was not a 'fundamental right', what it probably meant was that the right to social welfare, being social and economic in nature, was different from civil and political rights. The distinction between these two types of rights has been a matter of considerable debate, and the difference was increasingly acknowledged as one of degree and extent rather than of inherent character.

Due to the significant drop in the fertility rate in Hong Kong, the OWP Scheme became the most important immigration policy shaping the growth and composition of the population, accounting for some 93 per cent of population growth between 1997 and 2001. There was a daily quota of 150 new migrants from the Mainland who were allowed to come to settle in Hong Kong. The new arrivals comprised mainly children with a right of abode in Hong Kong and Mainland spouses coming to join their spouses who were already residents in Hong Kong. About half of the new arrivals were children under 18 years of age, and 65 per cent of all adult OWP migrants were females, mostly homemakers. The court pointed out that the humane and laudable purpose of the scheme was the promotion of family reunion. It also served the population needs of Hong Kong to have more young people to rejuvenate the population. Yet these young children required someone to look after them. Thus, it would be wholly irrational and counter-productive to the objective of family reunion under the OWP Scheme to increase the residence requirements for CSSA, as it would either deter the parents, usually the mothers, from coming, or the CSSA benefits for the young children, who were exempted from the residence requirement, would have to be thinly spread between the children and their adult parents who were ineligible for the benefits because of the residence requirement.

While Hong Kong has an aging population, the seven years' residence requirement had little to do with addressing this problem. Only a small number of new immigrants under the OWP Scheme were elderly people, and an even smaller number of them applied for CSSA (about 6.8 per cent). The saving, if any, arising from a longer residence requirement was insignificant. The root cause of the aging population was Hong Kong's low fertility rate, whereas the OWP Scheme, under which the majority of arrivals were children under 18 years of age, was the most significant contribution to population growth in Hong Kong. A rational response to the aging problem should be to encourage the entry of young immigrants to rejuvenate the population. The seven years' residence requirement was a counter-productive and irrational measure.

As to the rise in social welfare expenditure, it has already been pointed out that new arrivals represented consistently only 12–15 per cent of all CSSA claimants.[9] The overall increase in spending was obviously due to a whole range of other factors. Besides, as half of all new arrivals were children under 18 years of age who were exempted from the seven years' residence requirement, the saving that could be achieved was again insignificant and would represent only a small fraction of the overall expenditure on CSSA. Of the $14.4 billion overall expenditure on CSSA in 2001–2002, it was estimated that the saving arising from the seven years' residence requirement would be less than $7.64 million. Nor would this amount contribute in any significant manner to any suggested fiscal deficit, and no structural deficit was shown in evidence.[10] As

9. At [90].
10. Indeed, between 2001 and 2011, there were only two periods of fiscal deficit (2002–2003 and 2008–2009), which were more than offset by fiscal surplus in other years. The deficit in 2008–2009 was largely due to poor investment performance in the Exchange Fund: see [113]–[114].

Justice Ribeiro observed, the relatively insignificant level of savings achievable by implementing the seven-year residence requirement undermined the suggestion that the restriction was genuinely intended to be, or functioned as, a measure rationally designed to safeguard the sustainability of the social security system.[11] Indeed, the government itself had acknowledged that the saving was immaterial and the introduction of the seven years' residence requirement 'was not driven by the need to reduce CSSA expenditure on new arrivals'.[12]

That left the government with only a few other minor justifications. It was argued that the seven years' residence requirement was consistent with the grant of permanent residence and the entitlement to public housing benefit. Uniformity of requirements was a typical bureaucratic mode of thinking. The Court of Final Appeal described it as a 'somewhat bizarre suggestion that there is some intrinsic value in having uniform qualifying periods for welfare benefits where such benefits are heavily subsidized by the state'. The different nature of different kinds of benefits would require different qualifying periods, and 'symmetry for the sake of symmetry is hardly a legitimate aim'.[13]

It was then suggested that a seven years' residence requirement would reflect the contribution a resident has made towards the economy over a sustained period of time. This was weird as, first, it would be illogical to require a group who did not have the financial means to support themselves to make a contribution to the economy before they could be regarded as eligible for financial support; and secondly, it overlooked that most of the new arrival CSSA recipients (95 per cent being women) were looking after children who had the right of abode and were therefore unable to take up outside employment. They did make a valuable contribution to society by helping to integrate children with right of abode into our community and avoiding social problems arising from split families.

Finally, it was suggested that the new arrivals had been given prior warning that they would not be entitled to CSSA until after seven years of residence, that there were other charities available, and that the director had discretion to waive the residence requirement. The court was not impressed. The prior warning amounted to telling the potential immigrants who had been granted OWPs: 'If you are poor, stay at home. Don't come to Hong Kong if you can't afford it.' As the court pointed out, this has the effect of deterring potential new arrivals to settle in Hong Kong and ran counter to the avowed policies of promoting family unity. The support from other charities might supplement but could not be a practical substitute for CSSA, which operated as a safety net for basic needs. It might also amount to an abdication of constitutional responsibility by the government by shifting the burden to private charities. Finally, while the director had discretion to waive the residence requirement, the criteria were extremely restrictive and only a small number of cases were successful. The court was surprised at the very high proportion of applicants who withdrew their applications

---

11. At [96].
12. At [97].
13. At [102].

(62–78 per cent). The only explanation was that they had been told that they did not meet the criteria. Indeed, if the disposal of Madam Kong's case was anything to go by, and even the unexpected death of one's spouse would not qualify as exceptional circumstances, the discretion was unlikely to provide any real safeguard.

On these grounds, the Court of Final Appeal unanimously reversed the decision of the Court of Appeal and held that the seven years' residence requirement was not rationally connected to the legitimate aim espoused by the government and was manifestly without reasonable foundation.

It was a triumph for Madam Kong, who by then had satisfied the seven years' residence requirement. The judgment sparked off a great deal of public discontent. Many people continue to criticize the new arrivals for taking up the bulk of CSSA at the expense of hardworking and tax-paying Hong Kong residents despite the evidence that they either had not read or chose to ignore. Derogatory remarks against the new arrivals continued to be made long after the judgment. I received a number of anonymous letters accusing me of ruining Hong Kong's economy!

Madam Kong continued to make her living as a casual worker. She did not apply for CSSA.

7

The story of Eva

The foreign domestic helper case

The story of Eva

My name is Eva. I come from the Philippines and I'm married with three children. I have a college degree, but the economy in the Philippines is so bad that, like many others, I came to Hong Kong to work as a domestic helper. That was in August 1986. It was a hard decision, having to leave my family behind to go to a place where I had never set foot. I had heard many horrible stories about domestic workers being abused, and I didn't know anyone in Hong Kong. The job was introduced to me through an agent, who extorted a hefty introduction fee that was equivalent to the salary of my first six months. I later learned that the introduction fee was much more than what was allowed under the law, but what could I do when I desperately needed the job? It was rather ironic that, in order to improve our financial situation, I ended up heavily in debt before I even set off for Hong Kong. I was in tears when I left my children and set out on this journey of uncertainty. What would be waiting for me in Hong Kong?

My employer was a lawyer (I called him 'Sir'). His wife (whom I called 'Ma'am') was also a lawyer. Both of them were very busy and worked long hours. They lived in an apartment with two children. When I first joined them, the children were still toddlers. Of course they are a grown-up lady and a gentleman now. I am still working for them. They treat me well, as if I were a member of the family. I was fortunate to have a small cubicle of my own at the back of the kitchen. The bed hardly fitted in there, but at least it was my own little world. I had no complaint, as I knew that many foreign domestic helpers had to share a room with the children or just slept in the kitchen. I worked six days a week, normally waking up at 5:30 a.m. to prepare the children for school, and continuing till around 11 p.m., long after the children had gone to bed. Sometimes when Sir and Ma'am had to work late or had evening functions, I had to attend to them when they returned home. The parents of Sir and Ma'am came to visit very often, especially when the children were still young. They did not speak English, and we could only communicate through gestures though sometimes they behaved as if I knew Cantonese and got angry when I couldn't understand them. In the early days, Mai Mai (the mother of Sir) used to scold me ferociously. Sometimes she would accuse me of being lazy whenever I tried to take a break, because of working 18 hours a day. It hurt, but what else could I do? I needed the job to support my family. I could only cry myself to sleep, alone in my cubicle, having no one to talk to and missing my children in the Philippines. But as time passed, our relationship improved.

Sunday was my normal rest day, unless I was asked to take a weekday off instead. I usually left the apartment at 8 a.m. Not that I wanted to leave so early. I would have preferred to stay at home, but if I did, inevitably I would be asked to do various household chores. It was difficult to say no when I was at home, or more precisely, my workplace. And it wasn't a pleasant experience to lock myself up in a small cubicle at 'home' all day. I would usually join my friends in Central. There were not a lot of places to go, as most commercial buildings did not welcome us. I usually spent the day with some friends in the pedestrian tunnel leading from what used to be the Star Ferry Pier to Prince's Building in Central. It provided a nice shelter from the overwhelming dust and heat in the streets, though when it rained, the place could be flooded. We put some pieces of cardboard on the floor, and that became our temporary sojourn. We stayed there all day, eating, singing, talking, and even sleeping. To be honest, it was not a nice place, but strangely I felt I regained my dignity there, being treated and accepted as a person among my peers. At least, my friends and I were all in the same position, far from home and family. At times, some passers-by would give us derogatory stares, but I soon became used to that. After all, 'sticks and stones may break my bones, but words will never hurt me'. The section of Chater Road outside Prince's Building was normally designated as a pedestrian-only area on Sundays, and there were all kinds of performances and entertainment. Sometimes my compatriots organized various activities there, and when the weather was fine, there was a carnival-like atmosphere. I enjoyed being among people from home. Sometimes I would go with some friends to Lantau Island or go on a hike in the countryside. What we do in our free time is no different from what many Hong Kong people do. Like anyone else, we did need a social life and the support and friendship of one another. Yet some of my friends were required by their employers to take the day off only on weekdays, so that they could not mingle with other foreign domestic helpers and acquire 'bad habits' from them!

Every two years I had to renew my contract of employment. In the early days, this was always a period of great anxiety, as I wouldn't know whether my contract would be renewed. Many of my friends had their contracts terminated, and they were usually given short notice, sometimes even on the same day. Then we were only allowed to stay in Hong Kong for 14 days after the expiry or the termination of our contracts. That was hardly enough time to look for a new employer. There were also times when there was a dispute, and a friend of mine was dismissed immediately. We thought that this was unfair, but we couldn't get any help or redress within such a short time. I was fortunate that I had my contract renewed every time. I had to leave Hong Kong before I started a new contract. My employer would buy me the cheapest economy air ticket for my return home.

As there are more than 340,000 foreign domestic helpers in Hong Kong, no doubt there are some black sheep among us. However, they are a small minority only although the local media sometimes portrayed all foreign domestic helpers as dishonest, deceitful, and even violent individuals. In fact, the large majority of us are law-abiding people who work hard for our employers. We all work long hours, not everyone has a pleasant working/living environment, and this can be made even more difficult when there is a language barrier and a lack of understanding of our social, religious, or cultural backgrounds. In supermarkets, we might sometimes be treated as if we were shoplifters. We had nowhere to go on Sundays, and we were made to understand that we were not welcome to spend the day even in public places in Hong Kong. We had to stay on footbridges, under flyovers, on pedestrian pavements, and for a long time we were accused of having occupied Central or Victoria Park, which I thought were public places for everyone. At times, we could be verbally or physically abused. We came to Hong Kong to work, and as Sir used to say, we contribute a lot to the local economy too, particularly by allowing many working mums to continue to work instead of staying at home to take care of the young or elderly people. But this recognition was mostly just lip service. I must say that there are times we feel we are treated as an inferior class, as cheap labour, or in the worst cases, almost like slaves in a modern society.

I have lived in Hong Kong for almost 30 years now. Until recently, I did not realize that I was not regarded as having been ordinarily resident in Hong Kong. When I applied for permanent resident status, I was told by the Commissioner of Registration that, no matter how long I have been in Hong Kong, I would never be able to become a Hong Kong permanent resident. We were not part of Hong Kong community and were not welcome to become part of it.

I learned that Article 24(2)(4) of the Basic Law says that 'persons not of Chinese nationality who have entered Hong Kong with valid travel documents, have *ordinarily resided* in Hong Kong for a continuous period of not less than seven years and have taken Hong Kong as their place of permanent residence' shall be able to acquire permanent status in Hong Kong. But section 2(4)(a) of the Immigration Ordinance provides that any period when a person remains in Hong Kong while employed as a domestic helper who is from outside Hong Kong shall not be treated as ordinarily resident in Hong Kong. So, as long as I remain as a foreign domestic helper, even if I spend the rest of my life in Hong Kong, I will always be treated as an outsider and can never acquire the status of Hong Kong permanent resident. Is this fair? Isn't section 2(4)(a) of the Immigration Ordinance in contravention of the Basic Law?

As far as I could see, this was a simple matter of justice. Very few places in the world would shut the door to people who have contributed to the local economy over the years. Many of my friends had lived in Hong Kong for a long time. Yet the issue turned out to be far more controversial than I had thought. Many people in Hong Kong considered the idea scandalous and were worried that we would not be foreign domestic helpers as soon as we acquired permanent residence status after seven years. But so what, I asked myself? The employers could always decide not to renew our contracts after four or six years. They want our continued service, but they want us to be permanently locked in the status of foreign domestic helpers. There are plenty of foreign employees in Hong Kong, but they are not subject to the same constraint. Is this because they are considered to be contributing economically, whereas domestic work is not treated as equally valuable? It used to be the case that a divorced homemaker was regarded as not having contributed to matrimonial expenses, because housework and taking care of children were not considered to be of value. The court has long since rejected this argument as outmoded and discriminatory for the purpose of divorce and maintenance, but it appears that the same approach still holds good for the purpose of determining permanent residence! Isn't this a case of double standards?

I felt exhilarated when my compatriot Evangeline Vallejos decided to take the matter to court.[1]

The legal case

Vallejos had legal aid and was represented by Gladys Li SC, who was later joined by Michael Fordham QC, a leading London silk, at the Court of Final Appeal. The Commissioner of Registration was represented by Lord Pannick QC, also a leading London silk, and Anderson Chow SC. The arguments centred on the meaning of 'ordinary residence' in Article 24 of the Basic Law.

In the leading case of *Ex Parte Shah*,[2] the House of Lords had held that 'ordinary resident' referred to 'a man's abode in a particular place or country which he has adopted voluntarily and for settled purposes as part of the regular order of his life for the time being, whether of short or of long duration'. The focus of 'ordinary resident' was that the residence has to be in the course of the customary mode of life of the person concerned. A person was 'ordinarily resident' in a place where 'in the settled routine of his life he regularly, normally or customarily lives'.[3] *Ex Parte Shah* was a test case on whether foreign students were entitled to local authority education grants when they studied in the United Kingdom. Section 1(1) of the Local Education Act 1962 provided that the local education authority had to make available education grants to a person who had been 'ordinarily resident' in the United Kingdom throughout the three years preceding the first year of the course of study in question. The Court of Appeal held that a boy from overseas who came on a student visa, which was to be renewed every year, was not to be regarded as 'ordinarily resident' in the United Kingdom. On appeal, the House of Lords held that the Court of Appeal had erred in attaching decisive weight to the immigration status of the appellant. Lord Scarman pointed out that immigration status 'means no more than the terms of a person's leave to enter as stamped upon his passport. This may or may not be a guide to a person's

---

1. *Vallejos v Commissioner of Registration* [2011] 6 HKC 469 (CFI), [2012] 2 HKC 185 (CA), (2013) 16 HKCFAR 45 (CFA).
2. *R v Barnet London Borough Council, ex parte Shah* [1983] 2 AC 309, at 343.
3. *Thomson v Minister of National Revenue* [1946] SCR 209, at 231–232, per Estey J.

intention in establishing a residence in this country; it certainly cannot be the decisive test.' His Lordship then stated the test in an important passage:

> Local education authorities, when considering an application for a mandatory award, must ask themselves the question: has the applicant shown that he has habitually and normally resided in the United Kingdom from choice and for a settled purpose throughout the prescribed period, apart from temporary or occasional absence ... The relevant period is not the future but one which has largely (or wholly) elapsed, namely that between the date of the commencement of his proposed course and the date of his arrival in the United Kingdom. The terms of an immigration student's leave to enter and remain here may or may not throw light on the question: it will, however, be of little weight when put into the balance against the fact of continued residence over the prescribed period – unless the residence is itself a breach of the terms of his leave, in which event his residence, being unlawful, could not be ordinary.[4]

The *Ex Parte Shah* test has been adopted and applied to many other contexts. Before the Court of First Instance, Gladys Li SC relied on this test and argued forcefully that Ms Vallejos had satisfied this test. The Commissioner pointed to the restrictive immigration conditions applicable to foreign domestic helpers (FDH) and argued that their circumstances were so out of the ordinary that the residence of FDH could not be regarded as 'ordinary resident'. The Commissioner relied heavily on the following features: (1) their standard-form contract of employment was for two years only; (2) they were permitted to remain in Hong Kong for two years and must leave within two weeks after termination of contract; (3) they must return to their place of origin for home leave before commencing a new contract; (4) they were not allowed to change employer when the contract was terminated prematurely, save in exceptional circumstances; and (5) they were not allowed to bring in dependants, save in exceptional circumstances. It could be seen that all of these features were immigration conditions, which Lord Scarman had rejected as irrelevant in determining whether the residence was ordinary. The relevant consideration was not the conditions at the time of entry but the nature of stay after entry—whether the claimant had normally and habitually stayed in Hong Kong for a settled purpose, as part of the regular order of life for the time being. Applying the *Ex Parte Shah* test, Mr Justice Johnson Lam rejected these arguments. His judgment deserves to be quoted *in extenso*:

> 171. First, the permission to enter and remain granted to an FDH "[Foreign Domestic Helper]" is subject to the requirement that the FDH can only work as a domestic helper under a specified employment contract. An FDH is not allowed to change her employer in Hong Kong even though her contract is terminated prematurely. This can be considered together with the requirement that an FDH is required to leave Hong Kong within 2 weeks after the termination of the contract of employment if it is terminated before its expiry. In my judgment, these limits cannot alter the character of an FDH's residence in Hong Kong during the time she is permitted to stay.

---

4. At 349.

She resides here for a settled purpose, viz. employment, and she comes and stays here voluntarily. She is confined to a particular employer and has to leave after her contract ends. But it does not detract from the primary position: whilst she is here, she is here as part of the regular order of her life for the time being.

172. Second, whilst in Hong Kong the FDH has to work and reside in the employer's residence. The significance, Lord Pannick submitted, is that an FDH cannot establish a household or independent lifestyle of her own. I do not accept that an FDH cannot have a lifestyle of her own during her residence in Hong Kong. Much less am I persuaded that such a conclusion follows simply because of the requirement that an FDH has to work and reside at the specified residence of the employer. FDH, like other employees in Hong Kong, are protected by the Employment Ordinance and they are entitled to a rest day every week and statutory holidays in the same manner as other employees in Hong Kong. During their rest days and holidays, they are free to do whatever they like in terms of recreation, religious or social activities or other pursuit of life. It is a matter of private agreement between an FDH and her employer as to the spare time she could have during a working day. As demonstrated in the case of the Applicant, if her employer gives her sufficient spare time, she could pursue some part-time education. Alternatively, if she has the necessary spare time, there is no reason why she could not enjoy other aspects of life which other Hong Kong residents could enjoy during their spare time. Admittedly, there are activities which an FDH may have difficulties in pursuing due to her lack of access to an exclusive spacious residence. But the same constraint is experienced by many Hong Kong residents who do not have the resource to acquire such accommodation. Actually, it is not a foregone conclusion that the accommodation provided by an employer to an FDH is so limited that she could not enjoy the lifestyle of an average Hong Kong resident. There are certainly some FDHs in Hong Kong who worked for wealthy families and I would not be surprised that they enjoyed better living condition and have more spare time to themselves than some of our locals who have to work long hours to make ends meet. I stress I am not suggesting that this is a typical comparison. However, the reference to such atypical cases still serves the purpose in terms of demonstrating the fallacy in counsel's argument in this respect.

173. As regards the establishment of a separate household, this can be considered together with the last feature relied upon by Lord Pannick, viz. that FDHs are not allowed to bring dependants to Hong Kong. I do not think these features have any real bearing on the question of ordinary residence. It has never been an element of the *Shah* test that one has to have the capacity to establish a separate household or to bring his dependants along to a place before he could be regarded as ordinarily resident there. As recognized by Lord Scarman, education or employment can be the relevant settled purpose for staying at a place. I appreciate that the pursuit of such purposes is not mutually exclusive with the establishment of household or bringing along dependants to the place of residence. However, the point is that the inability to do the latter does not prevent one from pursuing the former as a settled purpose.

174. Third, Lord Pannick referred to the fact that an employer of an FDH is required to pay for her passage to and from her place of origin and make corresponding

arrangement in case of the death of the FDH. Further, counsel also referred to the prescribed home leave upon the completion of a contract. These measures are aimed at fostering and maintaining the FDH's link with her home country. Again, bearing in mind that the *Shah* test is the proper test to be applied instead of asking in a general sense whether an FDH's residence in Hong Kong has features which could be regarded as out of the ordinary, I do not think these features have much significance. The fostering of the link with the home country will have a bearing on the intention as to permanent residence. But that would only be relevant to the permanence requirement instead of the ordinary residence requirement. Using these features to support the Impugned Provision is equivalent to the confusion of the concept of ordinary residence with domicile, an error emphatically rejected by Lord Scarman in *Ex parte Shah*. In the context of Article 24(2)(4), it would be a confusion of the ordinary residence requirement with the permanence requirement. As pointed out by Lord Scarman, giving the expression its natural and ordinary meaning, a person can have ordinary residence at two different places at the same time. Thus, the mere maintenance of a link with her country of origin does not mean that she is not ordinarily resident in Hong Kong.

175. Though I have condensed Lord Pannick's list, I believe I have covered every item in the list of special features. On final analysis, these features whether taken individually or collectively cannot take an FDH's residence out of the concept of ordinary residence within the context of Article 24(2)(4) [*sic*].

Eva's voice

We were overwhelmed with joy and excitement. This reasoning is compelling. After all, FDHs live a life in Hong Kong no different from many other people in Hong Kong. We came here for a settled purpose; we work diligently and take statutory holidays. We do not have a big income but could enjoy ourselves in our own way. We go freely around Hong Kong when we do not have to work; we enjoy our liberty and freedom just like anyone else. We stay in Hong Kong as part of the regular order of our lives. Many of us have lived here for a long time. We have our families overseas, but so are many foreign employees in Hong Kong. If such residence is not ordinary, what is ordinary?

The case again: The appeal

Our excitement did not last long. The judgment of Mr Justice Lam sparked off very controversial responses in the community. His judgment was reversed on appeal, first by the Court of Appeal and then the Court of Final Appeal. The difference lies in whether 'ordinary residence' refers to 'how one organizes his habitual and customary stay as part of the regular order of life', or whether these immigration restrictions would affect the quality of stay to such an extent that they take the residence out of 'ordinary residence'. A hurdle that the Commissioner would have to overcome would be the *Ex Parte Shah* test.

At the Court of Final Appeal, it was agreed that the term 'ordinary residence' should be given its 'natural and ordinary meaning'. However, what that phrase means should depend on the context and the purpose of the relevant statute, so that the meaning of that expression in one context would not necessarily apply to a different context. Michael Fordham QC, who represented Ms Vallejo together with Gladys Li SC at this stage, argued forcefully that she came within the established meaning of 'ordinary residence' within the *Ex Parte Shah* test, just like many other persons who came to live in Hong Kong for business, education, or employment purposes and who had, unlike her, been treated as 'ordinarily resident' here. There was nothing in the way of life of FDH that would take their residence out of the ordinary. They were ordinarily resident in Hong Kong, not temporary sojourners.

Lord Pannick QC argued that the *Ex Parte Shah* test should provide only a starting point. He argued that the context for providing education grants to foreign students or for combating tax avoidance, where a broad meaning of 'ordinary residence' would be apposite, was very different from the context of immigration control and conferring the benefit of a right of abode on an alien. Given the highly restrictive conditions of stay of FDH, they were in an exceptional category and their stay could not be regarded as 'ordinary residence'. The Court of Final Appeal agreed with Lord Pannick QC. Chief Justice Ma held:

> 83. It is always necessary to examine the factual position of the person claiming to be ordinarily resident to see whether there are any special features affecting the nature and quality of his or her residence. If such features exist, one asks whether they result in that person's residence being qualitatively so far-removed from what would traditionally be recognized as 'ordinary residence' as to justify concluding that he or she is not 'ordinarily resident'. This is necessarily a question of fact and degree and the outer boundaries of 'ordinary residence' are incapable of precise definition.

Then after pointing out that Article 24(2)(4) of the Basic Law itself referred to the immigration status of the persons claiming a right of abode in Hong Kong and that it was implicit that immigration control was 'a constant feature in the process of building up eligibility when it stipulated a seven-year qualifying period [of ordinary residence]'—a point that is hard to understand, as it suggests that ordinary residence is determined at the point of entry—Chief Justice Ma concluded:

> 88. Adopting the aforesaid approach, it is clear that prominent distinguishing features have an important bearing on the nature and quality of the residence of FDHs as a class in Hong Kong... By way of summary, each time an FDH is given permission to enter, such permission is tied to employment solely as a domestic helper with a specific employer (in whose home the FDH is obliged to reside), under a specified contract and for the duration of that contract. The FDH is obliged to return to the country of origin at the end of the contract and is told from the outset that admission is not for the purposes of settlement and that dependants cannot be brought to reside in Hong Kong.

89. It is clear, in our view, that these distinguishing features result in the residence of FDHs in Hong Kong being qualitatively so far-removed from what would traditionally be recognized as 'ordinary residence' as to justify concluding that they do not, as a class, come within the meaning of 'ordinarily resident' as used in art 24(2)(4).

Back to Eva's story

Naturally, this judgment came as a great disappointment to us. It was disappointing, not so much in its conclusion but in its lack of sensitivity. The court was basically saying that, in view of those restrictive immigration conditions, our stay could not be regarded as 'ordinarily residence'. The immigration conditions were precisely the factors that Lord Scarman had rejected as decisive, as immigration conditions were stipulated at the point of entry, whereas ordinary residence was about the residence after entry. And the court hadn't even tried to explain why those immigration features were significant in the way Mr Justice Lam had done. Why was the fact that we could not bring in our dependants relevant to whether our stay was 'ordinary'?

My boss was also very disappointed at the judgment. He told me that Professor Wang Gungwu, the former vice-chancellor of the University of Hong Kong, was an Australian national when he was appointed by the university. He had no right of abode in Hong Kong, and he entered Hong Kong on the strength of an employment visa. Unless his visa was extended, he had no right to stay in Hong Kong on the expiry of his contract. Under the contract of employment, he had to reside at the University Lodge, which was also partly used for holding university functions. At the end of his employment, the university would provide him with air passage to return to his place of choice. Was there any real difference between his case and my case? Of course, the vice-chancellorship was a much more prestigious and well-paid position than that of a foreign domestic helper. His contract was initially for five years and was renewed once, whereas mine was for two years and had been renewed continuously in the last 30 years. He might apply to stay in Hong Kong even after the termination of his contract, but this was discretionary even though the discretion was unlikely to be exercised against him. My situation was the other way round. He could bring in his spouse, but again this was permitted as a discretion rather than a right. He had to stay at his employer's residence, like me, except that the University Lodge was a 4,000-square-foot house with a 5,000-square-foot garden overlooking the harbour, whereas mine was a 40-square-foot cubicle with a small window looking out at the wall of an adjacent building. In both cases, our employers would pay for our return air tickets, except Professor Wang was given a first-class air ticket, whereas I would get the cheapest economy ticket. I once saw him and his wife at Victoria Park on a Sunday. We both enjoyed our weekend in the same way! I had every respect for Professor Wang, who was an excellent vice-chancellor and a renowned scholar, but stripped of all the discretion and the financial differences, was there any real difference between our two cases? Yet his stay would be regarded as 'ordinary residence' and mine was not.

No doubt the judgment of the Court of Final Appeal was very learned. Most of the argument was about whether the *Ex Parte Shah* test should apply, but once it had reached the conclusion that it did not apply, there was little about what the proper test should be. I could understand that the meaning of the expression 'ordinary residence' must depend on context, but I couldn't understand how the context could lead to a different test, which was rather vague and imprecise and never expressly stated. How extraordinary before a stay could be considered out of the ordinary? The Court of Final Appeal said that it was a matter of fact and degree, but that did not tell us anything. The only case the court cited in support was a case about imprisonment. The issue was whether imprisonment would be regarded as 'ordinary residence'. Common sense would tell us that serving a custodial sentence could hardly be regarded as 'ordinary', but should our case be treated in parity with that of a prisoner who had to stay in a cell of 30 square feet for 22 hours a day for a crime for which he had been lawfully convicted? Yet that was the only authority that the court relied upon in justifying a different interpretation of the expression of 'ordinary residence'. Perhaps FDHs were regarded, in some people's subconscious mind, as being in the same league as prisoners!

The judgment was welcomed by at least some quarters of the community. The government was relieved with the result. But is it a just decision? Ironically, the judgment entrenches long-time discrimination against us as a class and reinforces the social prejudice that FDHs are an inferior class in Hong Kong, whatever might be said about our contribution to the local economy. Nothing was done before or after this judgment to address our problems or to eradicate or at least alleviate social prejudice against us. The judgment is treated as the final word on our inferior status, and the government could now sweep all forms of prejudice, discrimination, and maltreatment against us under the carpet. We know we are from a low-income group and don't have much influence, but that does not mean that we should be exploited. We just want to be treated fairly and with dignity. Is that too much to ask?

8

Big brother is watching

Covert surveillance

While I am generally known as a public lawyer, I started my career in private law. In my first ten years of teaching in the University, I taught personal property, mercantile law, contract, tort, and so on. The LLB curriculum at that time was closely modelled on the traditional LLB curriculum in the United Kingdom, which included, apart from jurisprudence, only subjects that are essential to legal practice. In 1987, my colleague Bill Clarke introduced an elective of civil liberties into the curriculum and invited me to join him to teach this course. Bill is a very learned colleague, from whom I have learned a lot. He is a tall and always well-dressed academic, a bit shy and inclined to blush, but very forceful in his argument. He later left the University and became a very successful solicitor. He continued with his academic work and was the chief editor of *White Book: Hong Kong Civil Practice*, the bible for all legal practitioners in civil practice. The course on civil liberties was very popular and attracted inquisitive and idealistic students like Eric Cheung and Benny Tai, both of whom later became my colleagues at the University; Kevin Lau, later a very successful journalist; and Anderson Chow, who took silk and later joined the Bench as a High Court judge.

In preparing for this course I came across a very interesting provision in the then Telecommunications Ordinance. Section 33 of the ordinance reads:

> Whenever he considers that the public interest so requires, the Governor, or any public officer authorized in that behalf by the Governor, either generally or for any particular occasion, may order that any message or any class of messages brought for transmission by telecommunication shall not be transmitted or that any message or any class of messages brought for transmission, or transmitted or received or being transmitted, by telecommunication shall be intercepted or detained or disclosed to the Governor or to the public officer specified in the order.

This may not be a very readable sentence. What it says essentially is that the governor may authorize any public officer to intercept any telecommunication message. I was curious how this section operated and decided to write to the Chief Secretary for further information. I was of course not interested in any specific case of interception but rather in how the system worked. In my letter, I raised a number of questions:

1. The governor may authorize interception on the grounds of public interest. I supposed public interest would include the prevention of crime but wondered if there were any more detailed guidelines on the meaning of public interest.
2. The governor may authorize any class of public officer to carry out the interception. I supposed the police and the ICAC were authorized, but I was curious to know whether other classes of public officers, and if so, what classes of officers, were also authorized to exercise this power.
3. Within the class of public officers who were authorized to exercise this power, was there any requirement that the power could only be exercised by officers above a particular rank, and if so, what rank?
4. In the course of surveillance, there were bound to be messages intercepted that had nothing to do with the objectives of the operation. How were these messages dealt with? Would they be kept, and if so, for how long? Who made the decision, and who would have access to such messages?
5. How long would messages that were relevant to the operation be kept? Who would have access to them? Were there any guidelines on the usage of the messages? Could they be used for purposes which had nothing to do with the operation?

To my great surprise, I received a letter of reply from the Chief Secretary a few weeks later. The Chief Secretary thanked me for my interest in the matter. He confirmed that there were detailed guidelines on all the issues that I had raised in my letter but that these guidelines were classified! So much for transparency!

When the Hong Kong Bill of Rights Ordinance was enacted in 1991, I wrote that section 33 of the Telecommunications Ordinance was at risk of being successfully challenged. The section was taken from an English Act, which has been successfully challenged before the European Court of Human Rights for being a violation of the right to private life under the European Convention on Human Rights.[1] As a result, parliament introduced a new Interception of Telecommunications Act 1985 in the United Kingdom. The 1985 Act did not apply to Hong Kong, which still retained the same law as that in the UK before 1985. I urged the Hong Kong government to review the Telecommunications Ordinance.

In late 1996, the Law Reform Commission in Hong Kong reached the same conclusion that section 33 was inconsistent with the Bill of Rights and unconstitutional. When the government refused to act, the Hon James To successfully introduced a private member's bill to amend the law. The amendment, modelled after the English Act, was opposed by the government. It was passed by a majority of the Legislative Council shortly before the changeover. As the government would need time to modify its own internal procedures in order to meet the requirements in the amendment, a standard clause that the bill should only take effect on a date to be appointed by the

---

1. *Malone v United Kingdom* (1984) 7 EHRR 14.

government was inserted. This was a common practice, and it was expected that the bill would be brought into effect within a reasonable time.

The government never specified a date of operation for the bill. In the event, this bill distinguished itself by being the first bill ever repealed before it even came into force! Covert surveillance continued to be carried out by the police and the ICAC, pursuant to procedures that were set out in internal guidelines. The practice erupted into an acute problem in early 2005, when the District Court began to review the constitutionality of the surveillance carried out by law enforcement agencies. It was held that the evidence obtained by such covert surveillance was unlawfully obtained.[2] In one case where the prosecution relied upon an audio recording of a conversation between a prosecution immunity witness, the defendant, and his lawyer, without their knowledge, the court held that the conduct of the ICAC amounted to an abuse of process and granted a permanent stay of the criminal proceedings.[3] This warning from the court finally pushed the government into action. Instead of bringing the pre-1997 amendments into force, the government decided to avoid the Legislative Council and introduced an Executive Order (titled 'Law Enforcement (Covert Surveillance Procedure) Order') that set out an administrative scheme and procedures to handle applications to carry out covert surveillance by law enforcement agencies.

The Executive Order was administrative in nature. This means that it could easily be changed without the sanction of the legislature and that failure to comply with the scheme would at best be an internal disciplinary matter with little transparency. Not surprisingly, the Executive Order, alongside section 33 of the Telecommunications Ordinance, was successfully challenged in court as a violation of both the Basic Law and the Bill of Rights. The challenge was brought by the Hon Leung Kwok Hung, one of the many judicial challenges that he has brought. Mr Justice Hartmann held that, while the Executive Order was 'entirely legitimate and of value as an administrative tool in regulating the internal conduct of law enforcement agencies', it failed to satisfy the requirement of the Basic Law that any restriction on the right to free communication under Article 30 of the Basic Law has to be 'in accordance with legal procedures'.[4] In response to the request of the government for time to introduce remedial legislation, Mr Justice Hartmann agreed exceptionally to suspend his declaration of unconstitutionality and made an order of temporary validity for a period of six months. This decision was itself highly controversial, as it appears difficult to reconcile a court order to uphold the validity of an act, even for a short period of time, which the court itself has unequivocally declared to be unconstitutional. It was a pragmatic compromise, and this issue was the subject of an appeal to the Court of Final Appeal, which confirmed

---

2. Unlawfully obtained evidence is not necessarily inadmissible. The court would still have discretion to consider if such evidence should be admitted: *HKSAR v Chan Kau Tai* [2006] 1 HKLRD 400; *HKSAR v Li Man Tak* [2005] HKEC 1309 (DCt) (22 April 2005).

3. *HKSAR v Shum Chiu*, DCCC 687/2004 (5 July 2005); remitted by the Court of First Instance for a full enquiry: [2005] HKEC 2139 (22 Dec 2005).

4. *Leung Kwok Hung v Chief Executive of the HKSAR*, HCAL 107/2005, 9 Feb 2005, at [127].

the existence of an exceptional power to stay a declaration of unconstitutionality for a short time to allow the government to take remedial action.[5]

Introduction of privacy

At the same time, the issue of privacy has received increasing attention from the community. While privacy is a well-developed concept in the United States, it has been a relative latecomer in English common law. Privacy interest was protected indirectly by various means, such as trespass when one's privacy is breached by a trespasser entering one's home or premises unlawfully, or breach of confidence when personal information is unlawfully disclosed. However, the concept of privacy itself was not recognized in the common law. When the right to privacy was first introduced into the territory by the Hong Kong Bill of Rights Ordinance in 1991, it was a relatively unfamiliar concept. Indeed, as a result of international pressure from the Organization of Economic Cooperation and Development (OECD) to have legislative regulation on the use of personal data, the Law Reform Commission was asked in the early 1990s to study and to recommend necessary legislation on this subject. The Law Reform Sub-committee on Privacy, which carried out the study and drafted the recommendation for consideration by the Commission, was chaired by my colleague Professor Raymond Wacks, an expert on privacy. The subcommittee swiftly produced its first report on Protection of Privacy (Personal Data), which was soon implemented to become the Personal Data (Privacy) Ordinance 1995. A law reform subcommittee would normally complete its work within a period of three to four years. However, the terms of reference of the subcommittee on privacy kept being enlarged so that it was probably the longest-lasting subcommittee ever appointed, spanning over 15 years! When Professor Raymond Wacks retired in or around 2001, the chairmanship was taken over by another of my colleagues, Professor John Bacon-Shone. John is a social scientist, but his knowledge in privacy matters is probably unrivalled even by any lawyer. I was then appointed to the subcommittee, which has since produced another five, albeit quite controversial, reports on privacy, only one of which has since been implemented.

Last-minute frenzies

By early 2006, the judgment of Mr Justice Hartmann had generated immense political pressure on the government to introduce new legislation. The Interception of Communications and Surveillance Ordinance was drafted. By this time, the Law Reform Sub-committee on Privacy was in the final phase of considering the whole subject of covert surveillance and was pushed to complete its study as soon as it could,

---

5. *Koo Siu Yiu v Chief Executive of the HKSAR* (2006) 9 HKCFAR 441. This power to stay a declaration of unconstitutionality has subsequently been invoked on a number of occasions, notably in the case on transgender marriage.

as Mr Justice Hartmann had granted a window of six months only. The subcommittee worked incredibly hard during that time, meeting practically every fortnight, and the very able secretary of the subcommittee was just wonderful in putting together a huge amount of research materials and producing version after version of draft discussion papers and draft recommendations after each meeting. The subcommittee shared its final draft report with the government, and most of the recommendations found their way into the Interception of Communications and Surveillance Ordinance. This was probably the first time that the recommendations of the Law Reform Commission were accepted by the government even before the commission had published its own report. Members of the subcommittee were of course very pleased to allow the government to take the credit!

The subcommittee recommended that covert surveillance carried out by private bodies should also be regulated, as many invasions of privacy were carried out by such bodies. This raised the touchy issue of investigative journalism. The government did not accept this recommendation, and this was one of the controversial issues in the consideration of the Interception of Communications and Surveillance Bill at the Legislative Council.

The temporary validity order made by Mr Justice Hartmann expired on 8 August 2006. The Interception of Communications and Surveillance Bill was finally passed by the Legislative Council on the morning of 6 August 2006, which was a Sunday. While a number of helpful amendments have been proposed by members of the Legislative Council, the government decided to push through the bill and refused to allow any of the 200-odd amendments put forward by pro-democratic members to go forward. As a result, the pro-democratic legislators decided to walk out of the council, and the bill was passed by a vote of 32 to 0.

A new regulatory regime

The Interception of Communications and Surveillance Ordinance introduced a framework to regulate both interception and covert surveillance. Under this ordinance, such activities could only be carried out pursuant to one of two types of authorization: executive authorization by a senior ranking officer for certain types of interception and covert surveillance, and judicial authorization for the more intrusive types of covert surveillance. Authorization could only last for a limited period of time, though it could be renewed, and a detailed code was drawn up governing the use of listening and optical surveillance devices. The ordinance also set up a Commissioner on Interception of Communications and Surveillance, who has the duty to oversee the implementation of and compliance with the ordinance.[6]

6. The first Commissioner was Mr Justice K. H. Woo, who, after his retirement from the judiciary, decided to run for the post of Chief Executive of the HKSAR in 2016.

Hong Kong has gone a long way in the last 30 years in protecting privacy, though, as my colleague Michael Jackson put it, 'the tale of privacy protection is not yet fully told'.[7] With the advance of modern technology, the world described by George Orwell in his famous book of *Nineteen Eighty-Four* is increasingly becoming a reality, and protection of privacy has become a more pressing issue than at any time before. Edward Snowden, the former US intelligence agent, confirmed that the threat is real and surveillance is carried out extensively and intensively by both national and international agents.[8] Can surveillance be eradicated? Probably not. Does it affect us? There is a nice story on the internet:

Mr A called a fast-food store to order his lunch. After he had placed his order, the shopkeeper told him, 'Mr A, according to our information, you should have four family members at home. Do you need to order more food?'

'No, thank you,' Mr A replied. 'I am having lunch with my mum only.'

The shopkeeper then said, 'Okay. Again, according to our information, your mother has high blood pressure. We would suggest a different soup.'

'Thank you,' Mr A said, 'that's a good suggestion. Can I pay by credit card?'

'Yes, of course,' the shopkeeper replied. 'According to our information, you are only about 5 minutes away from our shop. You can pay when you come to collect your order.'

---

7. M. Jackson, 'Right to Privacy, Unlawful Search and Surveillance', in J. Chan and C. L. Lim (eds.), *Law of the Hong Kong Constitution*, 2nd ed. (Hong Kong: Sweet & Maxwell, 2015), p. 817, para 32.187.

8. When Edward Snowden was in Hong Kong, there were rumours that I would be asked to represent him in court to apply for refugee status. There was of course no truth in the story, but within a few hours, I was told that the University had detected over 400 attacks on my computer system, some of which could be traced to North Korea and Mongolia.

IV

Equality before the Law: Law for the Rich and the Resourceful?

9

The Westies

It was an honour to defend a client who argued with her lawyer that she should plead guilty to a criminal charge because she was morally responsible!

My client is a good friend of mine, an elegant professor with an impeccable sense of righteousness. On a sunny Sunday afternoon, she and her husband had just taken their two lovely West Highland terriers for a walk and were about to leave. Their car was parked at the second level below ground of a nearby residential compound. As the two puppies seemed to be exhausted, she decided to unleash them next to her car and gave them some water before they departed.

At that moment, a family with a pram came out from another block at the far end of the parking lot. The baby suddenly screamed, and, provoked by the cries, the two Westies dashed towards the baby. Everyone was shocked and puzzled for a moment what to do. While my client's husband was able to hold back one of the Westies, the other managed to bite the baby on her forearm before it was subdued. Fortunately, the baby suffered only a nasty-looking but minor injury. My client apologized for the accident, and the incident ended as she and her husband drove away with the dogs.

A few months later, my client was charged with two criminal offences under the Rabies Ordinance. The offences alleged that my client, being the keeper of the Westies, permitted the dogs, which were not on a leash or otherwise under control, to be in a place from which they might reasonably be expected to wander into a public place.

This was the first time my client had come into direct contact with the legal system. Naturally she was anxious, not knowing what to expect. In our first conference, I tried to allay her anxiety by giving her an outline of what would be coming and then an analysis of the prospect of her being found guilty.

'It's not in dispute that you are the keeper of the Westies. It is also not in dispute that the dogs were not on leash at the material time. The wording of the offence suggests that the dogs were initially not in a public place, but as they were not under control, they might reasonably be expected to wander into a public place. Thus, the main issue is whether it is reasonable to expect that the dogs, not being under control, might wander into a public place.'

'Is the car park a public place?' My client asked sensibly, as you would have expected from a learned professor. 'It's the car park of a private residential block.'

'Good observation. Yet the mere fact that it is a parking lot in a private residential estate does not necessarily mean that it is not a public place.' I started to explain briefly the legal exposition of the meaning of 'public place'.

It sounded baffling to a lay person that the legal definition of a 'public place' could be so controversial, thanks to the ingenuity of generations of lawyers.

The parking lot in question was a huge underground parking lot for three residential blocks. These blocks were spaciously set apart from one another, and they formed a compound that was surrounded by a wall and fences so that outsiders could not enter the compound freely. At the entrance to the compound, which was staffed, there was a sign saying that this was a private place. Thus, whatever the intricacies of the case law might be, it is most likely that the parking lot was not a public place.

That was not the end yet. The offence would only be completed if it was reasonable to expect that the dogs, that were not in a public place, might wander into a public place. The site of the accident was a large low-density residential compound situated in a rather quiet part of Hong Kong Island. The accident took place at the second lower-ground-floor car park. There was only one exit driveway leading to the first lower-ground-floor car park. The dogs would have to run through about 30 parking spaces to reach the exit driveway to the first lower-ground-floor car park. From there, they would have to run through about another 80 parking spaces to reach the exit driveway leading to the ground floor and then another 100 metres to be out of the compound to reach the public road. Was it reasonable to expect the dogs to run that distance, with all the twists and turns through two levels of car parking space and driveway to get eventually into a public place?

I was fairly confident that there must be a reasonable doubt that the dogs might wander all the way to a public place, and therefore there was a good chance that the prosecution would not be able to prove its case. All that were needed were some nice photos showing the environment, and it would be a pretty convincing defence case.

After I had finished my analysis, my client looked at me with a puzzled expression.

'Are you telling me that I'm not guilty? How can that be? I am responsible for leaving the dogs unleashed, and as a result, one of the dogs bit the baby. I feel very sorry about this, and it is only responsible for me to face the consequences,' my client said, and she sounded serious.

'That's very noble of you, but,' I tried to explain, 'in criminal cases the burden of proof is on the prosecution, and it is for the prosecution to prove that you are guilty.'

'So? That doesn't change the fact that I am responsible and guilty of the offence!'

'Ah, whether you are morally responsible is one thing; whether you have committed a crime is quite another. A crime is defined by law and is committed only when every single element of the criminal offence has been established beyond reasonable doubt.'

'You talk like a lawyer! It sounds like split personality. So are you saying that I am not criminally liable even though I am morally responsible? The fact remains that I left the dog unleashed and it bit the baby. I have apologized for that and should live up to my apology. It is just morally wrong and irresponsible for me to walk away like that!' My client was obviously unconvinced.

'Well,' I tried again, 'there are civil liabilities and criminal liabilities. If the parents of the baby sue you later in a civil claim for compensation, it would be perfectly proper and indeed noble for you to accept your responsibility and to pay for whatever damages are appropriate to compensate for the injuries of the baby. Civil action is about rights and responsibilities between individuals.

'Criminal responsibility is quite different. It is about punishment, and the criminal justice system might be perceived as state machinery that allows systemic deprivation of the personal liberty of the citizens,' I continued. 'To protect liberty, a criminal offence is committed only when the conduct satisfies the legal definition of a crime. If the conduct does not amount to a crime, the individual should not be punished even though the conduct may be morally reprehensible. Many bad habits are disgusting, but they are not criminal conduct!

'Besides, we require the prosecution to prove guilt and not the defendant to prove innocence. It is true under this system some "guilty" defendants may walk away because the prosecution is unable to prove their guilt, but we think this is a better system. Therefore, the question is not whether you are morally wrong but whether your conduct amounts to a crime, and it is for the prosecution to prove that.'

'Are you saying that I have not committed a crime or that the prosecution will be unable to prove that I've committed a crime? That seems absurd to me! Well, if you say so, all right; you're the lawyer. I'll do what you suggest despite my misgivings! After all, you are trying to convince me that I am not guilty, whatever my conscience tells me.' My client was prepared to give up.

Fortunately, most crimes do involve morally reprehensible conduct. Yet law is not there to uphold morality, and it is unnecessary, and perhaps undesirable too, to try to uphold all moral behaviour by law.

In the end, we decided to prepare a submission to the prosecution setting out our arguments to show why we considered that there was no criminal offence on the facts of this case and to try to convince the prosecution not to proceed with the charges. The discussion took a few months, and eventually the prosecution agreed to offer no evidence and drop the charges.

When I told my office colleagues about this story, their reaction was not what I expected. 'Your client was lucky to have your service. Indeed, not only a senior barrister but also an experienced solicitor and some law students who did the background legal research.' One of my colleagues told me another story. A domestic helper of a friend of hers was shopping in a supermarket. She had just picked up some washing liquid when she received a phone call. As she talked on the phone and was carried away by the conversation, she inadvertently wandered beyond the precinct of the supermarket. She was immediately intercepted by the staff of the supermarket. They called the police and she was eventually charged with an offence of shoplifting. It was not in dispute that she was on the phone at the time and that she had enough money to pay for the washing liquid. She had a clear criminal record, and her employer, for whom she had worked for almost 8 years, was prepared to testify for her character. She had a lawyer, whom she met for the first time in court for a few minutes, and he convinced her to plead guilty. My colleague was very angry about the injustice in this case. She thought that there was a world of justice for the rich and the resourceful and another world for those who have no means and no access to lawyers.

I have to concede that there is no absolute equality between the rich and the poor. Yet the fact that the poor are not treated equally should not be a reason that the resourceful should be denied a fair treatment. Equality before the law should be equality for everyone, poor or rich, resourceful or otherwise. The Westies case just reminds us that there is a lot more we could do for people like the domestic helper in the shop-lifting case. One thing I keep telling my students is that what appears mundane to us may be the most important thing in the life of our clients, and we should always try to be generous with time for those who rely on our advice and service.

My client has since put on her profile page a picture of the two Westies in front of a court building, and in appreciation for my pro bono assistance, she sent me a book with a title from the famous words of Shakespeare: *The First Thing We Do—Let's Kill All the Lawyers*!

The Westies

10

The rich, the poor, and the sandwiched

Pro bono legal service

It has often been said that justice is only available to the rich and the resourceful. This is not to say that our court is biased in favour of the rich and the powerful. Indeed, our court is by and large fair and does live up to the ideal as represented by the Goddess of Justice—holding an impartial balance between the litigants, be they rich or poor. However, it cannot be disputed that those who are well off do enjoy some advantages in our legal system. They can afford the service of the best legal brains, and sometimes this enables them to manoeuvre the complex legal processes to their advantage, or simply to wear down their opponents through substantial financial resources. In one of the best-known probate cases in Hong Kong over the validity of some wills, rumour was that nearly all the silks in Hong Kong were briefed by one side, irrespective of whether they were in probate practice, so that they would not have been able to act for the other side!

Yet this is only half of the truth. Those who are sufficiently poor to qualify for legal aid are not necessarily in any worse-off position. With the state backing up their litigation, they are able to litigate at arm's length with the rich and the resourceful. The legal aid schemes run by the Legal Aid Department in Hong Kong are fairly generous. They offer legal representation at District Court or above. While the applicants have to satisfy a means test, i.e., their disposal income should not exceed a statutory limit, or an additional merit test in civil trials or criminal appeals, i.e., the applicants should have at least a reasonable prospect of success in the litigation, or whether it is in the interest of justice to grant legal aid in the case of criminal trials,[1] there is no ceiling of expense on a case once legal aid is granted. Reasonable expenses will be approved, and as long as there are reasonable grounds to appeal, legal aid will cover the costs all the way up to the Court of Final Appeal. In important cases, the Legal Aid Department is prepared to fund the best counsel, including London silks, to take up the case. As we moved to a new constitutional regime in 1997, it was particularly vital for our Court of Final

---

1. The merit test is more relaxed for criminal trials because everyone is presumed innocent in our system. It is not necessary for a defendant to prove his or her innocence, and all defendants are entitled to insist that the prosecution prove their guilt. The merit test for criminal trials requires the Director of Legal Aid to consider if it is in the interest of justice to grant legal aid, and the director can grant legal aid even if the accused person does not satisfy the means test if this is in the interest of justice.

Appeal to provide guidance and to lay down important constitutional principles in the early days of the new regime. Our Court of Final Appeal might not have been able to do that without the Legal Aid Department's generous approach to funding legal representation. Offering a generous legal aid scheme is challenging, not only financially but also in political reality, given that the Legal Aid Department is part of the government and most of the constitutional cases are brought against the government. In my professional life I have come across many legal aid officers. They are competent, dedicated, professional, and reasonable lawyers. They work behind the scenes and seldom get the recognition that they very much deserve in safeguarding the rule of law in Hong Kong.

The worst-off group in our legal system is the sandwich class—those who are neither rich enough to take advantage of the legal system nor poor enough to qualify for legal aid. Justice may well be too expensive for them! Unfortunately, Hong Kong does not have any good pro bono legal services that could assist those who for one reason or another fall outside the net of the state legal aid scheme. The Judiciary has set up a Legal Resources Centre, but given that the court has to remain impartial, the Resources Centre merely provides information on legal services available. The Hong Kong Bar Association runs a Free Legal Representation Scheme and may provide representation in meritorious cases or upon the request of the court. The Law Society has a pro bono legal service scheme that is not active at all. Many individual barristers and solicitors are willing to provide free legal service, but only a handful of law firms are willing to take up pro bono cases. The large law firms, especially those in the so-called magic circle, could have done a lot more in this respect when their London or US headquarters are far more active in taking up pro bono cases.

When I took up the deanship at the Faculty of Law, I decided that the law school should run a pro bono legal service. From an educational and pedagogical perspective, nothing could be better than engaging students in real cases to teach them how to apply the law to real situations, the soft skills of handling clients, and above all, professional ethics and conduct. At the same time, it could inculcate in our students in their early days of legal education the value of pro bono service, showing them that law students should and could use their legal knowledge to contribute to a fairer society. The service would also help to meet a huge and yet unmet demand for legal services in the community.

Having discussed this idea with a few colleagues who were very supportive, I first looked at the best practice in the common law world. Legal clinics have been prevalent in US law schools for many years, and a similar practice has been established in the United Kingdom and Australia. We then engaged a consultant from a leading US law school to advise us on how to set up a pro bono legal service in the university. Her advice was very encouraging. The initial response from Professor Tsui Lap-Chee, then the vice-chancellor of the University, was equally heartening.

Having taken these preparatory steps, I then approached the Hon Andrew Li, the Chief Justice, for his advice. Andrew is the first Chief Justice of the HKSAR and a leader with great foresight. Under his able leadership, the Court of Final Appeal has established itself as one of the finest courts in the common law world. He also managed to persuade a panel of most distinguished judges in the common law world to serve on our Court of Final Appeal as overseas judges, thereby enhancing the international reputation of the Hong Kong court. To me, Andrew has always been a great mentor.

Andrew immediately supported the idea and suggested that we approach the Small Claims Tribunal as a start. The Small Claims Tribunal has an exclusive jurisdiction over civil claims of not more than $50,000. In view of the small size of the claims, no lawyer is allowed in the Small Claims Tribunal. Thus, our service at the Tribunal would not affect any practising lawyers. The small size of the claims does not mean that the law involved is necessarily simple, and our assistance would no doubt be most welcome. Together with Eric Cheung, my colleague in the Faculty, we visited the Chief Adjudicator of the Small Claims Tribunal, who immediately welcomed our assistance. The Tribunal has a large number of cases, and as no lawyers are allowed, the claimants normally have little idea of how to proceed with their claims. Pleadings are not properly done, and the parties are often far from ready in preparing their case when they arrive in court, let alone having the evidence ready. More often than not, the judge at the first hearing has to brief the parties about what they need to do and what evidence will be required. The hearing would then have to be adjourned. The requirements of the court are rarely fully complied with at the adjourned hearing, and so a further adjournment is needed. The Tribunal was thus very enthusiastic about our assistance, which we hoped would result in more efficient use of the court's time and shorten the hearings.

Yet we soon ran into a formidable problem. Being the only body that offers legal assistance to the parties before the Small Claims Tribunal, we could only act for one party, hence leaving the other side without assistance. The court has to be impartial, and its active promotion of our services would mean putting one party in a disadvantageous position. We considered a number of options, but none seemed to be able to address this problem. Eventually, it was decided that we would assist one party only if the other party was 'represented', either by the Department of Justice or by an inhouse lawyer, provided that they consented to our assistance to their opponent. The Secretary for Justice readily gave his consent for any cases before the Small Claims Tribunal in which the government was involved, but there were not too many such cases. There were cases of major corporations being involved and being represented by their own in-house lawyers, but in none of these cases was consent to our acting for the other side forthcoming.

Our proposal was also warmly received by the Bar Association, the Department of Justice, and the Legal Aid Department. However, we encountered immense difficulties with the Law Society. To answer concerns about the quality of the service, I explained that all of our legal services would only be provided by qualified lawyers with valid practising certificates. The students would be involved in taking instructions from lay clients. They would do the necessary research and prepare a memo for their supervisor, who would be a qualified lawyer. The students would be given training in interviewing techniques and might give advice only in a mock session before their supervisors. The students would then join their supervisors in the real session when the supervisors were giving advice to the clients, and the students would be responsible for following up with the cases. If we had to take the cases further than just providing legal advice, a law firm on our list would be properly engaged, and the conditions for the law firms to be on our list included that they would provide the service on a pro bono basis and would take on our students to help with the cases. On the issue of liability, we would take out whatever professional insurance was required by the Law Society in the same way as any law firm. We would also adopt the Code of Conduct as prescribed by the professional bodies. The qualified lawyers on our scheme would be subject to the disciplinary jurisdictions of the professional bodies. We undertook to exercise similar disciplinary action against any students who might act in breach of any professional code of conduct. I further assured the Law Society that similar pro bono legal service schemes existed in many common law jurisdictions and that not only would such services not adversely affect the practice of any practising lawyers but they might in fact sometimes bring business to these lawyers.

The Law Society was not moved. They insisted that I should set up a law firm in the University. There would have been immense problems with this suggestion, as the legal definition of a law firm is an enterprise for commercial gain. Besides, the law at that time was that a law firm could only be set up by a person, not by a corporation, and this meant that, once the staff member who set up the law firm left the university, the law firm would go with him. None of the jurisdictions that we looked at required the university to set up a law firm to provide clinical legal services.

I appeared before a subcommittee of the Law Society and was met with a stone wall. Ten minutes into the meeting, it was clear to me that none of the members had even read our detailed proposal. The meeting did not take us anywhere.

My good friend Mr Huen Wong, the then President of the Law Society whom I have known for over 20 years, was sympathetic. Instead of pushing for an endorsement from the Law Society, his advice was that I try to find a way that would not contravene any regulation of the Law Society, and then just go ahead.

So, we turned to the existing practice. The Law Society and the Bar Association jointly run a Duty Lawyers and Free Legal Advice Scheme. Under that scheme, free legal advice is provided by qualified lawyers at various District Offices. The University was one of the accredited centres under this scheme though we had ceased offering advice at the University for some time, as only a handful of our staff were involved in that scheme. It was Eric's suggestion that we could revive the service under the scheme and try to model our service along the line of the scheme. We soon worked out a feasible model. The timing was right. We were about to move to the Centennial Campus. I included in the design of our new building a centre for clinical legal education, which is a small office with interview rooms where we could meet clients and conduct training for students. To avoid any unnecessary eyebrow-raising, the service, even up to this date, is officially called the Clinical Legal Education Programme rather than a legal clinic.[2]

It took me quite a few years to get through all these hurdles, and our legal clinic was formally open soon after the Faculty moved into the Cheng Yu Tung Tower on the Centennial Campus. Eric was appointed the director of the Clinical Legal Education Programme. We have recruited two other full-time lawyers to work on the Programme and have tried to keep the supervisor-student ratio to 1:8. We were also glad to be able to enlist the voluntary assistance of a number of practising lawyers as part-time supervisors and a number of law firms that are willing to partner with us to provide pro bono service. Given the history, we adopted a low profile with our service. Even so, we have handled over 1,000 cases since opening in 2012, which testifies to the strong public demand for legal services.

Apart from tendering legal advice, we would, if possible, assist lay clients to solve their problems. If legal aid has been refused, we can help them appeal against the decision of refusal if we are satisfied with the merits of the claim. The Legal Aid Department, which takes our assessment very seriously, has on a number of occasions reversed their decisions of refusal upon reading our analysis. There are also cases that we may take up in which the client would be represented by one of our staff through the associated law firms or by practising lawyers who agreed to take up the case on a pro bono basis. As an academic programme, we have introduced an appropriate system for training, supervision, and assessment of the participating students. I am pleased that the feedback on our service from clients, participating lawyers, and students has been consistently excellent. The students feel a sense of mission in taking up these cases. It is one programme in which students keep coming back to help long after they have completed it, and some even ask to retake it after they have already passed.

One of the early cases that was taken up by our programme involved a young boy from a working-class family in a public housing estate. One day after school, he was playing basketball along the long and winding Sau Mau Ping Road on his way back home. He threw the basketball against the wall on one side of the road but failed to catch it when it bounced back. At just that time a police officer on a motorbike was coming down along Sau Mau Ping Road. He swerved his motorbike to avoid the basketball, fell, and hit the wall along the Road and was injured. Sometime later, the government lodged a civil claim for negligence against the boy. The family was shocked by the claim, which they could in no way afford. The pressure of litigation seriously disrupted the happy life of the family. The boy's parents tried every possible means and managed to raise some money from friends and relatives. They offered a settlement, which was rejected as it was far below the claim. The government took the view that they could not justify to the Audit Commission accepting a much lesser sum of money than the claim and insisted on going ahead with the civil claim. The family was devastated. The matter dragged on for a few years. The boy, who had once done

---

2. Interestingly, the Clinical Legal Education Programme received the Law Society's Pro Bono and Community Service Award in December 2016.

very well academically, suffered mental depression. He became withdrawn and sullen. His academic performance deteriorated dramatically, and he was oppressed by a strong sense of guilt, as he felt he had let down his family. The case was referred to us by a pastor who had been counselling the boy.

Our legal team went through the papers, and after extensive research, we came to the view that the boy had a reasonable defence. We then made a written submission to the Secretary for Justice, urging him to consider dropping the case. After some discussion, the Secretary for Justice decided that the case should not proceed further.

Most of the cases taken up by our legal clinic are criminal matters. One of the weirdest cases involved a man who was charged with an offence of criminal damage.[3] He was the owner of a residential unit on the top floor of a building. His unit included the flat roof, and the water tank of the building was installed on the rooftop. He had a hobby of flying kites and often climbed to the top of the water tank to fly his kite. Apparently he had a dispute with the management committee of his building about his hobby. The management committee decided to set up some barbed wire on the railings above the flat roof owned by the defendant, to prevent him from accessing the water tank. One day, it was alleged that a section of the barbed wire had been cut away, and the defendant was seen flying a kite from the top of the water tank. The damage to the barbed wire led to the charge of criminal damage.

The defendant denied that he was on the rooftop or that he had damaged the wire fence. His defence was that he had been framed by the management committee. At the Magistrates' Court, the presiding magistrate apparently found this case relatively minor and not worth the time for a full trial. He invited the defendant to consider agreeing to be bound over. This would mean that the defendant voluntarily agreed to abide by good behaviour and the case would be dismissed with no criminal record. If the defendant agreed to this course, the case could be disposed of within minutes. The defendant, however, declared his innocence and said that this was a frame-up. He insisted on going to trial.

Not being a well-educated person, the defendant had no idea how to conduct cross-examination, and tended to 'make a speech' rather than asking questions in cross-examination. He was repeatedly interrupted and criticized by the magistrate, who was clearly getting impatient, for wasting the court's time. While the defendant had prepared a written statement of his defence, the magistrate repeatedly said that he would 'take no notice of it whatsoever' and did not give the defendant an opportunity to explain himself or to put his case to the witnesses. Part of the transcripts read:

Defendant: Your Worship, there is something which

Court: What is it?

Defendant: I hope you would approve.

---

3. *HKSAR v Chan Shu Hung*, Mag Appeal No 425 of 2011.

Court:	What is it?
Defendant:	If I speak a lot, too much of your time might be taken up, so I have written . . . I have written something for Your Worship to have a look at, so as to give you some idea of what this is about, to make it easier for you to reach a decision.
Court:	At this stage, I'll take no notice of it whatsoever. The trial is a cold-blooded (冷酷) process. Just now I have explained this process to you, because you said . . .
Defendant:	It is just about the facts of this case.
Court:	I will take no notice of it whatsoever.

Before the prosecution closed their case, the magistrate, without any prior warning, said that he found the defendant 'speaking in a somewhat incoherent and confused manner'. He decided to adjourn the hearing and remanded the defendant to Siu Lam Psychiatric Centre for 14 days for assessment of his mental fitness. At the resumed hearing two weeks later, the defendant decided to change his plea to guilty. He was convicted and fined $500.

The case came to us, and we were shocked at the rough justice that had been meted out to the defendant. We lodged an appeal on his behalf. There was no basis for the magistrate to suggest that the defendant was mentally unfit. Even if there was evidence to this effect, the magistrate had failed to consider the option of granting bail to the defendant pending psychiatric assessment. There was no justification to remand the defendant in custody. The criminal damage was of a minor nature, and the defendant had a clear record. Even if he was found guilty, there was no likelihood that the offence would attract a custodial sentence. Indeed, as the magistrate himself decided, the sentence was a fine only.

Eric conducted the appeal before the Court of First Instance. Madam Justice Barnes went through the audio recording and the transcript and agreed that there was no reasonable basis to conclude that the defendant was mentally unfit or incoherent. The court found that what the magistrate did was 'very unfair to the defendant' and that his repeated criticism and intervention had denied the defendant a fair trial. The appeal was allowed. We later helped the defendant to claim compensation for miscarriage of justice, and that process took almost two years!

These may not be glamorous cases, but each of them affects profoundly the life of an ordinary citizen. I often tell my students that, when they read cases, they should read them with compassion. These cases are not just law reports but sad or even traumatic events in the lives of real people. Law students should feel angry when justice has not been done and should find out why our system has failed to do justice.

When I stepped down as dean, I was sometimes asked what my greatest achievement was in my 12 years of deanship. I am not sure that there were any, but if I have to give an answer, I would unhesitatingly say I am most proud of setting up the clinical legal education programme. My wish is that one day it can be formally called a legal clinic and that every law student would have an opportunity to go through clinical legal education.

V

Presumption of Innocence

11

The Sham Shui Po drug addicts case

Life is full of irony. Sometimes what happens in real life can be more fictitious and incredible than fiction. One of the weirdest accidents that I have come across was a fatal injury case that I handled in my early years of practice. The deceased was a shopkeeper in Cheung Sha Wan. The shop was situated on the ground floor of busy Cheung Sha Wan Road. What it sold I cannot remember now. One afternoon the shopkeeper was sitting as usual at the cashier counter near the entrance of the small shop. A private vehicle that emerged from nowhere came along the road at high speed. The driver had apparently lost control of the car and tried unsuccessfully to slow it down. It hit a road sign outside the shop. The impact was so strong that the car bounced off into the outer lane, hit the concrete divider, and finally came to a halt some 300 yards away. The signpost was bent upon collision and fell towards the shop, hitting the shopkeeper on the head before he realized what had happened. He had joined the heavenly choir before the ambulance arrived.

It was a tragic and most unusual kind of accident. It was difficult to imagine that a fatal accident could have happened that way. Yet it also taught me that sometimes the weirdest and most incredible story might not necessarily be untrue.

In the late 1970s and early 1980s, the legal profession was concerned about the prevalence of a number of offences in the Magistrates' Courts. These offences, including loitering, unlawful possession, simple possession of a dangerous drug, and possession of a dangerous drug for the purpose of trafficking, share a number of characteristics. A lot of these offences had a similar factual pattern. The evidence was largely based on the oral testimony of one or two police officers and the defendant. It was the word of the police officers against that of the defendant. Most of the defendants came from the lower working class and were not well educated. Some of them might have criminal records. Most of them were unable to express themselves well in daily life, let alone in court. In light of frequent allegations of framing, the Bar Association and the Law Society jointly introduced a Duty Lawyer Scheme which, among other things, provided free legal representation to defendants charged with one of the nine specified offences in the Magistrates' Court (the scope of the scheme was later expanded to cover all criminal charges that carried a custodial sentence). This proved to be a most valuable service, as legal aid offered by the government's Legal Aid Department does not cover legal representation in the Magistrates' Court.

I was assigned by the Duty Lawyer Scheme to act for two defendants in a simple possession of drugs case. The prosecution case was fairly typical. At around 1 a.m. in Sham Shui Po, two police officers were doing high-rise patrol. When they reached the landing between the first floor and the street level, they found the two defendants on the landing, acting suspiciously. On seeing the police officers, the second defendant dashed out into the street. A police officer chased after him and arrested him in the street. He was found to be in possession of a small packet of powder that was subsequently certified to contain traces of heroin. The second defendant was recorded to have said, 'Ah sir, give me a chance.'

The first defendant was detained on the landing. The other police officer questioned him about what they were doing. He then conducted a body search and found a plastic packet with some powder, which was subsequently certified by the government chemist to contain traces of heroin. The first defendant remained silent.

The defence case was that this was a frame-up. They were street sleepers. They were on their way back to their usual dwelling place under a bridge after having some noodles that night. As it started to rain, the first defendant recalled that he had a friend who lived on the landing of the building in question, and he intended to borrow an umbrella from him. He did not find his friend there. At that time, the two police officers came down from upstairs. They questioned him and then said he was cheeky. One of the police officers took out a small plastic packet, slipped it into his pocket, and said that he was now going to charge the first defendant for simple possession. The first defendant protested to no avail. He said his friend was waiting for him downstairs. One of the police officers then went downstairs and found the second defendant. He told the second defendant that he was in trouble and arrested him. The second defendant denied that he had said anything about giving him a chance.

This was a classic case of the police and the defendants' versions of facts being diametrically contradictory. The defendants had not given any further statement at the police station. Apart from the exhibit of the plastic packet and the government chemist's certificate, that was basically the prosecution case.

At the conference with the two defendants, they basically affirmed their version of the defence. When asked if they could find their friend who was said to sleep in the building there, the answer was negative. They had tried but could not find him, which was not unusual with sleepers with no fixed abode. I noted that the first defendant walked with a slight limp and asked why he and not the second defendant went upstairs to borrow the umbrella. His answer was that the second defendant did not know his friend. I shrugged my shoulders. This was not a very convincing answer.

While this might well be one of those mundane, run-of-the-mill, drug possession cases that were tried every day in the Magistrates' Court, I somehow felt a bit uneasy with the case. The defence, I must say, was rather weak, if not hopeless, and I had warned my clients of the likelihood of conviction. Yet they stood by their defence.

Shortly before the trial, I decided to do a site visit. To make it as close to the event as possible, I visited the site at around 1 a.m. Like the day of the offence, it was a night with a new moon.

It was a Chinese building of eight storeys, which was fairly typical in that part of Sham Shui Po. The entrance was in an alley that ran at right angles to Fuk Wah Street, one of the main streets in that area, and was situated at about a third of the way down the alley. There were a few lamp posts along the alley, which gave a dim outline of the buildings along the dark alley, and on a night with only a new moon, one could easily vanish into the darkness. Not a soul could be seen around at that time of the night. The only access to the building was by climbing the stairs, and there was no gate at the entrance of the building. At the end of a flight of eight steps from the ground level there was a landing. Half of the landing was occupied by some kind of bed with a blanket and lot of used stuff. It appeared that the stuff had been there for some time, but no one was occupying that space then. The size of the landing was small, and the unoccupied part of the landing was barely enough for one person to pass by. The staircase was also quite narrow, just barely enough to allow two persons of moderate size to walk shoulder to shoulder together. After the landing, there was another flight of eight steps going in the opposite direction to the first floor. Of course, this type of building was not served by any elevator.

The trial was before an expatriate magistrate who had arrived in Hong Kong only a few months earlier. The prosecution first called one of the two police officers to give evidence. The police officer basically set out the prosecution case. On cross-examination, I first asked him to describe the surrounding and the details of the building. He was quite fair, accepting that the staircase was narrow and he and his colleague had to go in single file when they walked along the staircase. He also admitted that half of the landing was occupied by some kind of a dwelling.

Q: Officer, you and your colleague were on high-rise patrol at the material time and were walking downstairs from the top of the building towards the landing?

A: That's correct.

Q: You were in single file. You were in front and your colleague was behind you?

A: Yes.

Q: When you first saw the defendants, you were at the top of the flight of steps and your colleague was behind you?

A: Yes. The defendants squatted on the landing, acting suspiciously. We were only a few steps from the landing.

Q: Eight steps between the landing and the top of that part of the stairs, I reckon?

A: If you say so. I haven't counted, but it was a short flight and eight steps seem more or less right.

Q: There was bedding, blanket, a rice cooker, and some stuff on the landing?

A: Yes, apparently someone has been occupying that space.

Q: When you first saw the two defendants, they were squatting on the unoccupied part of the landing?

A: Yes.

Q: And you agree that with the two of them squatting on the unoccupied part of the landing, there was very little room left on the landing.

A: Agreed.

Q: It would be very difficult for anyone to go up or down the stairs unless the defendants moved to one side?

A: You may say so. No one was going up and down at that time.

Q: And you approached the first defendant and started to question him on the landing?

A: Yes. I found them acting suspiciously. So I ran down the steps to go to the first defendant who was nearest to me.

Q: And your colleague was still behind you when you ran towards the first defendant?

A: Yes, and the second defendant started to run towards the street.

Q: And your colleague immediately chased after him?

A: Yes, that's correct.

Q: The street was a pretty dark alley, and the second defendant could easily have disappeared into the darkness once he was in the street.

A: My colleague managed to arrest him on the street.

Q: How do you know, as you were still on the landing?

A: I was told by my colleague later.

Q: Were you told where exactly the second defendant was arrested by your colleague then? Right at the entrance of the building, or somewhere further down the street?

A: Right at the entrance of the building. My colleague ran fast.

Q: Your colleague was standing behind you when you first saw the defendants. You and the first defendant would be blocking his way. So he had to get past you and the first defendant before he could go down the staircase.

A: Yes, my colleague moved quickly. He managed to get through us and went into the street to chase after the second defendant.

Q: Of course he did, but it may take a little time. There were only eight steps between the landing and the street.

A: My colleague moved quickly.

Q: Did you have to push the first defendant to one side to make way for your colleague to pass through?

A: Not really. The first defendant was squatting on the floor. I held him down and my colleague just jumped over us.

[At this point, the magistrate was a bit impatient.]

Court: Mr Chan, where is this line of cross-examination leading us to? Are you suggesting that the police officer is lying?

A: Your Worship,[1] I am coming to that. The defence case is that this is a frame-up.

Court: Very well. You had better ensure that you can substantiate the defence.

[The hearing began to get rough at this point, with increasing intervention from the Bench. I came to the plastic packet. The witness was well rehearsed and stuck to his line. As part of my duty, I put forward to the witness the defence case for his response.]

Q: Officer, I put it to you that the plastic packet did not come from the first defendant.

A: I disagree. I found it in the possession of the first defendant.

Q: Mr Officer, I put it to you that the plastic packet came from you, and you wrongly alleged that it was from the first defendant.

'Come on, Mr Chan,' the magistrate intervened. 'Are you seriously suggesting that the police officer was carrying a packet of heroin to frame your client?'

'Your Worship, it is my duty to put the defence case to the witness.'

'Of course, but this is just ludicrous! Accusing police officer of planting heroin at your client? Mr Chan, give me a break!'

'Would your Worship be kind enough to allow the witness to answer my question?' It appeared to me that the magistrate had already made up his mind even though we were only halfway through the prosecution case.

The other police officer was called as the second prosecution witness. Like the first police officer, he basically recited his script and adhered to it faithfully; nothing more,

---

1. Magistrates are formally addressed as 'Your Worship' in court. District judges are addressed as 'Your Honour', and judges of the High Court and above are addressed as 'Your Lordship'.

nothing less. For anything that was outside his script, his answer was always that he did not know.

Q: Officer, when you first saw the defendants, you were at the top of the steps from the landing behind your colleague.

A: Yes. We were on high-rise patrol, and my colleague was in front of me as we came down from the top of the building.

Q: Your colleague came down the steps and started questioning the first defendant on the landing?

A: That's correct.

Q: And you ran down to go after the second defendant.

A: Yes. He began to run down the steps to the street when he saw us.

Q: As you came down the steps, your colleague and the first defendant would be blocking your way?

A: I got past them.

Q: It was a very narrow landing with stuff piled up on one side and two men were blocking your way.

A: I managed to get past them.

Q: Did you push them to one side?

A: A little bit.

Q: Did they move to one side to make way for you?

A: I can't remember the details. I managed to get past them.

Q: Could you still see the second defendant when you passed through your colleague and the first defendant?

A: He had run out of the building. I could not see him by then.

Q: When you ran out of the building, you saw the second defendant on the street?

A: Yes.

Q: The street was pretty dark.

A: Yes. I could see the second defendant on the street at a distance.

Q: How far away was the second defendant from you when you first saw him on the street?

A: I can't remember.

Q: Approximately? Would it be about the distance between where you stand now and the door to this courtroom?

A: About that.

Q: That would be about 10 metres.

A: Something like that, I suppose.

Q: And you ran after him and overtook him?

A: Yes. He ran fast, but I ran faster than him.

Q: So you arrested the second defendant on the street somewhere about at least 20 metres from the entrance of the building. Would that be correct?

A: I am not sure about the distance, but probably right. About 20 metres.

Q: The first witness has just told the court that you told him that you arrested the second defendant right at the entrance of the building.

A: I arrested him on the street.

Q: You found a small packet of drugs on him when you arrested him?

A: Yes.

Q: It was a dark alley. He ran 20 metres and at least 10 metres before you saw him. Would you agree that he would have plenty of time to dispose of the drug when he went down to the street?

'Mr Chan, this is speculative. Get on to your next question.' The magistrate was getting impatient.

Having done enough to show that the inconsistencies in the evidence between the two police officers, I let him go.

There was no re-examination, and the prosecution said, 'The case for the prosecution is closed.'

I rose. The magistrate stared at me and said, 'Mr Chan, if you are thinking of making a submission of no case to answer, you can spare it. I rule that there is a case to answer.'

'Your Worship, I don't intend to make any such submission. I am about to suggest to your Worship that maybe this is an appropriate moment for a mid-morning adjournment so that I can advise my clients accordingly!'

The hearing was adjourned for 15 minutes, during which I gave my clients my assessment of the situation. There were a number of discrepancies between the evidence of the two police officers, but the court apparently seemed to find outrageous the idea that police officers would frame anyone. The clients might choose not to give evidence, and the court would then have to rule on the existing evidence and consider whether the prosecution had proved the offence beyond reasonable doubt. If they chose to give evidence, they would be cross-examined by the prosecution. My view was that they would unlikely be able to improve their case by giving evidence, but the choice was theirs.

Just before we finished, the first defendant said to me, 'Mr Chan, thank you for what you have done for us. You know, we are drug addicts. We have criminal records and have been to prison a few times. So, if we were guilty of the offence, we would not mind pleading guilty. It does not concern us at all if we are to go to prison again. After all, prison provides better shelter than sleeping on the street. But we won't plead guilty this time because the stuff wasn't ours. We were framed. That isn't fair, and that's why we are pleading not guilty.'

I thought this was fairly convincing. Having heard the police officers, I was not as certain as before that my clients' version was incredible.

The first defendant decided to give evidence, and the second defendant decided to maintain his right to silence.

After the adjournment, the atmosphere calmed down quite a bit. There was little intervention from the Bench. Perhaps the magistrate felt that he had intervened too much, or was just determined to let me finish the case and then convict. The prosecution seemed to take the hint from the passivity of the Bench and did only minimal cross-examination. I closed the defence case and made the final submission.

'This case turns on the credibility of the evidence of the two police officers,' I began my final submission. 'The court doesn't need to be reminded that the benefit of any doubt goes to the defendants. Are there reasonable doubts? Yes, and plenty, in my submission. The evidence of the two police officers is contradictory in at least four areas. Minor each of them may be if they are looked at individually, but putting them together, they do cast considerable doubt on the credibility of their evidence. It was not in dispute that the size of the landing was so small that it could hardly allow more than two persons to stand there at the same time. With the first defendant and the first prosecution witness standing there, and with all the stuff on the landing, they would have completely blocked the staircase and obstructed anyone from upstairs heading downstairs to the street without considerable pushing. The first police officer's evidence of how the second police officer managed to get past him and the first defendant was most incredible and contradictory to the evidence of the second police officer and the evidence of the first defendant. The prosecution case was that the second defendant ran immediately when he saw the police officers. There were only a few steps to the street. He could have easily reached the street and vanished in the darkness. Yet the prosecution wants this court to believe that the second police officer, who was eight steps up the upper staircase when he first saw the second defendant, managed to run down eight steps, squeeze past his colleague and the first defendant, ran down another eight steps, and was still able to find the second defendant, who was said to have run as soon as he saw the police officers, who could easily have vanished in the dark alley that was only a few steps away, and who could have plenty of opportunities to dispose of the packet of drugs that was said to be found in his possession. And yet, he was there, "on the street", for the police officer to arrest him, with the packet of drugs in his pocket waiting to be found. There was also inconsistency in the evidence between the two police officers regarding the exact location where the second defendant was arrested. The truth is that the second defendant was never on the landing. He had always been waiting for the first defendant downstairs, right at the entrance of the building, and was arrested there and then. There were simply no drugs found. It was a frame-up. The court does not have to accept the evidence of the defendants. It is not for them to prove what actually happened. It suffices that there is reasonable doubt in the prosecution case.'

'Defendants stand up.' The clerk indicated to the defendants as soon as I had finished my submission. The magistrate was prepared to give his judgment.

'I have carefully considered all the evidence in this case and the submission of your counsel. I have also had the benefit of observing the demeanour of the witnesses. As your counsel rightly pointed out, this case turns on the credibility of the prosecution witnesses. Despite the discrepancies in the evidence between the two police officers that were eloquently pointed out by your counsel, which discrepancies I have considered most carefully, I found the police officers honest and reliable witnesses and the offence having been established beyond reasonable doubt. I therefore find both of you guilty.'

Though the verdict did not come as a surprise, I could not help feeling angry about it—not so much because I had lost the case but because the defendants had not been treated fairly. The court was not prepared to listen at all. I was then perhaps too young and too inexperienced to conceal my anger. There was not much to say in mitigation, as both defendants had a history of drug addiction and various previous convictions for petty crimes. Yet the magistrate was prepared to give an extremely lenient and non-custodial sentence. A cynical interpretation was that the sentence would ensure that the defendants would not appeal!

My clients thanked me. The lenient sentence would effectively mean an acquittal for them. Another criminal record would not add anything to their long and blemished background. And still, they maintained that they were innocent. 'Mr Chan, this is not the first time such a thing happened to us, and it won't be the last. Drug addicts, ex-convicts, the vulnerable, and the poor just have to accept that justice is not always on their side.' These were the last words of my clients.

No system is perfect. It would be naïve to pretend that miscarriage of justice does not exist in our system. Yet this is not a reason to accept, let alone condone, it. Most of the time, it is attributable to human fallibility. Cases like the one here remind us how heavy the responsibility of the lawyer is. We are entrusted with the liberty of a person, who has put his trust in us. Every case, no matter how mundane it may appear to be, deserves the best of our ability, for justice can never be taken for granted.

12

The best interest of the client

The MTR case

Is it more difficult to defend a client whom you believe is guilty, or a client whom you believe is innocent? Does it matter? Should it matter?

I was in my limited practice (that is, the second six months of my one-year pupillage) when I received a phone call from a solicitor who was a few years my senior in law school.

'I have a client who was my secondary schoolmate. He needs a barrister, but he can't afford one. Would you be able to help?'

'Of course.' For a very junior barrister, any opportunity to work was sufficiently attractive already.

'Thanks. I will bring him over for a conference at 5:30 this afternoon then.'

My client was a shy young man. He was charged with various offences of forgery and theft. It was alleged that he had stolen 500 used stored value tickets from the MTR and altered the magnetic programme of these tickets to restore them to the full value of $50 each and thus had made a profit out of the sale of those 'forged' tickets.

In 1984, the bulky desktop computer was the very icon of information technology. Steve Jobs had just launched his box-like Mackintosh desktop computers after his failed attempt with Apple Lily. The first generation of mobile phones, merely large bottle-like devices known commonly as 'Big Brother Water Bottle', had just appeared. Most law firms were still using electronic typewriters, and a desktop computer would attract envy from both bosses and secretaries.

Stored value tickets are similar to our Octopus cards today, except that these tickets could only be used on the MTR and could not be topped up once the stored value was exhausted. They came in different values, the maximum being $50. The fare was deducted each time the ticket was used. The advantage of the tickets was that commuters would be able to enjoy the last journey without further payment when the remaining stored value was insufficient to cover the fare of that journey. When the stored value was exhausted, the tickets would automatically be forfeited by the exit machines at the MTR station.

My client worked as a technician at the MTR. He once made some suggestions to refine the stored value ticket system, but his suggestions were rejected by his supervisor on the ground that they were impractical. Yet a few months later, he found that his supervisor had submitted his suggestions to the management as if they came from the supervisor himself. His protest led to nowhere, except that his relationship with his supervisor turned acrimonious.

Shortly after, the MTR encountered a problem of premature forfeiture of stored value tickets. These tickets were forfeited by the exit machines before the stored value was exhausted. Many engineers had worked on the problem but no solution was found. Rumour had it that whoever could solve the problem would get a promotion. My client decided to work on the problem. With his desktop Apple computer, he was able to identify the source of the problem even though he was not yet able to find a solution. Due to his unpleasant experience in the past, he decided not to inform his supervisor of his finding until he managed to find a solution, and he intended to present his solution directly to the management.

MTR common stored value ticket

By then the annual promotion exercise was taking place. He appeared before a promotion board which was chaired by his supervisor. The interview did not go well. He did not get a promotion. Worse still, he was put immediately under a promotion bar, which means he would not get a salary increment until he managed to get a promotion.

Not surprisingly, he felt he was a victim of jealousy and was treated unfairly by his supervisor. He was very upset by the decision. In the course of identifying the problem of premature forfeiture, he managed to break into the computer codes at the back of the stored value tickets. There were three sets of codes, totally about 256 different codes, the first set being the security codes and the second set being the remaining values on the tickets. In the midst of his anger and frustration, he decided to take away 500 used stored value tickets and restore them to their full value of $50. He then sold them to two former secondary school classmates at $25 each, claiming that, being MTR staff, he was entitled to purchase these tickets at a discount. His friends then resold these tickets to other people at $35 each, making a profit for themselves.

A few days later when he calmed down, he regretted what he had done. He had not taken any further tickets and spent the sale proceeds on computer books.

While he had successfully changed the stored values of those tickets, he did not manage to break the third set of codes, which were verification codes. When the value of these tickets was exhausted and forfeited by the exit machines of the MTR, the system was able to detect that these tickets had been tampered with. The matter was reported to the police. A few months later, my client was arrested and was charged with four offences. His case was then transferred to the District Court.

At our first conference, he readily admitted all the facts as alleged by the prosecution and was prepared to face the consequences.

Notwithstanding the confession of guilt, my duty as his counsel was first and foremost to ensure that he had actually committed a crime on the basis of the admitted facts. After some research, my conclusion was that, while there was no defence to the theft charge, it was arguable whether the forgery charge could be sustained. This was probably the first computer crime in Hong Kong, and there could be some novel legal arguments to make. However, I was not confident that the argument would carry the day, and if it were to have any chance of success, it would probably have to be put forward by a more experienced senior counsel than a junior counsel still in his days of limited practice! Yet it was equally clear that my client could not afford a senior counsel. At the same time, a conviction of forgery was likely to carry a custodial sentence.

Counsel has a duty to act in the best interests of his client. He has to give his client independent and professional advice, which on some occasions may not necessarily be what the client would like to hear. In criminal matters, the best interests of the client may not always be fighting the charges. Counsel has a duty to advise accordingly if he comes to an honest view that the chance of acquittal is dim. The decision whether to accept the advice is of course a matter for the client alone.

After I explained to the client the available options and consequences, he agreed to plead guilty. Not unexpectedly, he was troubled and depressed, especially at the not unrealistic possibility of being given a custodial sentence. The next thing was then to plan for the mitigation.

The defendant was charged with four offences, the most serious of which was forgery. It was probably a bit too much for mitigation to carry four offences. After some plea bargain with the prosecution, it was agreed that, if my client pleaded guilty to the forgery and the theft charges, the prosecution would offer no evidence on the remaining charges.

The first opportunity to plead guilty was on the plea day. That would be his first appearance in court. If he pleaded not guilty, the court would normally just extend his bail and adjourn the hearing to another day. If he pleaded guilty, the court would hear mitigation and might determine the sentence then or adjourn for necessary reports before the court decided on the appropriate sentence. The plea court was usually very busy, as the court would have to deal with a large number of cases in a morning. If a defendant was represented, the court would usually, as a matter of courtesy, deal with that case first.

As I had a fairly lengthy mitigation to make, I decided that it would be better to do it after the judge had cleared up all his business in court that morning. So, instead of having my case to go first, I asked the clerk to stand down my case until all other cases had been dealt with that morning. Fortunately, it was not a very busy morning. The court cleared all the cases by morning break, and the judge was refreshed and ready to hear the mitigation, probably after a cup of coffee during the break, knowing that mine would be the last case for that morning.

My client pleaded guilty to the charges of forgery and theft, the forgery relating to the 500 altered stored value tickets and the theft relating to the theft of 500 used stored value tickets (which technically were wasted paper of no value if nothing was to be done to the magnetic code). The prosecution agreed to offer no evidence on the remaining charges and confirmed that my client had a clear criminal record. Then it was my turn to do the mitigation.

Gradually I unfolded my client's story: his background, the previous unhappy experience with his supervisor, the frustration of not being promoted, the circumstances leading to the offence, his regrets and decision not to commit further offences which he could easily have done should he want to make a profit, as well as the fact of his spending the sale proceeds on computer books, his forthcoming guilty plea, his readiness to accept the consequences, the support from his family, his fiancée, his clear record, and genuine remorse. His pride drove him to solve a challenging problem, and the prejudice of his supervisor against him led him to the offence. After all, he was a bright and clever young man who managed to break a complex computer code with a simple Apple desktop computer! He could make good use of his talent to the benefit of the community if he were to be given a chance. In my later life, I have seen that mitigation was done all too often in courts as a matter of routine. Good mitigation, like any good submission, requires careful planning and a lot of preparation. It is to tell a story, and to tell it well, with appropriate compassion. It is not just about setting out the facts but setting them out in a way to persuade and win over the sympathy of the presiding judge.

The mitigation lasted for over an hour, and we finished just before the lunch break. My client was sentenced to two years' imprisonment, which were to be suspended for two years. That means he was allowed to go free, and if he kept himself in good behaviour for two years, the custodial sentence would be spent. That was probably the best sentence that he could have ever expected. His family and fiancée were in court and were happy and relieved that the matter had finally come to an end. I noticed that some senior staff of the MTR were also in the public gallery, not appearing too happy of course.

My client did turn to a new life. He was dismissed by the MTR. He started a small computer company and offered free classes to teach children how to use computers. A few months later, I received his invitation to his wedding ceremony. I went to City Hall, watching the newly wedded couple. They were happy, bathed with the blessings of the winter morning sun. Strangely, I decided to give them my good wishes from afar, and left City Hall, as I thought it was better for them to put the unhappy episode behind them.

13

A confession that came too late

How do you defend someone whom you know is guilty? Every law student has no doubt been asked of this question. There are of course many different possible answers. While we know who is guilty when we watch a movie or a TV series because we are at the crime scene witnessing the crime, facts and evidence are far murkier in real life. There is no independent witness in many crimes. The only persons at the crime scene are the victim and the perpetrator. The perception of victims may or may not be reliable. The same is true of the evidence of witnesses, if any, including both prosecution and defence witnesses. Sometimes there is documentary and independent evidence; sometimes the evidence is no more than the recollection of the victim, who may be giving evidence in court months or even years after the incident. It is not a straightforward task to determine, and to satisfy oneself beyond reasonable doubt, what happened at a particular moment in the distant past.

There are of course restrictions and guidance in the Bar's Code of Conduct on proper conduct in defending someone who has confessed his or her guilt. The first principle is that what constitutes a criminal offence is a matter of fact and law. The mere fact that a client has admitted guilt does not necessarily mean that the client has committed a criminal offence. The client's lawyer has to be satisfied that the client has in law committed a criminal offence. The second principle is that, in our system, the burden of proof is on the prosecution. It is for the prosecution to prove beyond reasonable doubt that a defendant is guilty, not for the defendant to prove his or her innocence. If the prosecution fails to discharge the burden of proof, the verdict of the court is that the defendant is found 'not guilty', not that the defendant is 'innocent'. Following from this principle, it is the right of the defendant to test the prosecution case. The third principle is that counsel owes a duty to the court. He or she must not mislead the court. In the case of a confession of guilt, counsel may test the credibility of prosecution witnesses in order to raise a doubt, but he or she may not put forward a positive case of not guilty, for example by calling witnesses to show the innocence of the client, or test prosecution witnesses on matters that are inconsistent with his or her instructions of guilt. Counsel's hands in conducting the defence are tied when there is a confession of guilt. The fourth principle is that counsel has a duty to provide independent advice to his or her client. If the client's case is weak, counsel has a duty to so advise the client and work out what is in his or her best interest. This best interest may not always be served by fighting the prosecution, especially when the evidence is overwhelming and when there is no credible defence. If needed, counsel may even use strong language to advise the client to enter a guilty plea. The decision, however, must remain that of the client.

So much for the principles. In reality, while there are many defendants who are prepared to accept their own wrongs and readily plead guilty, there are far fewer defendants who confess their guilt and yet insist on defending the criminal prosecution. Far more common is the situation in which a defendant comes up with some excuses, sometimes rather feeble, or sometimes with conflicting versions of defence, and swears to his or her innocence. I have had my share of such clients, and here is one of them.

The dark, narrow winding road leading to Bridal Pool in the New Territories was a popular venue for illegal car racing, an activity that is highly dangerous not only to the participants but also to other road users. The people who participated in such irresponsible conduct came from a variety of backgrounds and did so for different reasons. Some were car maniacs who enjoyed the sheer excitement; some were professionals or young people from relatively well-off families who could not think of a better way to spend their life!

At around 2 a.m. on a winter day, about 15 cars gathered outside a well-known congee restaurant at Tai Wai. With the waving of a towel, the cars roared off with a thundering noise and sped towards Bridal Pool. The wide section of the highway from Tai Wai to Tai Po was ideal for a start. The average speed could well be over 200 km per hour. They overtook other cars on the road and overtook one another from time to time. The dangerous part began when the cars left the highway and plunged into the narrow, winding Tai Po Road. They negotiated bends without slowing down and sometimes cut across at a steep corner to show off their skills.

The police had got wind of the race. A police van was waiting for the racers at a turning circle towards the end of Bridal Pool Road. Another police car was hidden somewhere on a branch road before the circle. The plan was that, once the racers had passed the hidden police car, it would then block the road so that the racers would be caught between the two police vehicles.

The operation went as planned. When the racers reached the circle and saw the police van, they tried to turn around and found that the road had been blocked by another police car. Seventeen people were caught and arrested. All of them were charged with illegal racing. Most of the cars were found to have been modified.

I represented one of them in the criminal trial. He emphatically denied taking part in the illegal racing and swore to the heavens that he was innocent. His case was that he was on his way home that night, and when he reached Tai Mei Tuk he suddenly found that he was sandwiched between several cars that were apparently in a race. The road was so narrow that he had no choice but to keep up with them, and he planned to leave the group when he reached the turning circle, which was the only place where he could leave the racers and turn around, but he was caught before he could do so. His car was not modified, and he did live in the vicinity. I told him that this was not very convincing, but he insisted that he was prepared to swear to Almighty God that he was telling me the truth, the whole truth, and nothing but the truth.

On the day of the trial, the seventeen defendants were represented by four different teams of lawyers. All defendants pleaded not guilty. The first prosecution witness was the police commander in charge of the operation. He was an expatriate officer and was unnecessarily arrogant. He tended to exaggerate his evidence at some points and was rather evasive on other points, sometimes totally unnecessarily. It was obvious that he could not remember some of the details. He could have easily admitted that he could not remember, for these facts were not vital to the case, but instead he insisted on his version, and this could not withstand cross-examination. This cast doubt on the reliability of his evidence on the key issues. By the end of the first day, it was clear that he had given conflicting evidence on a number of issues and was sufficiently discredited in the cross-examination.

On the second day, the prosecution case did not improve with the second witness. Among the defendants, some were drivers and some were passengers, and the police had failed to clearly identify who were drivers and who were passengers. By lunch time, discussions took place between the prosecution and the defence. An agreement was reached that, if all the defendants agreed to be bound over, the prosecution would offer no further evidence. What was originally expected to be a long trial of a strong prosecution case collapsed on the second day!

The case was finished in the afternoon. All the defendants walked free with a binding-over order. I still had my doubts if justice had been done, but as Patrick Yu once said, most criminal prosecutions failed, not because the defence counsel was good but because the prosecution witnesses were too eager to convict. As I left the court, my client came up to thank me, and then he told me, 'Now that it is over, I can tell you that I did take part in the race!' He even offered me a lift to my chambers, which I politely declined.

So much for 'the truth, the whole truth, and nothing but the truth' that he had insisted on so emphatically before the trial! I was not surprised, as I hadn't believed his version. Yet he had a constitutional right to put the prosecution to proof, and this right belongs to him, not his lawyer. If the prosecution fails to prove his guilt, he would be found not guilty (rather than innocent). In our system, we believe that it is better to let some guilty people go free than to wrongly convict an innocent person. So there are bound to be occasions when guilty persons have to be let free. This is the price we pay for a free society.

I had forgotten who the prosecution counsel was, until 15 years later when I received a warm congratulatory letter from John Reading QC on my silk appointment. John, in his usual charming manner, reminded me that we did this case against one another some 15 years earlier!

14

Disturbing the past and paralysing the future

One of the consequences of the presumption of innocence is that the burden of proof of a criminal offence rests with the prosecution, and this burden can only be discharged by proving the offence beyond reasonable doubt. Over time, the prosecution has experienced difficulties in proving certain elements of some offences. One of the solutions is to reverse, by statute, the burden of proof of these elements. These reversed onus provisions, as they are known, take a variety of forms and become quite widespread, as they considerably ease the burden of the prosecution. Before the Bill of Rights in Hong Kong came into force in 1991, there were hundreds of such reverse onus provisions in our law. Not surprisingly, they became obvious targets of attack based on the Bill of Rights.

Drug abuse is a serious problem and a major social concern. While drug trafficking is a criminal offence that carries a heavy penalty, it is quite difficult to prove actual trafficking. Hence, the law has introduced two other offences: simple possession of a dangerous drug, and possession of a dangerous drug for the purpose of trafficking. In order to prove the purpose of possession, the Dangerous Drugs Ordinance, as it was in 1991, contained some reversed onus provisions. If a defendant was found to be in possession of a certain quantity of dangerous drugs (0.5 grams or five packets), he or she was presumed to be in possession for the purpose of trafficking until he or she could prove to the contrary. To make the task of prosecution easier, it was further provided that, if a defendant was found to be in possession of a key to a wide variety of objects, be they a briefcase, a box, a vehicle, or even a house, the defendant was presumed to be in possession of whatever was found there and was further presumed to know the nature of the objects found there. If there were dangerous drugs which exceeded the above quantity, the defendant was further presumed to be in possession of dangerous drugs for the purpose of trafficking, that is, a presumption upon a presumption. The burden of rebutting the presumption was on the defendant. In those days, possession of dangerous drugs was a very common offence in the lower courts, and the framing of innocent defendants was not unheard of.

These statutory provisions were challenged for violating the right to be presumed innocent under the Bill of Rights, as soon as the Bill of Rights came into force in Hong

Kong.[1] In a leading judgment of the Court of Appeal, the court accepted that reversed onus provisions were a necessary evil in the fight against drug crime. But given the potential encroachment on personal liberty, the court established two important principles. In order to justify a reversed onus provision, there must be a rational relationship between the facts proved and the facts presumed; and the reversal of the onus of proof must be a proportionate response to the legitimate aims to be achieved. In simple terms, the government had to ask itself these questions: (1) Why is it necessary to have a reversed onus provision? What objective is to be achieved? (2) If there is a legitimate objective, has a proper balance been found between the objectives and the protection of individual rights? In particular, what facts have to be proved and what facts are to be presumed? Do the presumed facts follow rationally from the proved facts? (3) In considering if a proper balance has been achieved, what alternatives are there? Would the interference with individual rights go too far? The balancing exercise is to be approached with a starting point in favour of individual rights, and the government has to produce cogent and persuasive evidence in order to tilt the balance.

Under this statutory provision, the facts proved were that the defendant was in possession of 0.5 grams or five packets of a dangerous drug. The facts presumed were that he possessed them for the purpose of trafficking, which was a serious offence. Was there a rational relationship between the facts proved and the facts presumed? The prosecution produced evidence showing that the daily drug consumption of an average addict would be between 0.5 and 0.9 grams. Thus, possession of 0.5 grams was more consistent with the purpose of self-use than with trafficking. Likewise, the presumption based on five packets of a dangerous drug bears no rational connection with possession for the purpose of trafficking. Indeed, there could well be less than 0.5 grams of the dangerous drug in the packets, as there was no minimum quantity required under this presumption. Both presumptions were found to have failed the rationality test. The same applied to the presumption that was based on a key. There were too many occasions when it would not be rational to conclude that the objects found in a container belonged to the defendant on whom the key to the container was found or that the defendant should know the nature of these objects. Drugs found inside a taxi or a mini-bus, or drugs found inside a house when every member of the household had a key, were prime examples. The net of the presumption had been cast unjustifiably wide.

The judgment of the Court of Appeal in *Sin Yau Ming* was warmly received. Contrary to what some critics have suggested, the repeal of these presumptions has made little impact on the war against drug abuse. In most cases, the quantity of drugs found would speak for itself, and the packaging or instruments found (such as scale pans) would allow a reasonable jury to infer that the drugs were possessed for the purpose of trafficking. Indeed, in the *Sin Yau Ming* case, the defendant was found to be in possession of 337 grams of salts of esters of morphine! The case has triggered

---

1. *R v Sin Yau Ming* (1991) 1 HKPLR 88.

numerous challenges against different reversed onus provisions in our courts as well as a comprehensive review of all reversed onus provisions in our law.

A less obvious reversed onus provision was successfully challenged in the case of *Lee Kwong-kut*.[2] This case involved the offence of unlawful possession under section 30 of the Summary Offences Ordinance, another offence frequently found in the Magistrates' Courts. Under the ordinance, a person who was found to be in possession of anything that might be reasonably suspected of having been stolen or unlawfully obtained (in this case, $1.7 million) would commit an offence if he was unable to provide a satisfactory account. The purpose of the offence was to punish those in possession of stolen or otherwise unlawfully obtained goods. The prosecution was only required to prove that a police officer had reasonable suspicion that the goods were stolen or unlawfully obtained. At that point the burden of proof switched to the defendant, who had to provide a satisfactory explanation. Failing to do so would result in a conviction, which suggested that the reasonable suspicion would then be treated as proof beyond reasonable doubt. A Magistrates' Court found the offence in contravention of the presumption of innocence. This was confirmed by the Court of Appeal in June 1992. The Attorney General further appealed to the Privy Council, which confirmed in May 1993 that the offence was inconsistent with the presumption of innocence under the Bill of Rights.

Under the Bill of Rights Ordinance, any statute which is found to be inconsistent with the Bill of Rights is deemed to have been repealed by the Bill of Rights Ordinance as from 8 June 1991, the date when the ordinance came into effect. In 1994, Kwok Hing Man, who was convicted of the same offence as Lee Kwong-kut after 1991, applied to the court for an appeal 'out of time' with a view to expunging his criminal record.[3] His argument was that he was convicted of a criminal offence which was no longer in existence at the time of his conviction. It was found that, between June 1991 and May 1993 when the Privy Council confirmed the repeal of section 30 of the Summary Offences Ordinance, 364 persons were convicted of this criminal offence. Many of them had already served their sentence. The Attorney General opposed the application, arguing that there must be finality in criminal law. That is, the system could not work if settled convictions could be reopened later. There would be undue disturbance to the criminal justice system if criminal convictions in the distant past could be reopened many years later merely because the criminal offence was subsequently found to be inconsistent with the Bill of Rights. The Court of Appeal took the exceptional step of consulting all judges of the court and decided to exercise its discretion to allow an appeal out of time, the effect of which was that the criminal conviction of all of these defendants would be set aside, as the offence had already been repealed at the time of their conviction.

This case raises a difficult constitutional problem. If the court today finds a criminal offence inconsistent with the Bill of Rights or the Basic Law, the criminal offence would be deemed to have been repealed on 8 June 1991 in the case of the Bill of Rights,

---

2. *Attorney General v Lee Kwong-kut* [1993] 2 HKCLR 186.
3. [1994] 2 HKCLR 160.

or 1 July 1997 in the case of the Basic Law. What happens to all the criminal convictions in the interim? This problem is not confined to criminal law. Many past relations, such as those in family law, could be disturbed. What if a statutory procedure for admission to a mental hospital was found to be unconstitutional, resulting in unlawful admission of mental patients? It would not be a welcome prospect if the government were compelled to release hundreds of mental patients into the community.

The problem arose in the *Lam Siu Po* case, in which the court found that the statutory restriction on legal representation in police disciplinary proceeding was inconsistent with the Basic Law.[4] As a result of this case, over 80 police officers applied to the court to set aside their disciplinary convictions. In many of these cases the time limit for lodging an appeal had long expired, and the applicants had to apply for leave to appeal out of time. Different judges exercised their discretion differently to allow or refuse leave to appeal out of time. Eventually, the Court of Final Appeal held that the mere fact that the law had been changed in favour of a litigant who had previously lost on that view of the law was not a sufficient reason to justify an extension of time for appeal. While this decision dealt with part of the problem, the difficult situation in *Kwok Hing Man* remains unresolved.

The issue arose, and was ducked, in the *Hung Chan-wa* case.[5] This was another case involving the reversed onus provisions in the Dangerous Drugs Ordinance, which has since been amended. The amended provisions were still found to be inconsistent with the Basic Law, as the Court of Final Appeal found that a defendant could be convicted of trafficking or possession even if he could raise a reasonable doubt that he had legal possession or that he had knowledge that what he possessed was a dangerous drug. The burden could only be discharged if he could prove the absence of possession or knowledge on a balance of probabilities. The government had been concerned that this finding would result in setting aside the criminal conviction of many defendants of this offence in the past. The court, however, took the view that the mere fact that a defendant was able to rebut the presumption by a lesser standard of proof did not mean that his conviction was necessarily invalid. It preferred not to express a view on the validity of *Kwok Hing Man*.

The cautious approach of the court is understandable. It would be difficult for any court to uphold a criminal conviction for an offence that no longer exists. It would be even more difficult to ask the court to uphold the continued incarceration of a defendant who has been convicted of such an offence and is still in custody. While finality is highly desirable, it has to be balanced against any undue interference with personal liberty.

Not only could a decision on unconstitutionality unduly disturb the past, but it might also jeopardise the future by creating a legal vacuum. This happened in the covert surveillance case.[6] When the court found that the Executive Order authorizing

---

4. (2009) 12 HKCFAR 237. See Chapter 15 for this case.
5. *HKSAR v Hung Chan-wa* (2006) 9 HKCFAR 614.
6. *Koo Sze Yiu v Chief Executive of the HKSAR* (2006) 9 HKCFAR 441. See Chapter 8.

covert surveillance was inconsistent with the right to privacy under the Basic Law, the government argued that it would need time to introduce a new law to govern covert surveillance, and in the meantime, there would be serious consequences for the enforcement of law and order if the law enforcement agencies did not have the power to conduct covert surveillance. Mr Justice Hartmann was prepared to make an order of temporary validity so that the old law and the Executive Order would remain valid for six months, to allow the government to introduce the necessary remedial legislation. The conceptual dilemma faced by the court is that it is asked to hold some legislative provisions valid, albeit for a short period of time, when it has unequivocally held that the same legislative provisions are unconstitutional. On appeal, the Court of Final Appeal held that it has the power to suspend its declaration of unconstitutionality in exceptional cases. This is different from an order of temporary validity, as the government would be acting in peril under the old law in the interim period pending remedial legislation. But the difference is theoretical only, as it is difficult to envisage that the government would be visited with anything other than nominal damages for acting under the impugned legislation when the court has allowed a stay of its order of unconstitutionality on strong public interest grounds.

Likewise, in the transgender case,[7] the recognition of post-operation gender for the purpose of marriage gives rise to a whole range of issues that will have to be addressed. For example, should a gender-recognition procedure be set up to determine who qualifies as 'a woman' or 'a man' for marriage or other purposes? What happens to a marriage and the children of the marriage when one party of the marriage decides to change his or her gender during the marriage? To what extent is disclosure of one's former gender necessary in order to protect third parties? The government will need time to address these issues and introduce necessary legislation.

Although the court held that the power to stay a declaration of unconstitutionality would only be exercised in exceptional circumstances, it has invoked this power on several occasions. In the covert surveillance case, it gave the government six months to introduce remedial legislation. In the transgender case, it gave the government a year to introduce the necessary legislation to deal with the problems arising from the recognition of the post-operation gender for the purpose of marriage. Unfortunately, after 12 months the Legislative Council has still been unable to agree on the remedial bill. On the other hand, as the Court of Final Appeal observed, the jurisdiction to examine the compatibility of a statutory provision with the constitution is a matter of obligation, not discretion, and the injustice suffered by the applicant will be prolonged if the court is too ready to allow the impugned legislation to remain in force.

If a statutory provision is unconstitutional, it should have no legal effect. Yet this may have serious consequences for the distant past or the immediate future. In such situations, the solution is necessarily a compromise. It may not be philosophically neat or justifiable, but it highlights the pragmatism of the common law.

---

7. *W v Registrar of Marriages* (2013) 16 HKCFAR 112. See Chapter 30.

VI

Fairness in Public Administration: What a Mess!

15

Right to legal representation

The right to legal representation is said to be a fundamental right that goes to the rule of law. The reason is obvious. It is often difficult and painful, if not impossible, for a lay person to work through the complex tapestry of law without legal representation. The temple of law is supposed to be a place of justice for all, but the sacred temple may be inaccessible if one is not given assistance to navigate the legal labyrinth leading to it. However indispensable it may be, legal representation is not always welcome.

A characteristic feature of modern society is the existence of an array of administrative bodies in public decision making. They are called tribunals, committees, panels, boards, and so on. Invariably they are charged with authority to make decisions which may have serious or drastic consequences on the lives of ordinary people, be it an extension of a public housing tenancy, the renewal of a hawker licence, or the conviction of a student for disciplinary offences. Another characteristic of these administrative bodies is that they are usually staffed by members who do not have any legal training. They are also masters of their own houses, having power to determine their own procedures. More often than not, these procedures do not make provision for the right to have legal representation.

Ms Chua was a student at the then Hong Kong Polytechnic. She was required to withdraw from the Higher Diploma course in Hotel and Catering Management on the grounds of unsatisfactory performance. She appealed to the Academic Appeals Committee. On the date of the hearing, she was represented by Gerard McCoy, who later became a Senior Counsel. McCoy was accompanied by an articled clerk from his instructing solicitors, a shorthand writer, and a representative from the Students' Union. He demanded that the whole team be permitted to attend the appeal. The committee was apparently overwhelmed, if not also alarmed, by this formidable line-up. Someone was then able to point out that, according to their rules on appeal, a student was allowed to be represented by one person. So, one person only. The student would have to choose who she wanted to represent her. This presented some difficulty for her. No doubt she would have liked to have McCoy to represent her, but as a matter of the professional code of conduct, McCoy could only represent his client in the presence of a representative of his instructing solicitors, in this case, the articled clerk (who was a trainee solicitor).

After a bit of negotiation, the committee agreed that McCoy could represent the student with the articled clerk, provided that the articled clerk played no active part in the proceedings. The condition was both unnecessary and served no useful purpose. It was difficult to see what harm could have been done by allowing the articled clerk to do his job, if any, at the appeal. In the normal course of events, the role of an articled clerk in such a hearing would largely be passive, as the argument would be made primarily by the barrister. Surprisingly, McCoy then argued that he could not properly represent his client if his instructing solicitors could play no active part in the proceedings. He went further to argue that the condition would expose him to a charge of professional misconduct in violation of the Bar's Code of Conduct, an argument which was highly exaggerated and subsequently rejected by the court.[1]

The dispute was a classic example of a minor incident being unnecessarily escalated when it could have been easily resolved if common sense was allowed to prevail. The student then made a surprising move to withdraw the instructions to McCoy and to conduct the appeal in person. She sought an adjournment at the end of the hearing to raise further grounds of appeal. This request was refused. The committee then rejected her appeal. This decision became the subject of a judicial review application brought by the student.

On these facts, the court found that the absence of legal representation was a self-inflicted wound. The committee had not acted unreasonably when it accepted that the student could be represented by McCoy in the presence of the articled clerk. In any event, whether legal representation would be allowed depended on a number of factors, including the complexity of the proceedings, the nature of the issues, whether any legal issues would be involved, the seriousness of the consequences of the decision, and the ability of the student to represent herself. The issue here was relatively straight-forward. The main question before the Appeals Committee was whether her academic performance was such that a decision to ask her to withdraw from the course was justi-fied. There was no complex legal issue, and the committee was entitled to exercise its discretion not to allow legal representation in such circumstances.

It is not clear if judicial review could have been avoided if there were no condition to restrict the role of the articled clerk, a restriction that was totally unnecessary and would serve no useful purpose. There are too many instances when a dispute could have been avoided if the decision maker had been prepared to allow common sense to prevail. Unfortunately, common sense is by no means common. It is also far too often that what appears to be a legal dispute is in reality a personality issue.

To a large extent this was also true with Lam Siu Po although his case involved a systemic problem.[2]

Lam Siu Po was a police constable with a commendable record of service. The police force has long been concerned with police officers incurring huge financial debts, notably through gambling, as this could easily result in compromising their

---

1. *R v Hong Kong Polytechnic, ex parte Jenny Chua* (1992) 2 HKPLR 34.
2. *Lam Siu Po v Commissioner of Police* (2009) 12 HKCFAR 237.

duties. Hence, the force had introduced procedures and policies to deal with police 'officers with unmanageable debts' (known as OUDs). Police officers were not permitted to incur expenses that they were unable to afford, and there was 'no sympathy for officers who ... have had unmanageable debts due to financial imprudence, resulting in the impairment of the officers' operational efficiency'. Indeed, disciplinary action would be taken against those OUDs, often resulting in compulsory retirement with deferred or even forfeiture of pension rights.

Unlike some of his colleagues who had run up unmanageable debts through gambling, Lam Siu Po incurred a substantial debt through unsuccessful investment in red-chip shares in the stock market (though some may regard the stock market as the largest casino in Hong Kong!). He traded in the stock market in amounts that were about 80 times his monthly salary, initially relying on his own savings and later on credit cards and personal loans from different finance companies. When he incurred a loss in the region of over $500,000, he realized that his indebtedness had become unmanageable. He reported his indebtedness to his supervisor in or about May 2000 and petitioned his own bankruptcy.

No immediate action was taken against him. He was not allowed to handle money but was permitted to carry out his usual duties, including carrying firearms. In the few months between the report of his indebtedness and the time when he was adjudicated bankrupt, he succeeded in arresting a number of persons on the police wanted list. Eventually, he was charged with a disciplinary offence pursuant to PGO 6-01(8) of the Police General Orders, which provided:

> A police officer shall be prudent in his financial affairs. Serious pecuniary embarrassment stemming from financial imprudence which leads to the impairment of an officer's operational efficiency will result in disciplinary action.

As it turned out, there were two sets of disciplinary proceedings. The first took place in January 2001. Lam Siu Po was represented by a senior inspector at the disciplinary hearing. Witnesses were called and cross-examined. On 23 March 2001, Lam Siu Po was found guilty and was sentenced to be dismissed. This was the most severe punishment available, as it involved not only the loss of his job but also a forfeiture of his pension rights. However, five months later, he was told that, upon review, his conviction was set aside, as it was considered that there had been serious procedural irregularities or potential unfairness at the hearing. A rehearing was ordered.

The second set of disciplinary proceedings began in December 2001. There was a different adjudicating officer, but the prosecution and the witnesses remained the same. However, the senior inspector who represented Lam at the previous disciplinary proceeding was no longer available. Given the seriousness of the consequences, Lam was anxious to have proper representation. Under Regulations 9(11) and 9(12) of the Police (Discipline) Regulations, he could only be represented by a barrister or a solicitor who was also a serving police officer. There were not many police officers who had the necessary legal qualification and even fewer officers, among those with the appropriate legal qualification, who were willing to represent another police officer in a disciplinary hearing. As a disciplinary force, the strong and prevailing culture in the police force is strict obedience to the orders of seniors. No question and no query was expected or tolerated. Yet in representing a police officer in disciplinary proceedings, it would not be uncommon that the legal representative would have to cross-examine witnesses who might be senior to the legal representative himself. In fact, there were fewer than ten police officers in the entire police force who had put themselves forward as available to act as legal representatives.

Not surprisingly, Lam Siu Po faced immense difficulties in finding another police officer who was willing to represent him in the second set of disciplinary proceedings. Eventually he managed to secure the assistance of another senior inspector, but he soon lost confidence in him and dismissed his service. He asked the disciplinary tribunal if he could instruct a lawyer or an auxiliary officer or a civil servant from another department to represent him, and the answer was 'no'. So he represented himself at the disciplinary hearing.

It was soon apparent that he did not know how to conduct a defence or to cross-examine witnesses, and he made some incriminatory statements during the hearing. He was found guilty by the disciplinary tribunal and was initially given a suspended sentence of compulsory retirement, but the sentence was revised by the Assistant Commissioner to become one of immediate compulsory retirement with deferred pension rights. The sentence was confirmed by the Commissioner of Police on 21 October 2002. Lam Siu Po then lodged an application for judicial review to challenge the decision of his dismissal.

The original application, which was drafted by Lam himself, was rather messy. Fortunately he was granted legal aid and had the assistance of Margaret Ng, an able barrister and a legislator, who put the application in order. Among other things, it was argued that Lam had been wrongfully denied legal representation, in violation of his right under Article 35 of the Basic Law. Yet shortly before the Court of First Instance delivered its judgment, the Court of Final Appeal held in another case that Article 35 had no application to disciplinary proceedings! Lam's application was accordingly rejected by the Court of First Instance. On appeal, the Court of Appeal held that it was bound by its previous decision that no evidence was required to prove an impairment of operational efficiency, as it was a presumed result arising from serious pecuniary embarrassment. While Article 35 was no longer pursued, counsel continued to pursue the point, somewhat feebly, that Lam had been denied the right to legal representation and therefore his right to fair hearing under Article 10 of the Bill of Rights. The Court of Appeal rejected this argument, partly on the ground that his appeal was bound to fail, so that the availability of legal representation would not have altered the result.

Margaret, who has strong views on many things, felt very strongly about the case. We talked about the case one day when I happened to have afternoon tea in her chambers. Her exquisite high tea was always a delight and an attraction. I said while Article 35 had gone out of the window, the right to legal representation and the right to fair hearing under Article 10 of the Bill of Rights could still be a live issue. By confining Article 35 of the Basic Law to formal judicial proceedings, the Court of Final Appeal had left a major gap on the guarantee of a fair hearing in non-judicial proceedings, and this gap could have been filled by Article 10 of the Bill of Rights. This immediately brightened her day, and without my knowing, the conversation that afternoon had drawn me into a case with far-reaching implications before the Court of Final Appeal.

Appeal to the Court of Final Appeal is not as of right. Thanks to Margaret's careful drafting, the Bill of Rights was referred to in the original application for judicial review (even though the point was not taken before the Court of First Instance and not pressed before the Court of Appeal). We managed to persuade the Court of Appeal to grant leave to appeal and certify this Bill of Rights point as one of great and general public importance for the purpose of appeal to the Court of Final Appeal. One of the grounds of appeal was whether the statutory restriction to have legal representation before a police disciplinary tribunal under Regulations 9(11) and 9(12) was consistent with Article 10 of the Bill of Rights. Another ground was whether the decision of the Court of Appeal on the presumption of an impairment of operational efficiency was correct.

The hearing before the Court of Final Appeal took place on 10 and 11 March 2009, some seven years after the completion of the disciplinary proceeding against Lam Siu Po.

The Court of Final Appeal was then housed in the French Mission Building at the top of Battery Path. The building has been elegantly modified and has a most lovely library. The robing room was quiet and comfortable, with a window overlooking the entrance of the court and St John's Cathedral. The former chapel has been converted to become the main courtroom. It was a relatively small and cosy courtroom with a dome overhead. Usually, counsel on both sides fill the seats, leaving not much room for solicitors. For some big cases, counsel even have to bring their own trolleys for their files. There was only a short distance between the Bar table and the Bench. Yet the acoustics were far from perfect, and sometimes it was necessary to guess what a judge sitting at the far end was saying. Despite these limitations, the intellectual exchange between the Bar and the Bench more than made up for the inefficiency. It was always lively, courteous and challenging, which makes it a pleasure to appear before the Court of Final Appeal.

Presided over by Chief Justice Andrew Li, the Bench comprised Mr Justice Bokhary, Mr Justice Patrick Chan, Mr Justice Ribeiro, and Lord Woolf, the overseas judge whose reform of the civil justice system in England and Wales (best known as the Woolf Reform) has had an immense impact on similar reforms throughout the entire common law world. The Police Commissioner was represented by Anderson Chow SC, a most able counsel who was among my first batch of students and who subsequently joined the Bench. He fairly accepted that the effect of Regulations 9(11) and 9(12) was tantamount to a blanket denial of the right to legal representation, but he argued that Article 10 of the Bill of Rights was not engaged in the first place. The

Bill of Rights argument provoked a most interesting legal debate that required a good understanding of the differences between the common law system and the civil law system. I accepted that legal representation would not always be required. The determining factor was whether a fair hearing was possible without legal representation. Hence, the tribunal concerned should have discretion to decide whether it would be in the interest of justice to permit legal representation in the light of the circumstances of the case, but the legislature had taken away this discretion without sufficient justification, resulting in the denial of a fair hearing. The Court of Final Appeal accepted this argument and held that Regulations 9(11) and 9(12) were accordingly inconsistent with the Bill of Rights and repealed. This judgment became the leading judgment on the constitutional right to legal representation and the right to a fair hearing.

There was no question that Lam Siu Po had been prejudiced by the denial of legal representation in the disciplinary proceeding, as evidenced by the amateur way he conducted his defence. There was, however, still an obstacle to overcome, namely, that the availability of legal representation would not have altered the outcome. This depended on the second ground of appeal, namely whether Lam Siu Po could adduce evidence to show that his operational efficiency had not been impaired. As a matter of construction, PGO-6.01(8) clearly referred to three elements: 'serious embarrassment', that stemmed from 'financial imprudence', and that in turn led to 'the impairment of operational efficiency'. As a matter of both drafting and logic, the proof of the first two elements did not automatically lead to an impairment of operational efficiency. And how could Lam Siu Po's operational efficiency have been impaired, when he had still managed to arrest a number of wanted persons after he had filed his petition for bankruptcy? The Court of Final Appeal had no difficulty in overruling the earlier Court of Appeal decision to that effect.

After seven years, Lam Siu Po finally succeeded in overturning his disciplinary conviction. I have not heard further from him since the judgment of the Court of Final Appeal. Rumour has it that he underwent disciplinary proceedings for the third time, albeit with legal representation this time, and was convicted again with the same punishment. The victory at the Court of Final Appeal didn't change anything for him. Was justice done? While he had not managed his financial affairs properly, it was doubtful if dismissal was the right or proportionate solution. Hong Kong may have lost a good police constable as a result.

On the right to legal representation, the relevant regulations were repealed and the tribunal was given discretion to determine whether legal representation should be permitted on a case-by-case basis. The implication went well beyond the police force. The case led to an overhaul of the disciplinary proceedings of other disciplinary forces and even professional bodies.

Regulations 9(11) and 9(12) probably reflect a not uncommon attitude that lawyers tend to complicate matters and are not welcome before administrative tribunals. There may, sadly, be some truth in this. However, an argument that only police officers understand police disciplinary action was obviously unconvincing though the same argument is maintained in relation to investigation of complaints against police officers. The two cases here highlight different perceptions of the role of legal representation in lay tribunals, and lawyers are probably at least partially responsible for the adverse perception. Mr Justice Bokhary made a most pertinent observation on this point in his judgment:

> There are some disciplinary tribunals before which legal representation is quite common. Legal practitioners understand, as they should, that their duty is not only to their clients but also to the tribunals. Such are the traditions and responsibilities of professional advocates. Their role is a constitutional one, always to be approached as such and never to be abused. Most of them certainly need no reminder of that. But just in case some of them might sometimes need such a reminder, I have seen fit respectfully to issue one, meaning of course no offence thereby.[3]

The aftermath of this case was no less colourful. Many police officers who had been convicted of a disciplinary offence before this case then sought to reopen their conviction on the ground that they too had been denied legal representation because of the statutory restriction. There were over 80 such attempts, arguing that their convictions were unconstitutional and urging the court to grant them leave to appeal out of time, as the time limit to appeal had expired in virtually all of these cases. Once leave to appeal out of time was granted, the appeal would inevitably have to be successful. Thus, the issue turned to whether the court should grant leave to appeal out of time when the law was subsequently found to be unconstitutional. Some convictions dated back to five or six years. In some cases, the police officers did not contest the charges. In some other cases, there was no reliance on the Bill of Rights at all. The law was at one point rather confusing, as some judges were prepared to grant leave to appeal out of time, whereas other judges believed that there must be finality in litigation and it was wrong to reopen a conviction that was entered years ago. It took some time for the Court of Final Appeal to settle the issue. The court held that the mere fact that the law was subsequently found to be wrong was not by itself a sufficient reason to reopen an earlier decision. While the issue was eventually clarified, it does raise a more fundamental problem of what the proper approach should be when a statutory provision, which has been in existence for some time, is found to be unconstitutional and is repealed. Would such a holding disturb the peace of the distant past, or create a whirlpool of turbulence for the immediate future? This will have to be another story.[4]

---

3. At 254.
4. See Chapter 14.

16

The three sisters

Martin Lee SC has two well-known habits. First, he prefers to have conferences at home rather than in chambers. Second, when he is on a case, he will call up his junior for discussion whenever an idea dawns on him, and the hour of the day when the call is made is never one of his considerations. So it did not surprise me to get a call from him at 6:00 on a cold winter morning. He was very kind to me, as he used to call Alan Hoo SC at 4 a.m.!

It was a freezing morning shortly after the Chinese New Year. As usual, Mrs Lee kindly served me some heart-warming breakfast.

Our clients were three well-educated and elegant ladies. They owned a piece of land at Ma Wan, a small island between Tsing Yi and Lantau that was later to become one of the footholds of the world-famous Tsing Ma Bridge. The bridge was still at the planning stage at that time, and there would be an exit road to link Ma Wan with the bridge and the outside world. Ma Wan used to be a peaceful island with a few hundred inhabitants. Because of the Tsing Ma project, a major developer decided to build a middle-class residential estate on the island. In order to secure government approval for the private residential development, the developer offered to resettle the inhabitants to a new village on another part of the island and to build a theme park (this was before Disneyland came to Hong Kong). Our clients' land lay within the boundary of the proposed theme park. The developer was eager to acquire our clients' land because the theme park would be a major factor in securing the government's approval for the private residential project. Indeed, it later transpired that the developer was required under an agreement with the government, which was disclosed only in the court hearing, to use its best endeavours to acquire our clients' land. Notwithstanding this requirement, there was never any written offer from the developer to our clients regarding the acquisition of their land and the negotiation had gone to nowhere. At some stage of the negotiations, the developer indicated that it would invite the government to resume part of our clients' land if the parties failed to reach an agreement. The negotiations failed. In 1995, the Secretary for Transport proposed to construct the exit road from Tsing Ma Bridge (with an emergency access road to the proposed theme park) in such a way that it would cut through and divide our clients' land into quarters, hence depriving the land of most of its value. It also envisaged resumption of part of our clients' land for implementing such a road scheme. There was an odour of bad faith and collusion between the developer and the government to put pressure on our clients to accede to the developer's unattractive oral offer to acquire their land.

'I think we should consider amending our pleadings to include a ground of collusion and abuse of power on the part of the government.' This was the idea that had struck Martin in the early morning, and prompted his 6 a.m. call.

'Well, I am afraid that we don't have enough evidence to substantiate such a claim. This would be a very serious allegation, and under the Bar's Code of Conduct, we have a heavy duty to consider the matter very carefully before we make a claim like that,' I replied.

We spent a good hour debating the issue, and eventually I managed to convince Martin that it was not a good idea.

The Bill of Rights did not protect the right to property. As a result, we decided to mount a constitutional attack at the planning process on the ground that it did not provide for a fair hearing. The road scheme had been proposed by the Secretary for Transport and opposed by our clients. The objection was considered by the Chief Executive in Council, who decided to approve the road scheme without any modification. That decision was final and there was no further appeal. The law is relatively simple: the person who decides on someone's right must act fairly and impartially. This is a time-honoured principle. However, what could the law do if the legislation provides for a tribunal that is inherently unfair and partial because of certain systemic features in the process? As in this case, how could the Chief Executive in Council, being head of the Executive Government, be perceived to be a fair tribunal to hear a complaint against one of his secretaries? The common law could not help when the appeal tribunal was mandated by legislation, for legislation is supreme. However, under the Bill of Rights, our clients had a constitutional right to a fair hearing by a competent, independent, and impartial tribunal when their property rights were determined. Our submission was that they had not been afforded this right to fair hearing.

However, this apparently straightforward principle of a fair hearing has given rise to some difficulties when it is applied to administrative proceedings. The Bill of Rights suggests that this principle is more suitable for a court of law than an administrative tribunal that is composed largely of lay members and which transacts business on the basis of efficacy and policy rather than strict principles of law.

This was indeed the difficulty of the court when a similar point had been taken in an earlier case, *Kwan Kong Co Ltd v Town Planning Board* (in which Martin and I were also involved),[1] and the argument had been rejected by the Court of Appeal. Our major difficulty was that the right to a fair hearing in the Bill of Rights applied only to a determination of 'a suit at law'. On the face of it, 'suit at law' seems to suggest a lawsuit, or a formal legal process. This meaning is strengthened by the next sentence, which refers to the determination of a criminal charge. The proceeding before the Town

---

1. (1996) 6 HKPLR 237; [1996] 2 HKLR 363.

Planning Board in the *Kwan Kong* case, or the proceeding before the Chief Executive in Council in our case, was not a formal lawsuit but an administrative proceeding.

While it is true that administrative tribunals differ in many respects from a formal court, this does not mean that the principle of fairness has no application in administrative tribunals. This is an important issue, as many important decisions that have had a profound impact on the lives of ordinary members of the community are increasingly made by administrative tribunals these days. Just think about the decisions made by professional or disciplinary bodies deciding on the career or the pension of their members, or the decisions of the Housing Authority evicting a tenant of public housing, or the decisions of the Liquor Licencing Board not to renew a liquor licence of a small business on which income a family is dependent for its livelihood. It cannot be right that we have one set of principle of fairness in courts and another set of principle of fairness in administrative tribunals when important civil rights are at stake.

In order to get round the difficulty in the *Kwan Kong* case, we argued that the phrase 'suit at law' did not bear its natural meaning of 'a lawsuit' but that it carried a special meaning of 'civil rights and obligations' and hence, we maintained, the constitutional guarantee did apply to the present proceedings. We tried to make that argument by relying partly on the French version of the International Covenant on Civil and Political Rights, on which the English version of our Bill of Rights was based, and the identical French version (*droits et obligations de caractère civil*) and its English translation (civil rights and obligations) in the European Convention of Human Rights. In the *Kwan Kong* case, Mr Justice William Waung at first instance thought that this was a rather tortuous argument and rejected it, and he was supported by the Court of Appeal. In our case, at first instance, Mr Justice Keith found himself to be bound by the *Kwan Kong* decision. Thus, we now had to persuade the Court of Appeal not to follow its own decision in the *Kwan Kong* case.

We explained our assessment of the strengths of the appeal to our clients, who listened patiently and intervened only occasionally in a most gracious manner to clarify their understanding. It was clear that they had a thorough understanding of our arguments, and although we had lost before Mr Justice Keith, our clients were most understanding and placed full confidence and trust in their legal team. Somehow, they reminded me of the three sisters in a famous case on mistake in contract law decided by Lord Denning a few decades before.[2] In that case, the three sisters were deceived by a rogue and accepted a cheque for the sale of their car. As the story unfolded, the cheque was dishonoured and the car was later sold to an innocent third party, who fought with the three sisters on the rightful ownership of the car. In his characteristic anxiety to do justice, Lord Denning began his judgment by describing the plaintiffs as three innocent ladies, upon which description any reader could see that the judgment was a foregone conclusion. Would this happen to our clients as well?

---

2. *Ingram v Little* [1961] 1 QB 31.

The hearing before the Court of Appeal lasted for two days.[3] The Chief Executive in Council was most ably represented by Philip Dykes SC, the then Law Officer (Civil Law) at the Department of Justice and subsequently my chamber mate when he left government. The Bench was most courteous and patient. It took the Bench a month to reach its judgment. While it agreed with us on a more liberal interpretation of the phrase 'suit at law', it held that no civil right was engaged by the approval of the road scheme. Civil right would only be engaged if the government decided to make a resumption order, which it had not done, and in any event, the proposal of a road scheme was a decision of high policy content which would not be subject to the requirements of being reviewed on full merits by an independent and impartial tribunal. In one sense we won on the law and lost on the fact although this would not be much consolation to the clients.

Again, our clients accepted the decision in a most gracious manner and decided not to further appeal. I ran into our clients on a number of subsequent occasions. Every time they gave me a warm greeting which I know was for a friend rather than a lawyer who once intruded into their lives. I still remember the case and the three sisters every time I cross Tsing Ma Bridge. Would the outcome of the case have been any different had I not succeeded in convincing Martin to abandon the bad faith point on that morning?

The legal battle that we won in that case did not advance the law any further, save that there were now two conflicting Court of Appeal decisions. It took another ten years before I had a chance to argue this point again before the Court of Final Appeal.[4] My client, Lam Siu Po, was a police officer with an impeccable service record until he lost heavily in the stock market and had to declare bankruptcy. It was said that his pecuniary position led to embarrassment of the police force and an impairment of his efficiency (despite the fact that he managed to arrest a number of persons on the police wanted list during the period of his financial difficulty), and hence he was charged with a disciplinary offence. The relevant law at that time did not allow him to be represented by a lawyer before the disciplinary tribunal. He was convicted, dismissed from the police force, and lost his pension. The common law right to a fair hearing was not helpful, as the denial of legal representation was mandated by legislation. Our only chance was to challenge the constitutionality of the legislation in question. While the Basic Law does provide for a right of access to court, the Court of Final Appeal had decided in an earlier case that the provision in the Basic Law applies only to access to formal courts and not disciplinary tribunals.[5] So, our only hope to challenge the constitutionality of the relevant legislation would be to invoke the Bill of Rights, and we would face the same issue: Was the disciplinary hearing a 'suit at law' that would attract the protection of a fair hearing under the Bill of Rights?

---

3. *Ma Wan Farming Ltd v Chief Executive in Council* (1998–99) 8 HKPLR 386; [1998] 1 HKLRD 514.
4. *Lam Siu Po v Commissioner of Police* (2009) 12 HKCFAR 237. See also Chapter 15.
5. *Stock Exchange of Hong Kong v New World Development Ltd* (2006) 9 HKCFAR 234.

By then we faced a further obstacle, as there were two conflicting decisions of two international bodies. While the Human Rights Committee adopted a broad meaning of 'suit at law', it took the view that the phrase could not be extended to disciplinary proceedings against civil servants, as there existed a special bond of trust and loyalty to the government. The European Court of Human Rights disagreed, but the Human Rights Committee's decision was an interpretation of the relevant clause under the International Covenant on Civil and Political Rights from which our Bill of Rights was taken, whereas the European Convention on Human Rights was differently worded. Things were further complicated by a rigid distinction between private law and public law in the civil law system in Europe, a distinction that does not exist in the common law system.

As usual, the Court of Final Appeal was most patient and receptive. It has always been a pleasure to appear before our Court of Final Appeal where you could expect the highest level of intellectual engagement. As in the interpretation of any law, and particularly important for the interpretation of constitutional law, the interpretation should be guided by the constitutional values of our system rather than dictated by the literal meaning of the law. The Court of Final Appeal eventually ruled in my favour and accepted the arguments that we made a decade ago in the three sisters' case. The leading judgment was delivered by Mr Justice Ribeiro, with whom the rest of the court agreed. It is a judgment that deserves the most careful reading, as it expounds in detail the fundamental importance of the right to a fair hearing in a modern society. This is an important decision, as it means that a lot of administrative proceedings are now subject to the constitutional requirement of fair hearing, and any legislative interference with the right to fair hearing in these proceedings would have to stand the test of the Bill of Rights. It is a small step towards achieving greater fairness in many proceedings which are not formal legal proceedings but which make decisions that have grave consequences for the lives of many ordinary people.

When I read the judgment, I remember the three sisters and the early morning conference we had a decade ago. At least I have not let them down on the law even though it took more than ten years to prove the point. As for their land in Ma Wan previously gazetted to form part of the road scheme (which was vigorously challenged by us in Court in 1998), nothing has happened since then. Indeed, the government decided to de-gazette that part of the road scheme some ten years later. So it turns out that their land was after all not required for the theme park or any public purposes.

17

A duty to give reasons

In Shakespeare's *Henry IV*, the cowardly Falstaff is caught out in a lie. Asked by the Prince how he could have seen that his attackers wore green when it was so dark he could not even see his own hand, Falstaff refuses to explain, and blusters, 'If reasons were as plentiful as blackberries, I would give no man a reason upon compulsion' (*Henry IV*, Part 1, Act 2, Scene 4).

As early as 1971, Lord Denning said that 'the giving of reasons is one of the fundamentals of good administration'.[1] But in spite of tremendous progress in the last few decades in imposing on public administrators a duty to act fairly, the common law is curiously resistant to the introduction of a general duty to give reasons. Whether there is a duty to give reasons would depend on the context, including the statutory framework, what fairness required in the circumstances, and whether the decision appears aberrant in the absence of reasons although it is fair to say that there is a clear trend towards recognition of a duty to give reasons. Our Court of Final Appeal almost reached this point of introducing a general duty to give reasons but somehow just stopped at the threshold.[2] This arose in a somewhat unworthy context.

Oriental Daily Publisher Ltd (Oriental) was charged with publishing indecent articles in the *Oriental Daily Press* without the statutorily required safeguards of a cover or packing or warning notice, contrary to section 24 of the Control of Obscene and Indecent Articles Ordinance (the Ordinance). The subject matter involved three articles that reported on events that took place in Korea and Australia. One was about a human body painting exhibition; the second article was portrayals of different lifestyles and showed naked women dancing, and the third was about an annual naked shopping day. All these feature reports included photographs that showed nudity of female bodies although nipples were obscured by opaque squares and the pubic area was covered by various objects. Oriental pleaded not guilty. As a result, the magistrate referred the articles in question to the Obscene Articles Tribunal (the Tribunal) for determination, as he was obliged to do under section 29 of the Ordinance.

---

1. *Breen v Amalgamated Engineering Union* [1971] 2 QB 175 at 191.
2. *Oriental Daily Publisher Ltd v Commissioner for Television and Entertainment Licensing Authority* (1997–98) 1 HKCFAR 279.

We have a rather curious regime for determining obscenity and indecency. Under the Ordinance, the Tribunal exercises two kinds of jurisdiction. The first is an administrative jurisdiction, under which a list of persons can submit an article to the Tribunal for classification. The article can be classified as Class 1, which means it is suitable for publication to anyone; Class 2, which means it is indecent and not suitable for readers below the age of 18; or Class 3, which means it is obscene and cannot be published. Class 2 articles can only be published under certain conditions in relation to the packaging and a warning notice. The Tribunal will first give an interim classification, which will become final if it is not challenged; and if it is challenged, the Tribunal will give a final classification after hearing the parties. The majority of its classifications are not challenged. This procedure is intended to give the affected parties an easy means to ascertain the nature of the article before publication so that they can act accordingly. In practice, the classification process is usually initiated by public officers who pick up the publication after it has been published, and the process becomes a means to determine if there is a case to press with criminal prosecution.

The second jurisdiction of the Tribunal is to determine obscenity and indecency in the course of a criminal prosecution. It has an exclusive jurisdiction over such matters, so that whenever the issue of obscenity and indecency arises in any criminal proceedings, all courts (usually magistrates) will have to refer to the Tribunal for determination of such issues. On these occasions, the Tribunal acts as part of the criminal process. The Tribunal is presided over by a magistrate and two or more lay persons who are selected from a panel of adjudicators appointed by the Chief Justice. In exercising its criminal jurisdiction, the Tribunal has the same power as a magistrate.

It is a criminal offence to publish an obscene article or an indecent article to persons under the age of 18 or without proper covering up and warning notices. The statutory definition of 'obscenity' and 'indecency' is somewhat circular. Under section 2 of the Ordinance, 'a thing is obscene if by reason of obscenity it is not suitable to be published to any person and a thing is indecent if by reason of indecency it is not suitable to be published to a juvenile', meaning persons under the age of 18. A most helpful definition! 'Obscenity' and 'indecency' include violence, depravity, and repulsiveness. Section 10 of the Ordinance is more helpful and sets out some guidelines for the Tribunal to consider in determining the question of obscenity and indecency:

a Tribunal shall have regard to:

(a)   standards of morality, decency and propriety that are generally accepted by reasonable members of the community, . . .

(b)   the dominant effect of an article or of matter as a whole;

(c)   in the case of an article, the persons or class of persons, or age groups of persons, to or amongst whom the article is, or is intended or is likely to be, published;

(d)   in the case of matter publicly displayed, the location where the matter is or is to be publicly displayed and the persons or class of persons, or age groups of persons likely to view such matter; and

(e)   whether the article or matter has an honest purpose or whether its content is merely camouflage designed to render acceptable any part of it.

The hearing before the Tribunal

The prosecution pointed out that the newspaper was generally accessible to the public. The photographs occupied a large section of the page on which they appeared. They were published as part of the newspaper, without any warning labels or cover. Having regard to the articles and their dominant effect, it was submitted that they were clearly not suitable for publication to persons under the age of 18 and were by definition indecent.

Oriental, which was represented by Gerald McCoy SC, argued that, first, photos of partially naked people can be seen everywhere in Hong Kong; secondly, the nipples had been blocked out and the pubic area covered; thirdly, one could see things 'much worse than this' at MTR stations and in many newspapers; fourthly, the articles were informative and were about 'crazy things' that were happening around the world; they were genuine reports informing readers about what went on in other cultures; and finally, the photographs appeared in the adult section of the newspaper. They were not on the front page or the children's page. The articles were frivolous material and might be in bad taste, as counsel submitted, but they did not damage people and should not be made subjects of a criminal charge.

The Tribunal ruled against Oriental and gave the following decision:

> The tribunal has considered all the submissions advanced by defence counsel and has directed itself to s.2(2)(b) and s.10(1) of Control of Obscene and Indecent Articles Ordinance (Cap 390). This tribunal has also reminded itself that the standard to be adopted by it is the standard followed in criminal cases, namely, 'proof beyond reasonable doubt'. This tribunal unanimously determined that all the articles in the present two cases are indecent articles because:
>
> (1)   each and every photograph in these two cases violates and exceeds the standard of morality, decency and propriety that are generally accepted by reasonable members of the community;
> (2)   the dominant effect of each and every photograph as a whole in these two cases is indecent;
> (3)   by reason of indecency each and every photograph is not suitable to be published to a juvenile.

It can be seen that these reasons were simply a citation of the statutory criteria set out in section 10 of the Ordinance. Oriental appealed against this decision on the ground that no adequate reasons had been given.

The appeal

Both the Court of First Instance and the Court of Appeal agreed that the Tribunal was under a duty to give reasons. Both courts also agreed that the reasons given were adequate. Mr Justice Yeung of the Court of First Instance noted that the question of indecency was an extremely abstract matter and the giving of detailed reasons would impose an impossible task on the Tribunal. On appeal, the Chief Judge agreed that obscenity and indecency were notoriously abstract concepts and involved value judgments that were difficult to express. He found the photographs spoke for themselves, and the case for indecency was overwhelming so that, in the circumstances, the Tribunal's reasons were adequate. The case then went further to the Court of Final Appeal, the issue being whether the reasons as given by the Tribunal would, as a matter of law, satisfy the duty to give reasons.

The Court of Final Appeal

Before the Court of Final Appeal, Oriental was represented by Philip Dykes SC, and the prosecution was represented by Andrew Bruce SC, Senior Assistant Director of Public Prosecutions, and Wesley Wong, Senior Government Counsel, who later became the Solicitor General.

Both parties agreed that the Tribunal had a duty to give reasons as a matter of statutory construction. The Chief Justice, however, wished to go further to derive a duty to give reasons under the common law. He noted that there was a perceptible trend towards an insistence on greater openness in decision making, and a readiness of the courts to find a duty to give reasons in various contexts. While some decision makers might regard a duty to give reasons as an additional burden, the Chief Justice noted that the duty should be approached in a positive manner and urged decision makers to adopt a positive attitude towards it. He then set out in some detail the benefits of a duty to give reasons.

> First, it would impose desirable intellectual discipline and concentrate attention to the relevant issues. It would thus assist in ensuring that any decision is made on proper grounds and contribute to the effective disposal by the tribunal of its work.
>
> Secondly, reasons would assist in demonstrating to the parties that the tribunal has carried out its task properly and would enable them to decide on the appropriate course of action in the case at hand . . . It would also provide guidance in the future to the community and persons concerned in this area . . .
>
> Thirdly, the reasons given by the tribunal will promote and enhance consistency in its decision-making and assist the law enforcement and prosecuting authorities.
>
> Fourthly, the giving of reasons would demonstrate to the community that the tribunal is functioning properly and this would engender public confidence.

Chief Justice Li then concluded, in light of the character of the Tribunal, the kind of decision it had to make and the statutory framework in which it operated, the requirements of fairness demanded that the Tribunal should give reasons, there being no contrary intention in the statute. This came close to a presumption of a duty to give reasons unless the context suggests otherwise. However, as there was no issue regarding the existence of a duty to give reasons in that particular circumstance, and no argument had been put forward before the court on the jurisprudential basis of a more general duty, the court was not prepared to go further to lay down a general duty to give reasons.

While these reasons were framed in the context of the operation of the Tribunal, the same reasons applied to many other statutory bodies and decision makers in public law, including, for example, a publicly funded university. When parliament confers a power on a decision maker to make decisions that may affect others, it must be the intention of parliament that the power is to be exercised fairly, rationally, and for proper statutory purposes. The duty to act fairly and properly could hardly be discharged if the decision maker is not required to give reasons. Good public administration would require any public body to give reasons for its decisions. The provision of reasons marks the beginning of rationality, as it is only upon the reasons given that one can begin to consider the soundness of the decisions, let alone any grounds for appeal. It is just a matter of fairness and transparency, and it goes to the heart of the rule of law. It also enhances public confidence in the decision-making process. These points were powerfully made by Mr Justice Stock of our Court of Appeal in another case ten years later:

> Sound public administration requires that when reasons are required or are provided for an administrative decision, they should be clear as well as sufficient to the circumstances. The provision of adequate and clear reasons, where reasons are required by law, is a function of sound administration because transparency is more likely to promote confidence in public administration than is opacity, and also because the very requirement to provide clear reasons against the background of the particular issues raised itself encourages a disciplined approach to the issues at hand. But, most obviously, the requirement is based on fairness, so that the person or body adversely affected by a decision should have an adequate indication of the reasoning process, enabling him to know whether the decision-maker has addressed his grievance and whether there may be a basis for challenging the decision. So too clarity and sufficiency of reasons enable a supervisory court in judicial review better to assess the legality of a decision under challenge.[3]

This passage also highlights the requirement that the reasons given have to be intelligible and adequate. The court has accepted that many public administrators and members of administrative tribunals or statutory bodies are not lawyers. They are not expected to write a judicial thesis. Nor will the court approach their reasons with the relentless knife of a dissecting surgeon. The reasons can be briefly stated and in plain language. They need to refer only to the main issues and not cover every aspect of

---

3. *Capital Rich v Town Planning Board* [2007] 2 HKLRD 155, at [97].

the dispute. However, their reasons have to enable a reader to understand how the conclusion was reached, what evidence was taken into account, and how controversial issues or arguments were addressed. If specific arguments have been put to the decision makers, they would be expected to address these specific arguments in the reasons. In the *Oriental* case, the Chief Justice found that the 'reasons' given by the Tribunal were conclusions rather than reasons. Mere restatement of the statutory criteria was insufficient. After reading the decision, a reader would not be any the wiser in understanding why the Tribunal came to its conclusion that the articles were indecent. The Tribunal had to address the evidence and the main submissions made by Oriental. The Chief Justice gave a useful outline of what needed to be addressed in a proper 'reason':

> They are conclusions rather than reasons. They do not show that the tribunal has addressed the issues raised and why it came to the conclusion of indecency. It was pointed out to the tribunal that the nipples had been blocked and the private part covered and submitted that photographs similar to these are not uncommon in public places and newspapers. In other words, this is relevant to measuring community standards. Did the tribunal reject this submission? Or if [the Tribunal] accepted it, why did it conclude that the articles were indecent as violating and exceeding community standards. It was submitted to the tribunal in effect that these are newsworthy items to inform our community of others' cultures. What was the tribunal's view on that submission? It was submitted that the articles in question were in an adult section of the newspaper. Was this accepted or rejected? Did the tribunal consider that for a daily newspaper, there is no distinction between various parts of the newspaper?[4]

While the court has moved towards greater transparency and fairness, public administrators, whether in the executive government, statutory bodies or public institutions, are still reluctant to provide reasons for their decisions. They sometimes refer to an absolute discretion to make a decision as a justification not to give reasons. In law, there is no such thing as 'absolute discretion'. All public powers have to be exercised rationally and fairly, and the failure to give reasons is usually an indication of an arbitrary decision. In the *Oriental* case, the Court of Final Appeal rejected the argument that obscenity and indecency were notorious concepts and value judgments that could not be explained. The Tribunal would have to be able to defend its decision by showing that it was a rational decision and by applying the statutory criteria to the evidence. Nor will the court lightly accept a duty of confidence as an excuse. If someone is affected by the decision of a public body, fairness requires that that person be informed of the basis of the decision so that he or she can decide what to do next. Failure to do so would be a betrayal of public trust.

Perhaps the time has come when the law should require all public administrators and public bodies to give reasons, unless the context otherwise suggests that giving reasons is inappropriate, which should rarely be the case. This is what fairness requires; nothing more, nothing less.

---

4. At 293–294.

VII

The Labyrinth of Legal Process and Civil Justice Reform

18

Justice delayed is justice denied

Justice delayed is justice denied. While most people would expect the judicial process to take time, the average person may be amazed that it may take years before his or her case can be heard in court, let alone having it completed its journey across the abyss of litigation. It is easy to put the blame on lawyers' manipulation of legal procedures. There is of course some truth in this, but can they be blamed if the procedural skirmishing is done with a view to advancing their clients' best interest? The complex web of civil procedures does afford plenty of room for strategic moves, not all of which are compatible with the goal of achieving justice. On the other hand, one must not overlook the systemic issues. Justice and efficiency do not always go hand in hand.

Let's take a look at a rather messy case involving a well-known weekly magazine and a university in Hong Kong. In September 1994, the magazine published an article alleging that a university in Hong Kong had turned a blind eye to claims of false credentials by some of its academic staff. The university took out defamation proceedings against the magazine.[1] There were three plaintiffs: the university, its president, and an academic staff member who was named in the article.

The writ was filed in April 1995. The magazine filed its defence in the following month. The plaintiffs took the view that the defence was defective, and they applied to the court to strike out part of it. In October 1995, the court struck out part of the defence, but the magazine immediately applied for leave to amend the defence.

The plaintiffs also applied for specific discovery. As the article in the magazine provided very specific details, it was quite obvious that the source must be from someone inside the university. The plaintiffs wanted to have access to the records of interviews with the anonymous informers. The magazine admitted that there were a total of four audio tapes, but it claimed journalist privilege not to disclose them, as the disclosure would reveal their source. Another round of litigation ensued. By November 1995, both parties agreed that the discovery should be made on the basis that the identity of the informers should not be directly or indirectly revealed. On that basis, the magazine was asked by the court to provide a full transcript of the audio tapes and indicate which parts of the tapes should be excised to protect the identity of the interviewees. The court would then decide whether the excised part should be disclosed to the plaintiffs.

---

1. HCA No 3238 of 1995.

In the meantime, the magazine decided to strike back. Relying on an English decision that a minister has no right to bring defamation action and that his recourse should lie in political channels and not the court, the magazine argued there would be the same chilling effect on free speech if the university, as a publicly funded authority, was able to suppress a media report on matters of considerable public interest. The magazine applied to strike out the university and its president as plaintiffs on the ground that they had no right in the common law to bring a defamation action that would have the effect of stifling a report on a matter of public interest, or alternatively, they argued, to allow them to do so would be contrary to the protection of freedom of expression in the Bill of Rights. This striking-out application was no doubt a strategic move, for if the application were successful, the third plaintiff, the academic staff member who was named in the relevant article of the magazine, would have to pursue the case in his personal capacity and might not be able to rely on university funding to finance the litigation. The application was first made before a Master of the High Court, who dismissed it in April 1996. The magazine appealed, and Mr Justice Keith of the High Court, in a reserved judgment dated 7 June 1996, reversed the order of the Master and struck out the claims of the university and its president on the ground that, as public authorities, they had no right to bring defamation action in view of the Bill of Rights.[2] The plaintiffs appealed.

The appeal was heard in May 1997. The Court of Appeal reversed the judgment of Mr Justice Keith and held that the university must have a right to protect its reputation.[3] Mr Justice Litton of the Court of Appeal expressed his shock at the protracted litigation, as three years had gone by since the publication of the article, and the case had not gone beyond the pleading stage!

The case went back to Mr Justice Jerome Chan, the trial judge. Still pending before him was the decision on which parts of the transcripts of the interview records, which he had already heard, were to be excised, and the magazine's application for leave to amend its defence.

Before Mr Justice Jerome Chan had an opportunity to consider these outstanding procedural applications, he sadly passed away.

Justice delayed is justice denied. Unfortunately, delay is not uncommon. *Penny Bay* is another dramatic case.[4] It involved a claim for compensation arising from reclamation of foreshore and seabed for the purpose of constructing new container terminals on Lantau Island in the mid-1990s. The claim for compensation was made by a shipyard, which had been operating for many years on a site that could only be accessed by sea. The shipyard claimed that it could no longer operate as a result of the loss of its sea access. The government responded that any loss to the shipyard business

---

2. *Hong Kong Polytechnic University v Next Magazine Ltd (No 2)* (1996) 7 HKPLR 41, [1997] HKLRD 102.
3. *Hong Kong Polytechnic University v Next Magazine Publishing Ltd* (1997) 7 HKPLR 286, [1997] HKLRD 514.
4. *Penny Bay Investment Co Ltd v Secretary for Justice* [2016] HKEC 1078 (CA); [2014] HKEC 1695 (Lands Tribunal); (2010) 13 HKCFAR 287 (CFA); [2009] HKEC 22 (CA); [2006] HKEC 1145 (Lands Tribunal).

was adequately compensated by the benefit of road access to the site that would be constructed as part of the container terminal project. While the negotiation was going on, the government changed its plan. It abandoned the idea of constructing container terminals and instead decided to build a theme park, and the site is where Disneyland is today. One of the interesting issues was whether the government could maintain that any loss to the shipyard business would be compensated by the benefit of road work that has since been abandoned. The shipyard brought an action against the government, and this issue was taken as a preliminary point of law, which was argued all the way to the Court of Final Appeal. The Statement of Claims in the *Penny Bay* case was signed by Wong Yan Lung when he was still a junior counsel. He later took silk, and served subsequently for seven years as the Secretary for Justice. After he had stepped down as the Secretary for Justice, the case was still pending. The preliminary point of law was settled by the Court of Final Appeal in 2010, some 15 years since the authorization of the reclamation, and the litigation was back to the first stage! Likewise, in *Agrila Ltd*,[5] a preliminary point of law was taken as to the correct principles for assessing rateable value for undeveloped land. After the Court of Final Appeal had answered the preliminary points, the case went on to the stage of assessment of the rateable value. It went back to the Court of Final Appeal again on the assessment, through which the parties tried to revisit the principles of assessment laid down by the Court of Final Appeal in the first place. The case lasted for almost two decades and is still ongoing!

Well, these two cases involved commercial disputes over a very substantial amount of monetary claim. Delay can also happen in less glamorous cases. In *Kong Yunming*, the applicant, a new arrival in Hong Kong, complained that the seven-year residential requirement for Comprehensive Social Security Assistance was inconsistent with her right to social welfare under the Basic Law. Before the case reached the Court of Final Appeal, she had satisfied the seven-year residence requirement, so arguably the hearing of the Court of Final Appeal was academic by then.[6]

It is thus not surprising that cases of this kind led to a major review of the civil justice system. A striking characteristic of the civil justice system is the proliferation of interlocutory proceedings. Parties are able, if they wish, to have resort to all kinds of procedural skirmishes, some of which are no doubt justifiable, while others are less noble in nature, sometimes with a view to simply wearing out the opponents. The general direction of the eventual civil justice reform was to enhance judicial control of the progress of litigation so as to ensure the expeditious progress of cases—the so-called case management system. Parties are also required to do more preparation work at the early stage of litigations. Critics are quick to point out that such front-loading may lead to wasted costs when the litigation ends up in settlement without reaching

---

5. *Commissioner of Rating and Valuation v Agrila Development Co Ltd* [2001] 2 HKLRD 36(CFA). Subsequent litigation was taken out by another group of companies: see *Best Origin Co Ltd v Commissioner of Rating and Valuation* (2012) 15 HKCFAR 816.
6. *Kong Yunming v Director of Social Welfare* (2013) 6 HKCFAR 950. See Chapter 6.

the court for determination, and indeed this is the prevalent situation in many civil proceedings.

The civil justice reform has been in place for quite some years now. Has the system become more efficient? Many feel that over all there is little appreciable improvement. By the end of 2016, listing time has increased again to pre-civil justice reform levels. This is not surprising, as the civil justice reform addressed only some of the causes of delay, namely the adversarial nature of litigation and the tendency to strategize civil procedures to one's advantage. Yet there are also systemic factors. In the last few years, the courts have faced the new challenge of an increasing number of unrepresented litigants, whose unfamiliarity with court proceedings inevitably slows down the process. By mid-2015, there was a large number of deputy and acting judges at virtually all levels of courts. Many retired judges were brought back to serve as deputy judges. This is fine if it is just a short-term phenomenon, but it is worrying when a shortage of judges becomes systemic.[7]

Efficiency and fairness do not always sit well with one another. Thus, efficiency should not be the only consideration in case management. On the other hand, justice delayed is justice denied. These conflicting factors have to be carefully balanced in any civil justice reform. At the same time, it is important for all those involved in the civil justice system to bear in mind that procedural rules are there to serve and not to defeat the ends of justice. Ultimately the success or otherwise of the civil justice system rests upon the good sense of the people administering it—judges, lawyers, and the parties themselves.

---

7. A former High Court judge has voiced his concern over the prevalence of Deputy judicial appointment: see Anselmo Reyes, 'The Future of the Judiciary: A Reflections on the Present Challenges to the Administration of Justice' (2014) 44 HKLJ 429.

19

Vexatious litigants

While the right of access to court is a fundamental constitutional right that goes to the heart of the rule of law, there are occasions when some people have to be restricted from accessing the halls of justice when they try to abuse the system. They are known as 'vexatious litigants'. A common characteristic of this group of litigants is that they take out numerous applications to court and persistently refuse to accept the decision of the court. These actions may be directed at a person or a company, or sometimes a public official or even a judge. Most of these applications make wild allegations with no factual or legal basis; some applications are simply incomprehensible or unintelligible. They are typically written in the Chinese language. The litigants typically act in person, and their motives for so doing range from genuine grievances at injustice, to malicious attempts to harass, to simple mental deraignment. They are best described by Mr Justice Ribeiro as follows:

> There are many variants of such abuse and of what motivates it. It may represent a calculated attempt by a defendant to delay an inevitable judgment or its execution. Or it may be a malicious campaign of harassment directed against a particular adversary. Actions which are unintelligible or wholly frivolous may be commenced by litigants who are unfortunately mentally unbalanced. Sometimes the vexatious conduct springs from some deeply-felt sense of grievance left unassuaged after unsuccessful litigation. The vexatious litigant typically acts in person and characteristically refuses to accept the unfavourable result of the litigation, obstinately trying to re-open the matter without any viable legal basis. Such conduct can become obsessive with the litigant not shrinking from making wild allegations against the court, or against the other side's legal representatives or targeting well-known public personalities thought to be in some way blameworthy. Numerous actions may be commenced and numerous applications issued within each action.[1]

I have had my fair share of experience with vexatious litigants. In 2005, I received five writs within a period of two months, all coming from the same plaintiff whom I did not know. The writs were handwritten in Chinese, ran over many pages, and were

---

1. *Ng Yat Chi v Max Share Ltd* [2005] 1 HKLRD 473, at para 48.

simply incomprehensible. In the first writ, there were 72 defendants, and I was named as the 19th Defendant. As to what was alleged against me, I could not figure out.

It happened around that time that Mr Justice Ribeiro had agreed to speak at our Common Law Lecture Series. This is a series of prestigious public lectures given by eminent judges and scholars. As the Court of Final Appeal had just delivered an important judgment in *Ng Yat Chi v Max Share Ltd* on vexatious litigants, I invited Mr Justice Ribeiro to speak on the subject. Mr Justice Ribeiro was once my teacher when I was a student at law school. He later left the University and had a very successful practice at the Bar. He took silk and later was appointed to the Bench and was one of the longest-serving judges on the Court of Final Appeal. Throughout the years he has always been very supportive of the law school and has always been ready to share his wealth of knowledge and experience with law students. In *Ng Yat Chi*, the Court of Final Appeal laid down certain procedures to deal with abuse of court process by vexatious litigants. In essence, the court affirmed that it has power to make a restrictive order to restrain a vexatious litigant from taking out new applications in an existing action or fresh proceedings in a new action in the future without first obtaining leave from the court.

Mr Justice Ribeiro gave a wonderful lecture. I was so carried away by the subject that, in my introduction, I had gone to some lengths to explain the case of *Ng Yat Chi*. In his opening, Mr Justice Ribeiro generously accepted my lack of restraint and jokingly said that I had delivered half of his lecture already!

The lecture was very well received. A week later, I received another writ from the same plaintiff. There were seven respondents, including Mr Justice Ribeiro, the University, and me. The charge against Mr Justice Ribeiro was that he defamed the litigant. There was of course no truth at all in this; the lecture was directed at the general abuse of court process by vexatious litigants. The charge against me was that I created an opportunity for Mr Justice Ribeiro to defame the litigant by inviting him to speak on this subject!

A few more writs came in the following few weeks, and a number of other judges were named as respondents. Eventually, the Secretary for Justice took out proceedings to strike out these applications and to declare the plaintiff a vexatious litigant, so that he could not take out any more applications without first obtaining the approval of the court to do so.

Over the years, there has been no shortage of vexatious litigants. Restricting a person's right of access to court is a matter of grave importance which no court will undertake lightly. At the same time, as Chief Justice Andrew Li put it, the constitutional right of access to court does not include a right to abuse the court's process. The restrictive order strikes a proper balance: it does not forbid an applicant to take out legal proceedings; it simply requires the applicant to show the court that there is good reason for taking out proceedings. The right of access to court is not abrogated but merely restricted by a requirement to apply for leave from the High Court before any action is permitted to be taken out.

While restrictive orders have prevented vexatious litigants from abusing the court process, they have not stopped these litigants from staging public demonstrations and making derogatory remarks against individual judges. One of them has stood every day for years in front of the High Court building with placards defaming a few judges. The tolerance shown by the judiciary is the best testimony of the fine quality of our judiciary and the respect for freedom of expression in our society.

Having been a commentator on legal and constitutional issues over the years, I have managed to attract a good number of anonymous and abusive letters. These letters are typically handwritten in Chinese characters, without name or address of the authors, and contain nothing but wild allegations and defamatory and abusive accusations, if they are not outright unintelligible or offensive in the first place. They do not bother me at all though it is sad to see how far our community is prepared to descend to venomous and vicious personal attacks. Well, it is perhaps the price of a free society. When persons have to resort to personal attacks, it means they have run out of rational arguments. The best approach may be just to laugh them off while the letters land in the dustbin.

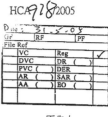

HCA918/2005

Date:	31.5.05		
Gr		RF	PF
File Ref			
VC		Reg	✓
DVC		DR ( )	
PVC ( )		DER	
AR ( )		SAR ( )	
AA ( )		EO ( )	

香港特別行政區
高等法院
原訟法庭
2005 年第978宗

馬桂珍　　　　　　　　　　　　及　　　　　　　　　　　　　　原告人

香港特區政府　　　　　　　　　　　　　　　　　　　第一被告人
前香港特首董建華　　　　　　　　　　　　　　　　　第二被告人
香港終審法院首席法官李國能　　　　　　　　　　　　第三被告人
香港終審法院常任法官李義　　　　　　　　　　　　　第四被告人
香港大學　　　　　　　　　　　　　　　　　　　　　第五被告人
香港大學校長徐立之　　　　　　　　　　　　　　　　第六被告人
香港大學法律學院院長陳文敏　　　　　　　　　　　　第七被告人

（姓名或名稱）香港特區政府、前香港特首董建華、香港終審法院首席法官李國能、香港終審法院常任法官李義、香港大學、香港大學校長徐立之、　香港大學法律學院院長陳文敏　。

（地址）中環下亞厘畢道政府總部（第1－2被告人）香港中環炮台里1號香港終審法院（第3－4被告人）香港薄扶林，香港大學（第5－7被告人）。

本傳訊令狀已由上述原告人就背頁所列出的申索而針對你發出。

在本令狀送達你後（14 天）內（送達之日計算在內），你必須了結該申索或將隨附的送達認收書交回高等法院登記處，並在認收書中述明你是否擬就此等法律程序提出爭議。

如你沒有在上述時限內了結該申索或交回送達認收書，或如你交回送達認收書但沒有在認收書中述明擬就法律程序提出爭議，則原告人可繼續進行訴訟，而判你敗訴的判決可隨時即在無進一步通知發出的情況下予以登錄。

本令狀於今天，即2005年 **27 MAY 2005** 月　　日由高等法院登記處發出。

司法常務官

重要事項

關於送達認收書的指示載於隨附的表格

A writ from a vexatious litigant

VIII

Free Speech

20

Human rights are not absolute

A right to defame?

In recent years we have regularly heard the argument that 'human rights are not absolute'. Those who put forward this argument are usually opposed to the exercise of human rights on a particular occasion, and more often than not, the argument is by itself put forward as a sufficient justification for the restriction of a fundamental right. Obviously this argument is not objectionable by itself though it tends to obscure the issue. Of course, human rights are not absolute. Yet the mere fact that human rights are not absolute does not mean that any restriction is permissible. As Mr Justice Bokhary put it, 'care must be exercised to ensure that it does not open the door too widely for those who are minded to curb human rights, whether for reasons of expediency or worse'.[1] The real question is what kind of restriction is justifiable and compatible with the high purpose served by the right or freedom engaged.

Take free speech as an example. Few people would argue that the right to free speech would include a right to make a defamatory statement, but what constitutes defamation, and what defences there are, would determine the scope of free speech. The more easily a comment would constitute defamation, the narrower the scope of free speech. The wider the defences to defamation, the greater the protection for free speech. In delineating the scope of defamation, the court would have to balance the protection of the reputation of an individual against the public interest of free speech. There are occasions when public interest is so overriding that a person is not even permitted to take out a defamation action. In February 2013, our then Chief Executive, C. Y. Leung, was annoyed by the criticism made against him by Mr Lian Yuet Tsang (練乙錚), a highly respected columnist, in the *Hong Kong Economic Journal Daily*. The Chief Executive threatened to take out a defamation action against the newspaper.[2] I heard the news on the radio that morning on my way to the University. I felt so upset that I decided to phone the radio programme and pointed out that the common law has held that it is against public interest for the government, and for that matter, the

---

1. K. Bokhary, *Human Rights: Source, Content and Enforcement* (Hong Kong: Sweet & Maxwell, 2015), p. 63, paras 7.026 and 7.027.

2. See 'Chief Executive demanded through his lawyer the retrieval of the comments on triad involvement; Lian Yuet Tsang criticized Leung's handling as failing to meet his responsibility' (特首發律師信要求撤回「涉黑」評論；練乙錚評梁振英：處理方式未盡其責), *Hong Kong Economic Journal Daily*, 8 Feb 2013, A10. See also *Ming Pao Daily News*, 8 Feb 2013, A1.

Chief Executive of the government, to bring a defamation suit to stifle criticism of the government. The redress of the government lies in the political arena and not in court. A few years later, the same Chief Executive was apparently furious about continuous media interest in alleged misconduct involving his receipt of a considerable amount of money shortly before his taking office as Chief Executive, an allegation which he considered unfounded. Instead of threatening a defamation suit, he threatened to take out a legal action against *Apple Daily* for jeopardizing his right to stand for re-election as the Chief Executive![3] The claim was difficult to understand, as he had not even expressed an intention to stand for re-election at that time, not to mention the fact that there's no legal bar to stand as a candidate merely because of an allegation! The interesting part is that, on this occasion, he at least refrained from threatening a defamation suit. In early 2017, he took out a defamation action against a member of the Legislative Council who has made remarks on the same subject matter.

When it comes to comments on public affairs, the court will usually accord a rather wide scope of free speech, as the transparency and accountability of public bodies are the foundation of modern civil society. Fair comment is a well-established defence to defamation. To run a defence of fair comment, it is necessary to show that the comment is based on true facts, that the comment is on a matter of public interest, that the comment is recognizable as a comment and not an imputation of fact, that the comment must explicitly or implicitly indicate what the facts are on which the comment is being made, and that the comment is a genuine opinion that an honest person could have formed on the basis of the established facts. For a long time, it was believed that this defence would be defeated if the comment was actuated by malice and not a genuine comment. In other words, the defence was available only to protect genuine public discussion and would not be a shield to those who attacked others by defamatory statements for malicious purposes: spite, ill will, personal vendetta, and so on. In this way, the law tried to balance the public interest of free speech by allowing a defence of fair comment and the protection of the reputation of a person by restricting the defence of fair comment to genuine public discussion.

This balance was, however, challenged in the case of *Albert Cheng v Tse Wai Chun Paul*,[4] which involved two local celebrities, and the judgment of the Court of Final Appeal has become a leading case on this subject in the common law world.

Mr Albert Cheng was the host of a popular morning radio programme on social and political affairs, known as 'Teacup in a Storm' (風波裏的茶杯). It was a very influential talk show programme and was said even to set the agenda of the day for the government. At one stage he was nicknamed 'the Chief Executive before 9 a.m.'. Mr Paul Tse was a lawyer and a Legislative Councillor. He was also the representative of the Tourism Industry Functional Constituency in the Legislative Council.

---

3. 'Leung criticized the Editorial of *Apple Daily* through his solicitors for obstructing his right to seek re-election; Journalist Association was shocked and expressed regret (梁向《蘋果》發律師信斥社論「阻連任權利」；記協表震驚遺憾), *Ming Pao*, 30 September 2016, A10.
4. (2000) 3 HKCFAR 339.

Mr Au Wing Cheung was a tour escort. He was instructed to lead a tour group to the Philippines after he had been working at his tour company for just a few weeks. As soon as he arrived at the Manila airport, he, together with Mr Wong, a member of the tour group, was arrested for drug trafficking. They were eventually convicted and sentenced to life imprisonment. The incident had attracted much publicity in Hong Kong. It was generally believed that they were innocent. Various groups were formed to secure their release. Both Mr Albert Cheng and Mr Paul Tse, who belonged to different groups, were involved in the attempt to secure their return to Hong Kong. After almost five years of continuous efforts, both were eventually released, and they returned triumphantly to Hong Kong, accompanied by Mr Cheng and Mr Tse. Not surprisingly, both Mr Albert Cheng and Mr Paul Tse claimed credit for their successful return.

Upon his return, Mr Au's employment was terminated by his employer. A question arose as to whether Mr Au should claim compensation from his former employer for the period of imprisonment in the Philippines, as he had been arrested and imprisoned in the course of his employment. Mr Albert Cheng encouraged him to do so, whereas Mr Paul Tse advised against it.

As the dispute between Mr Albert Cheng and Mr Paul Tse escalated, Mr Cheng, taking advantage of his position as a radio host, made a number of remarks on the integrity of Mr Tse on his programme. Mr Tse took exception to those remarks and responded by taking out a defamation suit against Mr Albert Cheng, his co-host Mr Lam Yuk Wah, and the Hong Kong Commercial Broadcasting Ltd., which broadcast the radio programme. Among other things, the defendants pleaded fair comment as a defence. In reply, Mr Tse argued that the statements were made maliciously and this destroyed the defence of fair comment. The jury found Albert Cheng and Mr Lam, but not Hong Kong Commercial Broadcasting Ltd, liable for defamation and awarded Mr Tse $80,000 damages. Their appeal was dismissed by the Court of Appeal. On further appeal to the Court of Final Appeal, the only issue was whether their defence of fair comment was defeated by the presence of malice.

Before the Court of Final Appeal, Mr Paul Tse articulated the malice as follows: (1) the defendants were reckless as whether their comments were true; (2) Mr Cheng made the comments to gratify his animosity against Mr Paul Tse and the employer of Mr Au and to belittle the efforts of Mr Tse in securing the release of Mr Au. Mr Tse argued that the defence of fair comment was to facilitate genuine public discussion on matters of public interest. If the defendants were to abuse the defence to further Mr Cheng's animosity against Mr Tse, the defence should not be available to them. He asked rhetorically why the law should protect a defamatory speech that was motivated by spite. In this regard he drew a comparison with the defence of qualified privilege, that is, when the law admits a defence to defamation under certain circumstances when there is a need, in the public interest, for a particular recipient to receive frank and uninhibited communication of particular information from a particular source, e.g., when writing a reference. Like fair comment, this defence of qualified privilege was destroyed by malice. The defence was a privilege, so Mr Tse contended, and this privilege would be lost if the defendants were to abuse it.

Mr Cheng and Mr Lam were represented by Martin Lee SC. They challenged the legal principle that the defence of fair comment would be destroyed by malice, a legal principle that has been in existence for over a century.

The judgment of the Court of Final Appeal was given by Lord Nicholls of Birkenhead, an overseas judge on the Court of Final Appeal who is also a member of the UK Supreme Court. His Lordship first set out the objective limits of fair comment, noting that it was restricted to comments on a matter of public interest and based on true facts and that the comment had to be what an honest person could have made in the circumstances. The court then examined the rationale for the defence of fair comment, which was 'to facilitate freedom of expression by commenting on matters of public interest'. The touchstone of this defence was that honestly held views should be allowed to be freely expressed, subject to the objective limits of the defence of fair comment, which limits ensured that the readers would have the materials to allow them to decide whether they agreed or disagreed with the comment. The court emphasized that untrammelled discussion of public affairs was a basic safeguard against irresponsible political power and a foundation supporting personal liberty. On this basis, the motive for the comment would be of little significance. After all, in the social and political fields, it was not unusual that those who made public comments might have some objectives of their own. This might be 'to publicize and advance themselves, or to hope to achieve some result, such as promoting one cause or defeating another, elevating one person or denigrating another'.[5] This was the political reality. As Lord Nicholls pointed out, 'in making their comments they do not act dispassionately, they do not intend merely to convey information. They have other motives.' But did it matter? Lord Nicholls held:

> The presence of these motives, and this is of crucial importance for the present purposes, is not a reason for excluding the defence of fair comment. The existence of motives such as these when expressing opinion does not mean that the defence of fair comment is being misused. It would make no sense, for instance, if a motive relating to the very feature which causes the matter to be one of public interest is regarded as defeating the defence.
>
> On the contrary, this defence is intended to protect and promote comments such as these. Liberty to make such comments, genuinely held, on matters of public interest lies at the heart of the defence of fair comment. That is the very object for which the defence exists. Commentators, of all shades of opinion, are entitled to 'have their own agendas'. Politicians, social reformers, busybodies, those with political or other ambitions and those with none, all can grind their axes. The defence of fair comment envisages that everyone is at liberty to conduct social and political campaigns by expressing his own views, subject always, and I repeat the refrain, to the objective safeguards which mark the limits of the defence.

---

5. At 352–353.

In this regard, Lord Nicholls distinguished the rationale for fair comment from that for qualified privilege. The latter was based on a notion of performance of a duty or protection of an interest, so that, for example, if a former employer put down a defamatory statement in a reference with a dominant motive to destroy the former employee, the former employer was misusing the privilege and this would vitiate his defence of qualified privilege. In contrast, fair comment did not rest on the existence of a special relationship; it was based on the high importance of protecting and promoting the freedom of comment by everyone at all times on matters of public interest, irrespective of their particular motives.

Lord Nicholls was at first troubled by the situation when the comment was made entirely out of spite. However, he found that in that case the comment would be unlikely to be able to satisfy the objective limits of fair comment, particularly that it was one that an honest person would have come to or that it was a comment that was honestly held. Besides, it would be difficult to disentangle a comment that was based entirely on malice and one that was made out of mixed motives, which was more likely to be the situation in real life. Thus, as long as the objective limits of fair comment were met, the defence would not be lost even if the comment were made entirely out of spite.

Having reached this position as a matter of principle, Lord Nicholls then took a survey of previous cases and found support for his conclusion. The court had previously held that irrationality, stupidity, or obstinacy did not constitute malice. Nor did a desire to embarrass or prejudice another person. What was important was that the opinion must be honestly held. His Lordship concluded:

> A comment which falls within the objective limits of the defence of fair comment can lose its immunity only by proof that the defendant did not genuinely hold the view expressed. Honesty of belief is the touchstone. Actuation by spite, animosity, intent to injure, intent to arouse controversy or other motivation, whatever it may be, even if it is the dominant or sole motive, does not of itself defeat the defence. However, proof of such motivation may be evidence, sometimes compelling evidence, from which lack of genuine belief in the view expressed may be inferred.

The appeal was allowed and a retrial was ordered. The matter was probably settled afterwards. However, what is more significant is that this judgment has reversed a principle that had lasted for at least 150 years that malice would destroy the defence of fair comment. It soon became a leading judgment on this point and has been followed in other parts of the common law world. It is exemplary of the approach of asking what the law is for. I have always told my students that law is not static; it exists to serve the ends of justice. The common law system is sometimes known as the system of precedents. We look to past decisions for guidance, and that is how certainty of the law is achieved. At the same time, our court breaks away from past decisions when the occasion arises. Every now and then, a leading case comes up that breaks new ground or steers a new direction of development. This happens because we are not prepared to accept precedents and authorities slavishly, because lawyers and judges dare to approach a matter from a new perspective, not being confined by what has been decided before, and because there is a burning flame and an unfailing duty to search for justice, which is always a matter of context and which is invariably the impetus for a change of direction in the development of law. It is inherent in our legal training that we accept authorities and yet we question authorities. It is a betrayal of legal training to accept uncritically whatever authority says. This is perhaps what makes lawyers a nuisance in a regime of compliant governance, be it a country, a government, or an institution.

This judgment also shows the fallacy of the argument that human rights are not absolute, if this is meant to support any restriction of human rights. Free speech lies at the core of a civil and democratic society, the hallmarks of which include plurality, broadmindedness, and tolerance. The right is highly valued, but it is not absolute. Yet this does not mean that a right can be restricted whenever there is a good reason. Protection of reputation is a good reason, but improperly confined, a defamation action could be abused to stifle freedom of expression. The reason to restrict a fundamental right provides only a starting point, and a much more sophisticated analysis is required before one can conclude what restriction of human rights is constitutionally permissible.

21

'I do not report the matter to him'

The paparazzi case

It is depressing when someone who you know is a scapegoat is sent to prison, and even more so when the defendant is a journalist of 24 years of experience.

The opening of our submission before the Court of First Instance, which was adopted by Mr Justice Patrick Chan in his judgment, summed up what the case was about:

> This is the most serious and flagrant contempt that Hong Kong has known. The attack on the judiciary was as unprecedented as it was persistent. For over a month, the people of Hong Kong were spoon fed with daily repetitive dosages of scurrilous abuse of not just one or two judges but the entire judiciary. The ultimate unparalleled challenge to the rule of law took the form of an 'educational' paparazzi trail which followed one of our appeal judges for three days around the clock.[1]

What led to these scandalous attacks on our judiciary? They were triggered by two series of cases. The first series involved a dispute between two rival media institutions over a photograph of a famous singer in Hong Kong. The second series of cases related to the Obscene Articles Tribunal's classification of various photographs published by *Oriental Daily News* as indecent.

Oriental Daily News is a widely circulated Chinese daily newspaper with a readership of about 2.3 million or 53 per cent of the vibrant newspaper market. From time to time it has published photographs that have been regarded as appealing to the prurient interests of some of its readers, with the result that it has been charged with and convicted of a number of offences of publication of indecent articles. *Oriental Daily News* felt aggrieved and considered that the members of the Obscene Articles Tribunal (OAT) were hostile and discriminatory against the press. There was some justification for its grievances, as some of the decisions of OAT have been difficult to support, such as its decision to classify a photograph depicting the statue of David by Michelangelo as indecent. In June 1996, *Oriental Daily News* published on two occasions some photographs of women in the nude. These photographs were classified as indecent. The same photographs were published in another local Chinese newspaper and were also classified as indecent. That newspaper successfully appealed and the case

1. *Secretary for Justice v Oriental Press Group Ltd* [1998] 2 HKC 627, at 640 (CFI).

was remitted to OAT, which, on reclassification, affirmed that the photographs were indecent. In contrast, the appeal by *Oriental Daily News* was dismissed, first by the then High Court and then by the Court of Appeal, which accepted that OAT had a duty to give reasons but considered that the reasons given by OAT were adequate.[2] The Court of Appeal also refused to grant leave to appeal to the Court of Final Appeal. Leave was subsequently granted by the Court of Final Appeal.

Lighting the fuse

There was at one time a rumour about the pregnancy of Ms Faye Wong, the superstar pop singer. One day a reporter from *Oriental Daily News* spotted Ms Wong in the VIP lounge of the Beijing airport. From the way she was dressed it was quite obvious that Ms Wong was pregnant. The reporter immediately took a photograph of Ms Wong, apparently without her consent. That photograph was then used as the front cover of *Sunday Weekly*, a weekly magazine of the Oriental Press Group, and was said to confirm her pregnancy for the first time.

On the following day, the same photograph, together with the front cover of *Sunday Weekly*, was reproduced in *Apple Daily News*, the rival of *Oriental Daily News*. Though *Apple Daily News* had acknowledged the source, it had not sought the consent of the Oriental Press Group for the reproduction. Not surprisingly, the Oriental Press Group threatened to take out a civil action against Apple Daily Ltd. for breach of copyright. *Apple Daily* did not seriously dispute liability and, instead, asked how much the Oriental Press Group would demand for compensation. The Oriental Press Group initially asked for a compensation of about $270,000, which was reduced to $195,000 at the hearing, plus $100,000 legal costs, whereas *Apple Daily* counter-offered $10,000 as agreed compensation. No agreement could be reached, and the Oriental Press Group pressed ahead with the civil action.

As a matter of tactics, *Apple Daily* made an open offer of $10,000 as settlement, which was later treated by Mr Justice Rogers as in effect payment into court. This meant that the Oriental Press Group could at any time accept the offer and discontinue the legal action. However, if the Oriental Press Group did not accept the offer and insisted on going to court, and if the eventual judgment made an award less than the sum offered, there would be serious implications for legal costs. In civil actions, the general rule is that the losing party will have to pay to the winning party the costs incurred by the winning party in bringing the action. The most substantial part of these costs would be the legal fees. If the sum offered for settlement is greater than the damages eventually awarded by the court, this shows that the defendant's offer was a reasonable attempt to avoid litigation. Instead of accepting a reasonable offer, the plaintiff dragged the defendant into court and forced the defendant to incur legal costs to defend itself. In this situation, the general rule on costs will not apply. Instead,

---

2. [1998] 1 HKLRD 253. For the details of this case, see Chapter 17.

the losing party may be able to claim the legal costs from the plaintiff, as the plaintiff's insistence to go ahead with the legal action was both unnecessary and unreasonable. Payment into court is a familiar tactical move. To be effective, the amount offered has to be such that it would face the plaintiff with a difficult choice of either accepting the amount, which will be lower than what it claims, or taking the risk of pressing on with the legal action, hoping that the eventual award of compensation will be of a larger amount. The offer would of course be kept away from the trial judge so as not to affect his or her judgment on liability.

Following his decision on liability, Mr Justice Rogers then focused on the assessment of compensation for breach of copyright.[3] The Oriental Press Group suggested that the value of the photograph of Ms Faye Wong was comparable to a photograph of Princess Diana with some hypothetical new lover, or a photograph of the pregnant Madonna, or a photograph of Deng Xiaoping showing him on his deathbed. The court found those comparisons unreal and unhelpful. Eventually, the trial judge ordered a compensation of $8,001, which was lower than what *Apple Daily* had offered.

At this point, *Apple Daily* revealed to the court its offer for settlement and successfully asked for legal costs even though it had lost the case.[4] Thus, the Oriental Press Group won the case with a compensation of $8,001, but in return had to pay the legal costs of *Apple Daily* for unreasonably dragging it to court. These legal costs far exceeded the compensation awarded. Not surprisingly, the Oriental Press Group appealed.

On 19 September 1997, the Court of Appeal upheld the award made by the trial judge.[5] At the end of his judgment, Mr Justice Godfrey observed that the picture was obviously obtained without the consent of Ms Wong, who would most likely have refused to give her consent if asked. Mr Justice Godfrey then queried whether a picture that was obtained in a manner that constituted a violation of other people's privacy deserved the protection of copyright law. This kind of statement is known in law as *obiter dicta*, meaning 'something said by the way'. It is not intrinsic to the decision but is a personal reflection of the judge on the state of the law. It is intended to draw to the attention of the government some deficiencies in the law. The remarks of Mr Justice Godfrey were important in understanding the subsequent development of the matter and are worth quoting in full:

> The taking of photographs of public figures on *public* occasions (for example, when emerging from limousines on first nights) is and must remain legitimate. But the taking of photographs of public figures on *private* occasions without their consent is quite another matter. It has been held, on public policy grounds, that no copyright can subsist in matter which is normally offensive, although, nowadays, the work

---

3. *Oriental Press Group Ltd v Apple Daily Ltd* [1997] 2 HKC 515.
4. Mr Justice Rogers was prepared to treat the letter of settlement as in effect a payment into court. This was not accepted by the Court of Appeal although it accepted that the letter of settlement would be a relevant factor to be taken into consideration in awarding legal costs. As a result, the Court of Appeal set aside the costs order of Mr Justice Rogers and replaced it by an order that each side be responsible for its own costs.
5. [1997] 2 HKC 525.

would have to be considered as having a grossly immoral tendency before it would be excluded from copyright protection. The point is that the law should, and can, reflect public sentiment. Public sentiment has turned, or seems to be turning, against those who are guilty of invasion of the privacy of public figures by taking their photographs for large sums which reflect the cupidity of the publishers and the prurience of their readers. The time may come when, if the legislature does not step in first, the court may have to intervene in this field (as Lord Bingham of Cornhill LCJ has recently suggested in England); for example, by holding that the protection of copyright will not be extended to photographs of public figures taken on private occasions without their consent.[6] [italics in the original; references omitted]

It was on the basis of this paragraph that Mr Justice Godfrey was subsequently criticized by *Oriental Daily News* for accusing the reporter of *Oriental Daily News* as paparazzo. There was of course no reference to paparazzo in this paragraph at all.

In September 1997, a few days after the judgment of the Court of Appeal, a series of articles began to appear in *Oriental Daily News*. They made personal attacks against Mr Justice Godfrey, describing him as 'ignorant and unreasonable', 'ridiculous and arbitrary', 'prejudiced', and 'arrogant'.[7] The attack was soon extended to cover judges of OAT and then the entire judiciary. It was said that the judiciary was unfair to the Oriental Press Group and that the previous British Hong Kong government had intensified its persecution of the Oriental Press Group through the police and OAT. Members of OAT were individually identified and publicly reviled, described as 'stupid, despicable and ignorant' and 'scumbags'.[8] These rumblings of discontent continued, almost daily, in the few months that followed. The newspaper also republished photographs which had been classified and confirmed by the court as indecent, an act which the court described as 'nothing less than a defiance of the court's decision and a challenge to the rule of law'.[9]

Stepping up the attacks culminating in the paparazzi chase

On 9 December 1997, the Court of Appeal set aside the costs order of Mr Justice Rogers and ordered that each side be responsible for its own costs for the hearing at the court below but that the Oriental Press Group be responsible for two-thirds of the costs of the appeal.[10] A month later, on 8 January 1998, the Court of Appeal refused to grant leave to appeal to the Court of Final Appeal in the Faye Wong case.

Meanwhile, on 10 December 1997, the Court of Appeal refused to grant leave to appeal to the Court of Final Appeal in the above OAT case about the nude photograph,

---

6. At 529H–530B.
7. [1998] 2 HKC 627 at 643.
8. At 644.
9. At 644.
10. This means that while Oriental Press Group had won the Faye Wong case, it could not recover its costs at the Court of First Instance and had to pay two-thirds of the costs of *Apple Daily* at the Court of Appeal. The amount of legal costs far exceeded the compensation of $8,001.

thus bringing an end to that litigation. Soon after, the Kung Fu Tea column in *Oriental Daily News* stepped up its attacks against the judiciary. A series of articles appeared between 11 and 15 December 1997, and they formed the subject matter of the first set of charges of contempt of court. These vitriolic attacks singled out Mr Justice Rogers and Mr Justice Godfrey, and then extended to the entire judiciary. As described by the court, these attacks were 'abusive, offensive and scurrilous', with persistent racial slurs, made without any justification or basis for such remarks, and contained an alarming threat to do something harmful or unpleasant to members of OAT and the judges.[11] The language of the attacks is too vulgar to be reproduced here. The titles of the articles, including 'The Swinish White-Skinned Judges and the Canine Yellow-Skinned Tribunal' and 'Rogers' Despicableness and Godfrey's Derangement' are sufficient to give a flavour of the tone of the attacks. I may add that much of the vulgarity in these articles was indeed lost in the English translation.

On 12 January 1998, a few days after the Court of Appeal refused to grant leave to appeal to the Court of Final Appeal in the Faye Wong case, a full-page statement was published in *Oriental Daily News*. It accused the judiciary of conspiring with the former colonial government to persecute the Oriental Press Group and protested against Mr Justice Godfrey for wrongfully calling their journalist a paparazzo. It vowed to destroy the public authority of OAT. As described by the Court of First Instance, the article 'ended almost like a declaration of war'.[12]

On the following day, another article in the Kung Fu Tea column announced the launch of a 'paparazzi chase' against Mr Justice Godfrey in order to 'educate' him on the true meaning of paparazzi. These attacks on Mr Justice Godfrey were most unfair, as it could be seen from his judgments, quoted above, that he had never accused the reporter of being a paparazzo and indeed had never used this term in his judgment. This article also set out how the pursuit of the judge would be organized.

This well-publicized threat of a paparazzi chase was put into practice. For three days, reporters of *Oriental Daily News* were outside the residence of Mr Justice Godfrey early in the morning and kept him under surveillance around the clock. They followed him to work, sat in his court, followed him to lunch, and trailed him after work. The pursuit was carried out in an intentionally conspicuous manner. Mr Justice Godfrey was publicly warned that 'any false steps' taken by him would be immediately captured and published. The paparazzi chase attracted a lot of other media to cover the story. On the first day of the chase, a large number of reporters gathered outside Mr Justice Godfrey's home with a view to reporting the pursuit. At one stage, the chase became dangerous when members of the *Oriental Daily News* tried to overtake the judge's car to take photos of him; the car swerved to avoid the pursuit and nearly knocked down some other reporters who were following.

The paparazzi chase lasted for three days and was covered extensively by all media in Hong Kong. At the end of the third day, *Oriental Daily News* announced that the

---

11. At 645, 646, 647, and 648.
12. At 650.

chase had achieved its educational purpose and called a halt to the operation. The community was shocked. The Secretary for Justice decided to charge the Oriental Press Group for contempt of court by scandalizing the court.

Enough is enough: The contempt charges

Given the politically sensitive nature of the charge, especially when it was directed against a newspaper shortly after the handover, the Department of Justice decided to instruct counsel in private practice to advise on the matters. Ronny Tong SC and I were instructed to act for the Secretary for Justice in the prosecution.

The first question was to decide who the defendants should be. There was practically no way that the chief editor could escape liability. The poor man had been promoted to that position only shortly before the launch of the attacks. From the very beginning, he was represented separately from the rest of the defendants and was prepared to accept full responsibility.

The owner of the newspaper would be another obvious defendant. Under the Registration of Local Newspapers Ordinance, the proprietor, the publisher, and the printer of the newspaper was Oriental Daily Publishing Ltd., a shell company with two nominee directors. This company was in turn wholly owned by *Oriental Daily News* Ltd., another shell company, which was 99 per cent owned by the parent company, Oriental Press Group Ltd., a substantial listed company.

Although Oriental Daily Publishing Ltd. was described as the proprietor, publisher, and printer of the newspaper, it was not responsible for any of the expenditure incurred in publication. The printing was carried out by OPG Printing Ltd., another shell company. The newsprint was paid for by OPG Finance Ltd., and the staff of the newspaper were indeed employed by OPG Human Resources Ltd. and apparently seconded to the newspaper. All these companies came under the Oriental Press Group. The parent company, Oriental Press Group Ltd., was at least two tiers removed from the newspaper.

Given the unprecedented attacks on the judiciary, it was apparent that public interest would not be adequately served by just prosecuting a shell company. Yet if the prosecution was to go after people behind the scene, it would have to lift the corporate veil of a number of intermediate companies, which was not easy. Eventually, six defendants were charged: The Oriental Press Group (D1), Mr Ma, chairman of its board of directors (D3), Oriental Daily Printing Ltd. (D2), its two nominee directors (D4 & D5), and the chief editor of *Oriental Daily News* (D6).

There are two types of contempt of court. The classic type of contempt of court is about interference with the fair trial of an ongoing or pending case. The rationale behind contempt of court is that a litigant is entitled to a fair trial by the court, not by the media or the community. Therefore, any attempt to interfere with a decision of the court on an issue that is to be determined by the court is a violation of the right of the litigants to a fair trial. In this regard, there is always a tension between contempt of court and freedom of expression. Over the years, the scope of contempt of court has been gradually reduced. The so-called 'gagging writ', whereby a person could stifle public discussion on matters of public concern simply by issuing a writ in court, has been abolished. Contempt is unlikely to be committed unless the comment or interference takes place in close proximity to the trial and therefore poses a real risk of undermining a fair trial. It is also presumed that a professional judge is less likely to be influenced by popular comments, and hence contempt is unlikely to be committed if the case is before the Court of Appeal or above. In contrast, members of a jury are more susceptible to the influence of popular comments, and most contempt charges are related to jury trials.

Unlike the classic type of contempt, in which the interference is directed at a particular trial, the second type of contempt, of 'scandalizing the court', is designed to preserve public confidence in the due administration of justice. The interference is not directed at any particular trial but to the administration of justice as a whole. The tension of this type of contempt with freedom of expression is particularly acute. While it is important to preserve public confidence in the administration of justice, any judgment of the court is open to public criticism. Justice is not a fragile flower that will wither in the heat of criticism. The court has also recognized that not all criticisms are going to be sweetly reasoned, particularly if they come from the disappointed party in a case. It is part of the price of a free society. On the other hand, the judiciary has no means to defend itself in the face of scurrilous attacks, as it is not appropriate for the judiciary to engage in public debates. If the attacks become sustained, widespread, and exaggerated, public confidence in the administration of justice will be eroded, and this will eventually endanger the rule of law. It was thought at the end of the nineteenth century that this kind of contempt would soon become obsolete. This prediction did not come true, as this kind of contempt continues to be invoked in our own time in different parts of the common law world. It is not easy to draw the appropriate line between free expression and criticisms of the court on the one hand, and protecting public confidence in the administration of the justice system on the other.

The trial

The charges of scandalizing the court were based on eight articles published mainly in the Kung Fu Tea column in *Oriental Daily News* and the paparazzi hounding of Mr Justice Godfrey. The chief editor accepted full responsibility and made an apology at the outset. He was represented by Cheng Huan SC. The rest of the defendants contested the charges and were represented by John Griffiths SC, the former Attorney General. In view of the significance of the case, it was heard by a Divisional Court of two judges, Mr Justice Patrick Chan, a bilingual judge who would be able to read the articles in their original language and later a judge of the Court of Final Appeal, and Mr Justice Keith. Not surprisingly, the court was packed with reporters.

It was quite clear at the outset that the strategy of the defence was to put the blame on the chief editor so as to exonerate Mr Ma, the chairman of the Board of Directors of Oriental Press Group Ltd.[13] While the Oriental Press Group Ltd. was the parent company, it said in defence that it fully enshrined the policy of editorial independence in the running of its publication subsidiaries. As Mr Griffiths submitted in his final submission, 'I accept, of course, that *Oriental Daily News* is an important tabloid newspaper and the most widely read in Hong Kong, but Homer nodded and it may be occasionally the chief editor of that newspaper nods and make mistakes.' It was submitted that the attacks against the judiciary were so outrageous and preposterous that 'no reasonable or right thinking member of society would take it seriously for a moment'. The articles were said to be written by a 'disgruntled or, indeed, perhaps, even paranoid litigant'. In light of the high level of public education on the rule of law in Hong Kong, the population, it was submitted, was unlikely to be affected 'by articles in a tabloid paper'. It was sad to hear that a newspaper with one of the highest daily circulations in Hong Kong had to admit through its counsel in open court that it was just a tabloid newspaper, the articles of which were not to be taken seriously.

The prosecution case was that, while the chief editor might enjoy editorial independence, it was unthinkable that the attacks were just the frolic of the chief editor without any involvement of the group. There was of course no direct evidence, and the prosecution rested on inference. The attacks were primarily a complaint against the treatment of the Oriental Press Group as a whole and not just *Oriental Daily News*. There were various references in the articles under complaint to the Oriental Press Group. Indeed, the prosecution case went further to say that it was the chairman who had connived if not consented to the attacks against the judiciary.

Mr Mak, the assistant to the chairman of Oriental Press Group, was tendered for cross-examination. The gist of his evidence was to dissociate the chairman from any involvement in the articles and the paparazzi chase. It was said that the chairman did not have the regular habit of reading the *Oriental Daily News* or other publications of the group in detail. Indeed, he did not spend much time on these publications even though the newspaper contributed at that time the most significant source of income to the group. Mr Mak's evidence was quite comical, not to say absurd. To the best of my memory, part of the cross-examination went like this:

Q: Mr Mak, your title is 'assistant to the chairman'?

A: Yes.

Q: Do you agree, therefore, that the main duty is to assist the chairman?

---

13. The Divisional Court expressed in its judgment its suspicion that the chief editor 'might have been instructed or at least encouraged to mount this campaign by members of the Board of Directors of the Oriental Press Group Ltd., including Mr Ma, even if the detailed implementation of it was left to Mr Wong and his editorial team' (at 683) and that 'a deal has been done for Mr Wong to take full responsibility on himself, and in doing so to enable others to be exonerated' (at 684).

A: But when talking about the responsibility, being the assistant, of course I have to assist the chairman, but that does not mean that I could not do other things.

. . .

Q: Mr Mak, is it correct that Oriental Press Group Limited is very concerned about its image?

A: Yes.

Q: To the extent that one of your major responsibilities is to head a team of people to review television and radio programmes and newspapers and magazines in Hong Kong: is that right?

A: The so-called team of persons who view these things is merely the same group of personnel working in the library, and it is a sort of by-the-way job—they watch all this.

Q: Are you sure you are not underplaying their job, the significance of their job?

A: How do you mean?

Q: If you would please go to your statement at page 592, this is a statement that you gave in the action involving Mo Man Ching?

A: Yes.

Q: It says here that you have to report to the chairman and the management of OPG on all matters of interest concerning the operation of OPG and its subsidiaries:

'In order for me to keep abreast of the said matters, there has been, and still is, a special team of OPG staff, whose function is to review television and radio programmes and newspapers and magazines, and to specifically report on all matters concerning or touching OPG and its subsidiaries.'

That is correct, is it not?

A: Yes.

Q: They report to you?

A: Yes.

Q: You report to the chairman?

A: No—as I have told the court earlier on, for those matters that have to be dealt with by the chairman, I would report to him. Other than those, then I would report to the management.

A: Who is the 'management' in this case?

Q: About this statement, let me say this: because we had two chairmen: before 1 July 1996, it was Mr Ma Ching Kwan who was the chairman. When I made this statement, when I mentioned 'chairman', it was the then chairman. Mr Ma Ching Kwan, and the management here mainly refers to me.

After 1 July 1996, we set up the post of general manager, so, from then on, when I say 'management', I mean the general manager's office.

...

Q: What if you come across a matter which is of great importance to the group; would you have reported to the chairman?

A: It depends on the importance.

...

Q: Let me be more specific with you. Mr Mak, if it has come to your attention that Oriental Press Group Limited might have committed a crime and is about to be prosecuted, do you say that is a matter that you would draw to your chairman's attention?

A: I would report to the general manager.

Q: You would not report it to the chairman?

A: No.

...

Q: At the time in question, the paparazzi trail of Mr Justice Godfrey received very widespread coverage by other media, correct?

A: I think so, yes.

Q: It was even covered by television?

A: Yes.

Q: So, did your special team report or draw your attention to this matter?

A: I am not sure, but I think so, yes.

Q: What did you do? Did you report to the chairman?

A: If I had seen it, and if I thought that there was something in it, then I would pass it on to the legal department. If nothing was in it, then I would just pass it on to the general manager's office.

Q: Mr Mak, I am not asking you a hypothetical question; I am asking you as a matter of fact: Did you report that matter to the chairman?

A: First of all, I am not sure if I read all those newspapers referred to in this paragraph, but I think I did and, if I did, and if I thought that there were serious criticisms or libellous comments, then I would pass them on to the legal department for further handling. If not, then I would pass it on to the general manager.

Q: 'Mr Mak, I do not understand that answer. I thought it was a very simple question. Did you or did you not draw the attention of the chairman to those matters?

A: . . . but I did not tell the chairman.

Q: So, you did not?

A: True.

Q: You thought it was a rather trivial matter. Is that right?

A: At the time, there was a large number of these sorts of reports or articles.

Q: You have territory-wide coverage of something done in the name of the group, and you thought it was not appropriate to refer to the chairman?

A: As I said earlier, for things outside my responsibility in assisting him, then I need not report to him.

Q: So, what did you do, if anything?

A: I did nothing—as I said, if I find that there was no criticism, then I would just pass it on to the general manager for handling.

Q: You did not even refer this matter to your legal department where there are three qualified lawyers?

A: I am not sure if I did or not.

. . .

Q: But we have evidence in this case that the other newspapers were carrying interviews with various people, like the chairman of the Bar Association, the chairman of the Democratic Party, who all say, 'You have done something gravely wrong.'

A: Yes.

Q: Did those matters not concern the image of the group?

A: I think—well, let me say I am not well acquainted with the law, so I based it only on my own opinion, my own view, whether in my view it is a criticism or not, then I would pass it on to the general manager. It is only purely on my own view.

...

Chief Judge Chan: I have a few questions. On 12 or 13 January this year, did the chairman speak to you about the paparazzi operation?

A: No.

Chief Judge Chan: Was he not concerned?

A: He did not mention it to me.

Chief Judge Chan: Did he mention it to you on 14 January?

A: I do not think so.

Chief Judge Chan: The 15th?

A: No.

Chief Judge Chan: When was the first time, or did he ever talk to you about the paparazzi operation?

A: No, he did not mention it to me at all. What I knew about this paparazzi team was from what I read from the newspaper.

Chief Judge Chan: As far as you know, did he know about this operation at that time?

A: I do not know if he knew or not, because he never mentioned it to me.

Chief Judge Chan: Up to now, have you ever talked to him about it?

A: Until this case came about, I told him that he had to attend court on such and such a day.

Chief Judge Chan: What was his reaction?

A: I did not see any reaction from him, because I was on the phone—I mean, I was talking to him on the phone.

The suggestion that the chairman knew nothing about the sustained campaign against the judiciary or the paparazzi chase was preposterous. Mr Mak's repeated line that 'I do not report the matter to him' began to sound like the famous 'Brutus is an honourable man' in Shakespeare's *Julius Caesar*!

Apart from denying responsibility, the defendants argued that the common law offence of scandalizing the court constituted an unjustifiable restriction of the right to freedom of expression under the Bill of Rights. The court was not impressed. At one stage the court suggested that if a person engaged in conduct of scandalizing those responsible for the due administration of justice and hence jeopardized the rule of law, that person could not be said to be exercising the right to freedom of expression at all.[14] Therefore, it would not even be necessary to consider the constitutionality of the restriction on the right to freedom of expression. We declined the invitation to take this point. Instead of arguing that the right to freedom of expression did not apply and hence creating rooms for unnecessary and undesirable arguments in future on what constitutes an exercise of the right to freedom of expression, it is better to justify the restriction on its merits. It may be tempting to take up an invitation from the Bench to adopt a particular line of argument. Yet it is equally important in our system that the duty of the prosecution is not to win a case at all costs.

The verdict

The court found the chief editor guilty of all contempt charges. It pointed out that 'the campaign which the *Oriental Daily News* had waged against the judiciary was without parallel in modern times. The features of this prolonged and sustained campaign which made it so unique include the venom of the language which was used, the outrageousness of the motives which it ascribed to its targets, and—if the numerous letters of support which the *Oriental Daily News* claimed to have received from its readers is anything to go by—the impact which the campaign had on public confidence in the ability of Hong Kong's judges to dispense justice conscientiously and impartially.'[15] The real purpose of the paparazzi chase was to take revenge upon the judgment of the court against the Oriental Press Group and to punish a judge for his decision.[16] It was 'to teach the judge a lesson'. The court did suspect that the campaign against the judiciary was not the chief editor's own idea; he might even have been instructed to carry out the campaign.[17] Although the chief editor had accepted full responsibility, the court suspected that a deal might have been done for him to take full responsibility on himself so as to exonerate others.[18] Taking into account all the mitigating factors, the court took an eight-month imprisonment as a starting point and reduced it to a four-month imprisonment. This was the first time in the history of Hong Kong that the chief editor of a newspaper was sent to jail for contempt on the basis of what had been published in his newspaper.

The chief editor was motionless when he heard the sentence. I looked into his eyes as he was taken into custody. There was no life, no hope, and no future. He suddenly reminded me of a scene in *The Devil's Advocate*, a movie in which Al Pacino sold his soul to the devil.

How about the others?

Notwithstanding the complex corporate structure, the court, giving the word 'proprietor' its natural meaning, found that the real proprietor of the *Oriental Daily*

---

14. [1998] 2 HKC 627 at 668D-H.
15. At 681.
16. At 666–667.
17. At 683.
18. At 684.

News was the Oriental Press Group Ltd. Among other things, the court noted that, in the photograph of the Faye Wong case, the Oriental Press Group Ltd. was the plaintiff, and it was alleged that the copyright of the photograph was vested in the Oriental Press Group Ltd. As Mr Justice Chan remarked, 'to hold that a shell company, with nominee directors and no assets or operational functions, could be the proprietor, publisher and printer of a newspaper—simply because of the fact of registration—would be to fly in the face of reality.'[19] In the event, the court also found that the printer of the newspaper was OPG Printing Ltd., whereas the publisher was likely to be *Oriental Daily News* Ltd. In light of this finding, Oriental Daily Printing Ltd., the second defendant registered as the proprietor, printer, and publisher of *Oriental Daily News*, and its two nominee directors, were acquitted, though Mr Justice Chan added that 'we leave it to the Secretary for Justice to decide whether a prosecution should be commenced under section 11 of the [Registration of Local Newspapers] Ordinance against the person who certified the correctness of those particulars'.[20]

The court found that the Oriental Press Group Ltd., as proprietor of *Oriental Daily News*, was guilty of contempt for the publication of the articles but not for the paparazzi chase. It could not be argued that the Oriental Press Group Ltd. was unaware of the publication of the articles, which lasted for over two months. Even if it had entrusted the responsibility of publication to the publisher and the editor, and even if it had had full respect for editorial freedom, the Group could not escape from its responsibility when it took no notice and no action on the publications, which were sustained and intense. The articles gave the impression that they spoke on behalf of the Group. There were various references to the Group both in the articles attacking the judiciary and the subsequent notices defending its position. The court rejected any suggestion that the proprietor of a popular daily newspaper could just stand back and do nothing when the newspapers committed the very grave contempt of subjecting the judiciary to an unparalleled campaign of vilification and abuse to achieve its own ends. On the other hand, even though the pursuit of Mr Justice Godfrey was part and parcel of the campaign, it was not part of the normal activities that would be carried out by a publisher and an editor. In the absence of any evidence of active participation, the Group could not be responsible for acts that were outside the normal scope of duties of the publisher and the editor, to whom it had entrusted the duties of publication.

The court found this case a most outrageous contempt. It asked for an analysis of the consolidated accounts of the Oriental Press Group. To a corporate body, the best the court could do was to impose a fine. As the court noted, fines were intended to punish and were meant to hurt. Notwithstanding the publication of an unreserved apology by the Oriental Press Group, the court imposed an unprecedented fine of $5 million and ordered the Group to pay the legal costs of the Secretary for Justice on an indemnity basis.

How about the chairman of the Oriental Press Group?

---

19. At 676.
20. At 676.

The court had no difficulty in rejecting the suggestion that the chairman did not know about the campaign against the judiciary. It was naive even to make such a suggestion, as Mr Justice Chan remarked.[21] While the evidence of Mr Mak was most preposterous, mere knowledge of the campaign or an absence of any attempt to prevent its commission was insufficient to find the chairman guilty of contempt. Some degree of involvement would be required. The prosecution was not able to show, let alone beyond reasonable doubt, that Mr Ma instigated the campaign and procured the publication of the articles. He was acquitted.

The appeal

The chief editor appealed. The sentence meted out to him was probably more severe than had been expected. On appeal, he was represented by Sydney Kentridge QC, a well-known London silk.[22] He argued that the offence of scandalizing the court was inconsistent with the guarantee of freedom of expression under the Bill of Rights, as it could be committed without any interference with any present or pending legal proceedings. The Court of Appeal was not convinced. The rationale behind the offence of scandalizing the court was not to protect judges from criticism but to protect the due administration of justice as a continuing process. The path to criticism was a public way whereby the court would have to accept complaints, which might on occasion exceed the boundary of courtesy, from disappointed litigants or their lawyers. But sustained, scurrilous, abusive attacks made in bad faith, if unchecked, would almost certainly lead to interference with the administration of justice as a continuing process. This was particularly so because Hong Kong is a small jurisdiction, and maintaining public confidence in the administration of justice and the rule of law is of the utmost importance. The contempt would be committed only if there was a real risk of interference with the due administration of justice, and there was plenty of evidence in this case to show that there was not only such a risk but a very great likelihood that the due administration of justice was undermined. In light of the unprecedented gravity of the contempt of court, the Court of Appeal found that a starting point of eight months' imprisonment was indeed 'in all respects moderate', and the final sentence of four months' imprisonment after taking all the mitigating circumstances into consideration was 'temperate, proper and in all the circumstances necessary'.[23] The appeal was dismissed.

Four months later, the Appeal Committee of the Court of Final Appeal refused to grant leave to appeal to the Court of Final Appeal.[24] Mr Justice Litton, delivering the judgment of the Appeal Committee, held that the suggestion of there being a substantial and grave injustice was absurd, and the sentence appeared extremely lenient.[25]

---

21. At 679.
22. *Wong Yeung Ng v Secretary for Justice* [1999] 2 HKC 24 (9 Feb 1999).
23. [1999] 2 HKC 24 at 48.
24. *Wong Yeung Ng v Secretary for Justice* [1999] 3 HKC 143 (25 June 1999).
25. At 147.

This decision finally brought to a close this inglorious chapter in the history of freedom of the press in Hong Kong. Should the offence of contempt of scandalizing the court remain in our law? It was abolished in the United Kingdom in 2013 but has vigorously been applied in Singapore. The offence has been upheld in Canada, New Zealand, and Australia, and in all these jurisdictions, the offence is, like the situation in Hong Kong, reserved for those situations in which there is a real risk that public confidence in the judiciary would be undermined. This is right, so that freedom of expression would not be unduly hampered. The offence is not designed to protect individual judges. The reasoning of the court must be open to public scrutiny and public criticism. There is nothing wrong with criticizing a judgment once it is delivered, and it has to be accepted that not all criticisms would be sweetly reasoned. However, in recent years, there has been a tendency to criticize cases in a strictly result-oriented manner, and judges have been subject to personal attacks and scurrilous abuses for no reason other than that their judgment was not favoured. These attacks are unwarranted and only serve to undermine our legal system. By undermining public confidence in our judiciary and hence the rule of law, we will soon find that we are destroying the very institution that protects our freedoms and liberty.

Freedom of the press is another pillar of our society. It is not something to be taken for granted. I have always held journalists in Hong Kong, including those from Oriental Press, in high regard. In my professional life, I have come across many journalists. Some of them have become good friends; a number of them have been my students. Their commitment, enthusiasm, and dedication are unparalleled. Thus, it is a particularly sad moment when an experienced journalist is sent to jail. The date was 25 June 1999. The summer sun had set in. As I walked down Battery Path after the last court hearing, a reporter asked me how I felt about the case. I sighed, believing that this was only an aberration, and hoped that tomorrow would be a better day.

IX

Fair Hearing and Personal Liberty

22

Trial observers and humanitarian missions

The right to a fair trial is one of the most widely recognized rights in the world though many jurisdictions pay only lip service to it. The moral appeal of a fair trial is so powerful that even the most oppressive regimes find it necessary to put on show trials to justify the detention or sometimes persecution of political opponents. Sometimes a regime may even accede to the request of an international body to send an observer to observe a trial in order to dispel the speculation that the trial is a political show. The observer is usually an expert from a foreign jurisdiction. He or she will just be an observer and will not take part in the trial, but the person's presence will impose some kind of discipline on the court so that everyone will try harder to observe at least procedural justice.

I have had the honour of serving as a trial observer on a few occasions. My first mission was at the request of the headquarters of Amnesty International to observe the retrial of some former political prisoners in Taiwan in the late 1980s.[1] The two defendants were convicted of various political offences under the martial law in Taiwan. Upon their release, they joined an association of former political prisoners. At the Inaugural General Meeting of the association, they put forward an amendment to the constitution to suggest that Formosa should become independent. For this act they were charged with various offences of secession. The trial went on till 10 p.m. and continued even after one of the defendants physically collapsed and needed medical care. Not surprisingly, both of them were convicted and received respectively a custodial sentence of 10 and 11 years of imprisonment. On appeal, their conviction was set aside on grounds of procedural unfairness, and the Court of Appeal ordered a retrial. I was asked to serve as an observer at their retrial.

It required a lot of preparation. As the trial date was announced on relatively short notice, I had to familiarize myself with the trial procedure and the relevant law in Taiwan within a short time. There are strict codes of conduct governing the role of a trial observer. In general, a trial observer, as the title suggests, is to be present at the trial and to report on its fairness. The presence of a trial observer will usually attract a lot of media attention, and the trial observer has to be careful about what can and cannot be said.

---

1. The case was generally known as the Xu and Cai Formosa Independence case (許曹德、蔡有全台獨案).

As a non-governmental organization, Amnesty International has only limited resources. So do not expect a five-star hotel or any VIP reception. It was indeed my first visit to Taiwan. The trial took place on a Friday. I arrived on Thursday evening and was met at the airport by a lady named Chen of the Democratic Progressive Party, the then opposition party. On the day before my arrival there had been a massive demonstration by farmers from the south. The demonstration had resulted in some violent confrontations with the police, and many demonstrators were arrested. Not surprisingly, Ms Chen immediately briefed me about the arrest and urged me to visit the demonstrators who were in custody. This was something entirely outside my brief. Upon consultation with the London headquarters, I was told to go ahead with the meeting on a fact-finding basis but should absolutely refrain from making any public comment.

I was put up at a small hotel at Ximending (西門町), which was not far from the court. This was then (and still) a trendy area with a lot of barber shops. The porter who led me to the room asked me if I needed a haircut. I was at first puzzled by this strange suggestion, especially as it was almost 10 p.m., and declined it. With a lot of reading to do as a result of the last-minute instruction to meet the demonstrators, a haircut would be the last thing on my mind. Of course, as I later found out, anyone familiar with the situation in Taiwan at that time would understand that a haircut was a euphemism for sexual services!

The trial began at 9 a.m. The court was packed with supporters and journalists. The court was notified of my presence, and I was provided with a designated seat in the public gallery. As a matter of courtesy, I greeted the prosecution counsel briefly before the trial. I didn't have a chance to speak to the defendants, as they were denied bail and were remanded in custody. The judges nodded politely to me as they came out to note my presence. The prosecution case contained largely documentary evidence. The prosecution counsel went through the evidence carefully, which was probably a result of my presence, and spent a disproportionate amount of time on the significance of the amendments to the constitution of the association. This seemed to me to be overkill. All three defendants pleaded not guilty and defended themselves in person. As the case was about Formosa independence, the defendants decided to make their speeches in the local Minnan dialect (閩南話). Fortunately, I spoke the Chiu Chow (Chaozhou) dialect (潮州話), which bears some similarities to the Minnan dialect, and with some familiarity with the context, I was able to understand about 60 per cent of the speech.

The court was patient and afforded the defendants full facilities to defend themselves. The hearing was adjourned in the early afternoon. I had a chance to talk to the defendants briefly and was then escorted by Ms Chen to the detention centre to meet the demonstrators. I spent the rest of the afternoon at the detention centre and then went straight to the airport to return to Hong Kong. Thus, on my first trip to Taiwan, all I had seen was a courtroom and a detention centre!

The trial was resumed two months later and then adjourned for verdict. This meant another short overnight stay. I returned to Taiwan for the third time for the verdict. All three defendants were convicted (again) and were sentenced to seven years' imprisonment. This was pretty harsh, given that all they had done was to propose an amendment at a general meeting. At this time, martial law was in force. The law was harsh, but as far as the trial process was concerned, there was not much that I could criticize. They had had a fair trial, but was that sufficient to achieve justice?

Given the sensitive nature of my visits, I did not meet any friends, and I didn't have much chance to see Taiwan. Since then I have visited Taiwan many times and have witnessed great changes there in the following decades. It has become a more civilized and more open society, especially after the lifting of martial law. I have not met the defendants again and have heard that they were pardoned before serving the full sentence. One of them passed away in May 2017. Nor have I met Ms Chen again though I recognized her many years later as a high-ranking official when the DPP was in power.

Some years later, I was asked to join an international team to monitor the general election in Sri Lanka. I knew very little about Sri Lanka and immediately asked my then PhD student, Jayantha Jayasuriya, who was from Sri Lanka, to give me a crash course on the country. The first thing he told me was that the last few presidents of Sri Lanka had been assassinated! And outside Colombo, virtually everyone except foreign visitors was armed! A civil war had broken out in 1983, and when it came to an end in 2009, it was estimated that about 80,000 to 100,000 civilians had been killed. There were allegations that both the Sri Lankan military and the Tamil Tigers were guilty of war crimes. I was asked to cover an area in the north, which was the base of the Tamil Tigers. Two weeks before the general election, martial law was declared, and soldiers were given a licence to kill any suspicious person on the spot. Eventually I did not make it, much to the relief of my family. Since then I have been to Sri Lanka for conferences and meetings and was glad that law and order had been restored. My student, Jayasuriya, was appointed a judge of the Court of Appeal of Fiji in 2015 and then Attorney General of Sri Lanka in 2016.

Shortly after the changeover, I was on an audit team of the Hong Kong Red Cross to audit the rehabilitation and reconstruction work in Yunnan a year after a major earthquake. A huge amount of money had been donated by the people of Hong Kong through the Hong Kong Red Cross to help with the rehabilitation work after the disaster. The delegation was led by Mrs Betty Tung, the wife of the then Chief Executive of Hong Kong and the then president and director of the Hong Kong Red Cross. We were received by the provincial government of Yunnan, and a lavish welcoming dinner was arranged by the mayor on the first day of our arrival. It was pretty ironic. I suspect the banquet would have been sufficient to feed a lot of people for some time, and, after all, we were an NGO doing relief work! The banquet did not finish until 11 p.m. A group of minorities from Xishuangbanna (西雙版納) wanted to meet us to discuss certain water projects. They had travelled for eight hours to Yunnan and had been waiting for us for a few hours. While my colleagues and I were quite exhausted by the end of the banquet, we felt that we should meet them. We had a good discussion, and by the time I managed to get some sleep, it was well past midnight. My colleagues and I had to take an inland flight to Lijian, the site of the earthquake, at around 5 a.m. the following day. Mrs Tung returned to Hong Kong that morning and decided to visit a market before she went to the airport. The mayor sent a whole team of escorts to take her to the market.

Our first port of call was a local hospital at Lijian. We arrived there shortly before 7 a.m. and were treated with a simple but most delicious breakfast with buns and soya milk, which I thought was far better than the sumptuous dinner the night before. After a short meeting at the hospital, we set off for the mountainous area in a jeep. The road was bumpy, and we started going up to about 6,000 feet above sea level. The scenery was breath-taking, but all of us were too exhausted to enjoy it by the time we reached a village at midday. A local clinic had been built, but contrary to the construction plan, a part of the ground floor, which was supposed to be used as a treatment area, had been converted to a small shop selling souvenirs and various miscellaneous items. We had a good discussion with the people in charge. We were assured that the total floor area had not been reduced, but they needed a shop to subsidize the operation of the clinic. This was the only clinic in the region, and patients might have to be carried, sometimes on foot, for hours to come here for treatment. There were also personnel issues that needed to be addressed. While lawyers are pretty useless at the frontline of a natural disaster, some lawyering skills would at least be of use in the follow-up actions.

We visited a few more sites, spent an evening at a remote village, and took a long journey in the same jeep back to Lijian, followed by another day of meetings with the local Red Cross at Yunnan before we caught the return flight to Hong Kong.

While some of these overseas humanitarian trips may sound exciting or even romantic, most of them are very hectic, with a lot of meetings and a very tight schedule. They can be mentally and physically exhausting and sometimes dangerous. They also require a relatively mature personality, as one is bound to deal with many different types of people on the trips, some very unpleasant situations, and sometimes the dark side of humanity. This is what real human rights and humanitarian work is all about.

I am only an amateur in human rights fieldwork and have a lot of respect and admiration for my colleagues who are on the frontline all the time. It is their strong faith in humanity that keeps them going.

23

Liberty of the person

Under the spreading chestnut tree
I sold you and you sold me;
There lie they, and here lie we
Under the spreading chestnut tree.

—George Orwell, *Nineteen Eighty-Four*

Many of the younger generation may not know what USSR stands for—the Union of Soviet Socialist Republics—once the largest country in the world, covering one-sixth of the earth's land space, spanning across freezing Siberia from picturesque St Petersburg in the west to Vladivostok in the east and the Afghan border in the south, bordering no less than 12 countries, 6 in Asia and 6 in Europe. It was the laboratory of Marxism-Leninism, the country that sent the first man into space, the land that both Napoleon and Hitler failed to conquer. Yet the USSR collapsed dramatically into a number of independent countries on Christmas Day 1991.

I have always found Russian culture and history fascinating. So when I first learned about a Soviet state-organized tour to the USSR, I immediately jumped at the chance to go. It was in the late spring of 1983, and the tour was no doubt part of the Soviet Union's propaganda effort targeting young people in the West. It was a 15-day tour, 5 days in each of the three cities of Moscow, Kiev, and Leningrad, and departed from London, on Aeroflot (of course). There was a guided tour on the first day in each city, and the group would be on its own for the remaining four days. The price was extremely attractive (and no doubt subsidized), and it was sold out within two days.

The tour took place during the Easter break. There were about 30 members, most of us students. Our first stop was Moscow. We were put on a tour bus as soon as we landed. Our tour escort was a Russian lady who spoke fluent English. We were taken to all the usual tourist spots: Red Square, the colourful St Basil's Cathedral, the imposing Kremlin, the magnificent iconostasis of the Cathedral of the Annunciation, and so on. My first impression of the USSR was that it was a much brighter and more affluent country than China, the only other socialist country that I had visited. The boulevards were lined with trees, and the columns of statues supporting the Stalinist style buildings were magnificent. Buses and cars were old. There were not many interesting shops on the streets, but the supermarkets seemed well stocked. People dressed in bright colours, much more attractive than the monotonous grey, dark blue and green in China at that time.

We were put up at a small hotel near Red Square. I was assigned to share a room with a gentleman in his early fifties. He told me he was a pastor. Apparently he had been to Moscow before.

After the hectic first day, we were on our own for the remaining four days in Moscow. Each day at breakfast everyone was excited, planning the day ahead, or exchanging information and sharing experiences of the day before. We went on our own adventures shortly after breakfast, and most of us didn't return to the hotel till late at night. The Moscow underground is famous for its marble architecture. Each station is decorated differently and looks like a palace. One common experience was that we were approached in the street to exchange US dollars, and the things on offer for exchange ranged from dubious artefacts to fashionable jeans with holes (yes, these 'distressed' jeans were the fashion in Russia at least three decades before they became fashionable in Hong Kong)! A few young men from Liverpool in our group went to see a Russian ballet performance one evening, and on their way back one of them was pickpocketed and lost his wallet. Instead of reporting to the police, he searched for two hours the refuse bins in the vicinity, and surprisingly, he managed to recover his wallet in one of the bins! The money was gone, but his identity documents and some precious photographs had not been taken.

Red Square is a fascinating place to spend some time. At one end is the picturesque St Basil's Cathedral. At the other end stands the largest department store in Moscow. The towers rising from behind the imposing wall of the Kremlin overlook one of the best-known squares in the world. It symbolizes power, politics, history, and Russian identity. Standing in the square, one can feel the unbearable burden of history and the intense political atmosphere in this country. Red Square was within walking distance of our hotel, and I spent a few nights there, just watching the people coming and going. One late night I saw a few young men emerge from the far side of the square. They were chanting and singing loudly. Very soon a police car appeared from nowhere, and the young men became quiet and left the square after a few police officers talked to them. I was writing down what I had seen when an old couple came up to me and said, in fluent English, 'That's the effect of vodka.'

On the third day I found out that my roommate was on a mission for Amnesty International to visit a prisoner of conscience in Moscow. As a student studying human rights at that time, how could I miss such an opportunity? With some difficulty, I managed to persuade him to take me along. At first he suggested that we should go the following morning. The prisoner of conscience was a writer who had been critical of what was happening in the Soviet Union. He had managed to leave the country unlawfully but was arrested when he arrived in Finland and was repatriated to the Soviet Union. He was then sent to a mental hospital where he was remanded for a few years before he was released. The pastor's mission to find out about his present situation. He was living in a Moscow suburb. After breakfast, the pastor told me that he had changed his mind. He now suggested that we should go in the early afternoon.

The writer lived in some kind of public housing. It was like a public housing estate in Hong Kong except that there were only six units on each floor (there can be about 40 units on each floor in Hong Kong's public housing estates). Each block has about eight floors and its own entrance to the block. A row of eight to ten blocks forms a larger block. We arrived in the early afternoon and found the writer without much difficulty.

He invited us in. It was a one-bedroom flat of about 300 square feet. There was a working stool in the dining/sitting room, and it looked as if the author was also a carpenter. At least this was his job since his release from the mental hospital. The furniture was simple, and there was almost no decoration on the walls. We caught a glimpse of a little girl, who immediately retreated into the bedroom, and we did not see her again, or anyone else, in the flat. The pastor spoke little Russian, and the author spoke little English. We had to use our ingenuity in trying to communicate with one another. When he learned that I was from Hong Kong (I'd shown him where I came from on a map), he showed me a book which was apparently a Russian translation of the Chinese classic, *Romance of the Three Kingdoms*. As time passed, the writer became nervous and restless. He kept pacing around and was smoking non-stop. The pastor asked him to put down in writing any request that he might have. We stayed there for about 30 minutes, and the writer handed the pastor a letter. Before we left, he gave me a bronze knife and an ivory knife as souvenirs.

On the last day in Moscow, I decided to visit a palace on the outskirts of the city. It turned out to be a bit run down and not particularly exciting. After eating my packed sandwich in the garden of the palace, I decided to take a bus to go back to Moscow. On the way back, I noticed a village where there were some interesting Russian cottages. I immediately got off the bus and soon found myself at the entrance to a small village. The floral decoration along the window frames suggested that these were traditional Russian houses. I took some pictures of the houses and was about to walk into the village when I was stopped by two strongly built Russian women. They shouted at me in Russian and looked distinctly unfriendly. Apparently they were not pleased with my taking pictures. As their attitude seemed hostile, I thought it would be best to leave the place. I returned to the bus stop where I had got off the bus. The two women followed me.

It was a hot afternoon, and I could sense the tension as we stood at the bus stop. A single-decker red bus, not unlike those we used to see in Hong Kong in the late 1960s, arrived about 15 minutes later. It was full of passengers. I expected some resistance from the two women, who did try to stop me from boarding the bus, but I managed to get on board. They then asked the driver not to go and ordered me to get off the bus. I refused and was clinging to the iron rail, as I thought it would be far better to get back to Moscow to deal with this matter than to get stuck in this remote village when

I could not speak the language. A passenger tried feebly to push me off the bus. After a while, the two women got on board and the bus moved off.

After a while, we stopped. The door opened and I saw a uniformed police officer, who asked me to get off the bus. I thought for a second, and decided that I'd better do as he said. The bus had driven to a nearby police outpost, which was a small office at the roadside. The police took away my passport and my camera, and I asked for an interpreter. The two women got off the bus as well and gave a statement at the police outpost.

Forty minutes later, two men in grey suits arrived. At first I thought they were interpreters, but they spoke little English. After talking to the police officer in charge, they signalled me to follow them. I had no choice, as they had my passport. We got into a car driven by a man in uniform. From what I could make out of their conversation, I figured out that the two gentlemen were from the KGB. It seems that I had really got myself into trouble!

It was another three-quarters of an hour before we arrived at a building in the middle of nowhere. It was a two-storey structure which stood in a place like a park off the main road, and there was no other building around. All the windows had iron bars. There was no sign, no flag, and no emblem to indicate the nature of the building. I was told that it was a police station. There were indeed a few police officers in uniform around. As I went in, I passed a few rooms which looked like detention cells. The door of one of these rooms stood open, and I could see a single bed inside. A shiver went down my spine! No one knew where I had gone. I had no idea where this place was. Would I be detained in a place like this for the rest of my life? Might I just 'disappear'?

I was led to a waiting area outside a larger reception area and was told to wait there. About an hour later, I was taken to a small interview room for questioning. I felt like a suspect. Soon, two gentlemen in dark suits came in. Both of them spoke fluent English. One of them introduced himself as the representative of the office of State Tourism, and another was a representative of the USSR—I suppose a State official. They tried to figure out why I, a stranger, had gone to a remote village outside Moscow. I explained to them the nature of the tour and that I was on my way back to Moscow from the palace. Fortunately I had kept the entrance ticket to the palace.

'Do you know that your visa is limited to visiting the cities of Moscow, Kiev, and Leningrad?'

'Yes, I do. We are not allowed to travel more than 40 kilometres beyond the city.' Before the tour, we had been told in a briefing about the nature of the visa and its limits. 'I don't think I have travelled beyond the limit,' I added. I knew the palace was about 36 kilometres from the city, and I was travelling back towards Moscow.

'Do you know that there are places that tourists are not expected to take photographs?'

'Yes, we are not allowed to take pictures of airports, bridges, or anything that might be of military significance. I was taking pictures of some ordinary houses, which I didn't think are of any military significance.'

They kept questioning me, trying to figure out why a foreigner who could not speak any Russian would turn up alone in a remote village on the outskirts of Moscow. At some point, the State Tourism official asked me, 'Have you ever visited China?'

'Yes, twice as a tourist some years ago.' I answered promptly without giving it much thought. This answer unexpectedly triggered a long list of new questions. When did I visit China? Where did I go? Why did I go? Did I meet anyone there? Where did my parents come from? Did I still have relatives in China? What did they do? Where did they live? When did I last meet them? Sino-Soviet relations were not particularly good at that time. Was I suspected of being a Chinese spy?

After some exhaustive questioning, the two gentlemen said that they were going to take me back to the village and ask me a few more questions on the site. It was already getting dark, and I had absolutely no idea where I was. The only consolation was that the attitude of my two questioners appeared more relaxed than when they first started the interview.

When we got to the village, I showed them where I stood and took the pictures. One of them went into the village, apparently to speak to the two women who had reported me to the police. I waited at the entrance of the village with the state official. He agreed with me that decorative motif on the window frames was indeed typically Russian. He even jokingly asked me if I would consider marrying a Russian woman!

After a while, the other gentleman came back from the village. They spoke to each other for a while and told me that they believed me. They warned me not to wander around and returned the passport and the camera to me. The films were, however, gone. They told me that the bus was still running and I could catch it back to Moscow. I had arrived at the village shortly before 3 p.m. By the time I reached the hotel in Moscow, it was almost 12:00 midnight.

We left Moscow for Kiev the following day. My story was soon known to the entire group. As soon as we arrived in Kiev, my roommate said that he would like to share the room with another member of the group and he hoped I would not mind having the room to myself (as we had an odd number of tour members, one of us would be occupying a room by himself). I suppose the real reason was that I was the only person who knew that he was carrying a letter from a prisoner of conscience. If the police had found out who I had visited the day before, I cannot imagine what might have happened to me.

Kiev is the capital of Ukraine and not far from the site of the Chernobyl nuclear disaster some years later. The astounding dome of St Sophia Cathedral, with its mosaics and frescoes carefully positioned according to Byzantine decorative schemes, stood as an iconic symbol of the Orthodox world order. Even so, five days in Kiev seemed more than enough.

Leningrad, which used to be and is again known as St Petersburg, was completely different from Moscow and Kiev. It was a lovely, relaxed, and romantic place, a city of many bridges and canals, known as the Venice of the North. There was the Hermitage, which rivals the Louvre in both architecture and collections; the richly decorated

Summer Palace; the brightly coloured Orthodox Church of the Saviour on Spilled Blood; the lovely tree-lined garden; and an elaborate system of fountains in Peterhof that may well dwarf Versailles. Gold-leafed statues standing on the marble stairways on both sides of the Grand Cascade, the equally lavishly decorated Grand Palace at the back, and a long reflection pool in front stretching all the way to the Gulf of Finland, greeted visitors with delightful showers of waterfalls. As dusk fell, lovers strolled along the river; couples danced in the street. There was nothing to remind one that this was a socialist city, save perhaps the Peter and Paul Fortress on an island in the river, where many political prisoners were imprisoned.

While enjoying this lovely city, I kept pondering if I should dispose of the knives given to me by the writer in Moscow before I left the country. The security check at the airport had been very tight when we arrived in Moscow. Eventually I decided to take the risk, and thank God, the security search at the departure point at Leningrad was more lax. Years later, I donated the bronze knife to an auction to raise funds to help our students to go to Washington, DC, to participate in the final round of Jessup International Mooting.

Even after many years, the scene of the detention room has remained vivid in my memory. Every year I used to meet the new members of the executive committee of the Student Law Association. When they asked me for advice about activities, I always recommended that they should organize a visit to our prisons. Only when you have seen a real prison, and have heard the echo of clanging keys turning in the lock of iron doors, will you begin to appreciate the true value of freedom and personal liberty.

X

Law and Politics

24

The whole is more than the sum of its parts
The Shen Yun case

In contrast to both the Legislative Council and the executive government, which have been consistently poorly rated by the public in recent years, the Judiciary in Hong Kong remains a highly respected institution. This is no doubt due to the independence and the impartiality of the Judiciary, a core value that lies at the heart of the rule of law. The Judiciary earns its legitimacy, not through the ballot box but through the transparency of its process and the rationality of its reasoning. The independence of the Judiciary means that the court will make its decisions only in accordance with the law. The court can and will only address legal issues, not political issues. This does not mean that the court should not be sensitive to the political context or political consequences of its decisions. The dividing line between law and politics can be blurred, and sometimes artificial. Nonetheless, the court will have to draw the line somewhere, beyond which is the realm of politics that the court is not and should not be concerned with. On the other hand, the mere fact that a decision may have policy or political implications does not by itself render the decision beyond the bounds of judicial review. While the court will fully respect a decision of the executive government when it involves an exercise of discretion in policy areas, it is also the duty of the court to ensure that the executive government abides by the law and that the exercise of public powers is in compliance with the requirements of public law. The government cannot hide behind the cloak of politics or policy if its decision is unlawful. The rule of law requires this; nothing more, nothing less.

Epoch Group Ltd. is the publisher of a newspaper, the *Epoch Times*. It is also an organizer of public activities including performing arts events, and has been involved in the organization of many public activities for the Hong Kong Association of Falun Dafa, a local organization that represents Falun Gong followers in Hong Kong. While Falun Gong has been outlawed in the Mainland, the association is a lawful body under Hong Kong law and is treated in the same way as any other lawful organization in Hong Kong.

In 2009, Epoch Group invited Shen Yun Performing Arts (formerly known as Divine Performing Arts) to perform at the Lyric Theatre of the Hong Kong Academy of Performing Arts. Established in 2006, Shen Yun is a performing group that is based in New York. It seeks to revive Chinese classical and traditional dance and music traditions while producing entirely new performances of dances, songs, and musical scores. Its choreography and routines range from 'grand processions to ethnic dances with dancers moving in synchronized pattern'.[1] A key feature of the performances is the 'state-of-the-art digital backdrops, often animated, and designed to match the story line, lighting and choreography of particular dancers'. It established its fame as the premier Chinese dance and music company on its first performance in 2006. It conducts world tours and has been invited to perform in over 100 cities around the world, including at the Royal Festival Hall in London, the John F. Kennedy Center in Washington, and the Palais des Congrès in Paris. In the year 2009 alone, it attracted a total audience of 800,000.

I received two complimentary tickets to the performance. The shows, which were to run from 27 to 31 January 2010, were publicly announced in October 2009. Ticket sales opened on 2 December 2009, and within a few days, tickets for all seven shows were sold out. Having heard about the success of Shen Yun, I very much looked forward to seeing the show, but to my great disappointment, it was cancelled at the last minute. Tickets were refunded, and the amount was said to involve over HK$5 million. What had happened?

Between October and December 2009, Epoch Group had submitted a total of 95 employment visa applications on behalf of the members of Shen Yun to take part in the performance. There was apparently no special category of visas for short-term travelling performing groups in Hong Kong, be they dance groups, orchestras, chorus, opera or musical companies, pop music groups, or even sports teams. As a result, all the members of Shen Yun had to apply for 'entry for employment as professionals in Hong Kong' under the General Employment Policy Scheme, which is applicable to talents and professionals, irrespective of the duration of the employment. Under the then policy, a visa applicant had to possess 'special skills, knowledge or experience of value to and not readily available in Hong Kong'. The same visa requirement applied to Manchester United, the world-renowned football team, who were invited to play in the Chinese New Year Celebration Soccer Match, or the Berlin Philharmonic, one of the finest orchestras in the world, that came to perform in the Hong Kong Arts Festival.

By mid-January 2010, the Director of Immigration had approved the visa applications of all except six members of Shen Yun. These six members were involved in backstage work and included an audio engineer, a production staff/lighting engineer, a project engineer, two dancers/audio assistants, and a dancer/projection assistant. Their applications were rejected on 21 January 2010, barely a week before the scheduled performance. The reason for the rejection was that they did not meet the visa requirements, as similar local expertise was readily available. The standard letter of rejection said:

---

1. *Epoch Group Ltd v Director of Immigration* [2011] 3 HKLRD H2, para 4 (9 Mar 2011).

Under existing policy, a person seeking to enter the Hong Kong Special Administrative Region (HKSAR) for employment should among other things, possess a special skill, knowledge or experience of value to and not readily available in the HKSAR. Besides, other criteria to be considered include whether the job can be filled locally and whether it is justified for the employer to bring in an expatriate staff.

Having considered the information made available and all circumstances of the case, we are not satisfied that [their] case meets the aforesaid criteria. [Their] application is therefore refused.

Epoch Group and Shen Yun maintained that the group had come as a group. As a team of performing players, they had had to rehearse many times before their arrival, and though these individuals were responsible for backstage work, their participation was crucial to the performance. Indeed, three of them doubled as dancers. Further information about their role was supplied to the Director of Immigration. When the Director of Immigration continued to refuse their visa application upon two further requests for reconsideration, the Epoch Group and Shen Yun found it impossible to go ahead with the performance, which was then cancelled. They subsequently brought an application for judicial review against the decisions of the Director of Immigration.

According to the director, the Department of Immigration, in processing these applications, would consider information on the background of the performance group, the nature and characteristics of the shows intended to be given in Hong Kong, the venue facilities, and the financial arrangements of the sponsor, to establish whether the invitation to an overseas performing arts troupe could be justified. Each individual would then be considered separately, taking into account their education background, relevant working experience, details of the position and their role in the show. There should also be no security objection.

The internal minutes that were disclosed had some passages blacked out. Given the close association of the Epoch Group and Shen Yun with Falun Gong, it was not surprising that the Group suspected that the refusal was due to their political affiliation. They sought disclosure of the redacted information. The director refused to release it, on the ground that it was sensitive information and irrelevant to the application. Without seeing the information, it would be difficult for the applicants to argue otherwise. Hence, the trial judge ordered that the information be made available to him for consideration first. After reading the information, he decided that the information was prima facie relevant to the application. The director was then afforded an opportunity to persuade him otherwise. The director filed a supplemental affidavit to explain the content of the information and argued for non-disclosure on the ground of public interest immunity, which means that the disclosure of this class of documents would not be in the public interest. Having further considered the supplemental affidavit and the submission of the director, the trial judge accepted that he did not fully understand the original materials, pointing out that they contained abbreviations whose meaning he did not fully appreciate, and came to the view that the materials were not relevant to the application and therefore not required to be disclosed. It was also unnecessary, as a result, to decide whether the materials were protected by public interest immunity. Once these matters had been disposed of, the court was able to dissociate the political context from the merits of the claim. The arguments proceeded on the basis that the decisions of the Director of Immigration had nothing to do with the dance company's Falun Gong background.

The hearing focused on the reasons provided by the director in refusing to grant visas to the six members of Shen Yun, namely that their expertise was available locally and that they could be replaced by local recruits. The director had great difficulty in sustaining this argument. It was clear at the outset that it was artificial and inappropriate to rely on the General Employment Policy to determine the visa application of members of a travelling performance group. The requirements under the General Employment Policy are designed to deal with applicants who come to take up employment or otherwise work in Hong Kong as professionals. Thus, it is necessary to demonstrate that 'there is a genuine job vacancy' in Hong Kong and the applicant has to have a confirmed offer of employment and to be employed in a job 'that cannot be readily taken up by the local work force', or that the applicant's remuneration package has to be 'broadly commensurate with the prevailing market level for professionals in the HKSAR'. These requirements are designed to protect the local workforce and are ill suited to deal with applications for entry by members of a travelling performing group who are to perform in Hong Kong for a short duration and will leave Hong Kong soon after the performance. As Paul Harris SC, who represented the applicants, forcefully argued, the director had ignored 'the simple but obvious fact that being able to operate the lighting, sound effect or backdrop for a stage event is not just a matter of knowing how to operate them, but is also a matter of knowing when to operate them. Knowing when to operate them can only be achieved by rehearsing together with the dancers and knowing extremely well the sequences of the performances they are to perform.'

The director argued that the court should not lightly interfere with the director's exercise of discretion or his policies. Hong Kong is a small place with a huge population, a relatively high per capita income and living standard. It is an attractive place for migrants. The director has the unenviable task of maintaining very restrictive and tough immigration policies and control. The legislature has entrusted the director with very wide discretion in exercising immigration control, and the court, as the director contended, should only adopt a supervisory role and should not step into the shoes of the director in the exercise of his discretion.

All these arguments, however, did not mean that the decisions of the director are beyond the control of the courts. His powers, wide as they may be, are still subject to the principles of public law governing the exercise of discretion and the decision-making process. This means that he has to take into account all relevant considerations and disregard all considerations that are irrelevant. His decision must not be unreasonable (in the public law sense), perverse, irrational, arbitrary, unlawful, or motivated by bad faith, and the decision-making process must be fair. This is what the rule of law requires, and this is how the dividing line between executive powers and judicial supervision is drawn.

For a dance troupe that has achieved its fame in part by its lighting and stage effects, it seems to be just too obvious that the backstage work is as important and crucial to the performance as the performers at the front of the stage. As the court pointed out, a group is a group. By definition, different members of the group have different duties. What brings them into a group is that each member is not an individual performer but part of the ensemble, and what makes them a group is the rigorous rehearsals and practices. The whole is more than merely the sum of its parts. It would be incongruous and indeed impertinent for a local organizer to invite just part of the group to come to Hong Kong to perform on the ground that the rest of the group could be replaced by locals. As an analogy, it would not make sense for the director to refuse the entry of the goalkeeper or the reserve goalkeeper of a foreign soccer team to play in a tournament in Hong Kong on the ground that there would be many excellent local goalkeepers available to play for the team. Thus, the proper question was not whether the individual's job could be filled by local people but whether his or her role formed an integral part of the performance as a team member in whom the group reposed trust and confidence. Unlike any individual applying for an employment visa, each of the visa applicants in this case was applying to come as a member of a visiting cultural or arts performing ensemble that had been invited to Hong Kong to perform or otherwise take part in a cultural or artistic activity for a very short time. They were not here to seek employment. In applying the general requirements under the General Employment Policy, the director had, as the court held, failed and indeed refused to consider this relevant and peculiar factor in this case and had therefore simply been asking the wrong questions.

Accordingly, the court set aside the decision to refuse to grant visas to the six members of Shen Yun. By then it was of course too late for the Group to revive its performances, and a claim for damages was separately dealt with. As the refusal of the application for entry of the six members was made only on 21 January 2010, barely a week before the scheduled performance, and given that the court found that they were an integral part of the group, it was hardly surprising that the Group had had to cancel the performance. It is also highly likely that, subject to the duty of Shen Yun to mitigate its loss, the government must have had to pay a substantial amount of damages for its wrongful decisions. The refund for ticket sales alone already exceeded $5 million. There is no information about the claim for damages, but it would not be surprising if the public had to foot a substantial bill for the government's blunder.

Were the decisions of the director disguised political decisions to sabotage the performance of a Falun Gong–related group? On the evidence, I tend to believe that they were just a blunder of the bureaucracy. If there is an obvious explanation for a decision that is devoid of common sense, there is usually no need to speculate if there are political or other motives. Time and again, such decisions are a consequence of a bureaucratic, inflexible, over-cautious, paternalistic, or even arrogant attitude rather than a result of political bad faith or manipulation. The court in this case had no difficulty in disentangling the merits of the decisions from their political context. In the next case, which also involved Falun Gong, the court had to address the more sensitive political issue of national security, and once again, it had to strike a delicate balance between law and politics.

25

The mysterious case of the missing documents

The mysterious disappearance of crucial documents is a familiar plot device in detective movies. When it happens in real life that the government says that some crucial documents have disappeared, the claim will more often than not attract more questions that it can answer.

On 21 February 2003, four Falun Gong practitioners from Taiwan came to Hong Kong to attend the Hong Kong Falun Gong Experience Sharing Conference, which was to be held at the Sheraton Hotel on the following day. They were stopped at the Hong Kong International Airport by immigration officers, and after an interview, they were denied entry to Hong Kong for 'security reasons' and returned, forcibly in some cases, by the same plane. All four were in possession of valid multiple-entry permits, and three of them had been to Hong Kong on previous occasions for purposes unrelated to Falun Gong events. When they demanded to know why they had not been allowed in, all they were told was that it was for 'security reasons'. On the same day, another 76 Falun Gong practitioners from Taiwan who came for the conference were turned back at the airport.

On 3 April 2003, judicial review proceedings to challenge the decisions of the Director of Immigration in refusing their entry to Hong Kong were taken out.[1] Their case was simple. They said that the Director of Immigration had not been able to provide any details to substantiate his claim of 'security reasons'. All along the director had chosen to obfuscate the issue, and he had been deliberately vague and ambiguous on the precise reason for denying their entry. They argued that the director had been so lacking in candour that the court ought to find as a matter of fact that no or no proper reasons existed for the denial of entry. They firmly believed that they had been banned from Hong Kong solely because of their beliefs, and that the Mainland authorities had exerted pressure on the Hong Kong government in this regard. The fact that some 80 Falun Gong members who arrived at the airport that day were turned back pointed clearly to a blanket refusal policy against entry by Falun Gong practitioners. Indeed,

---

1. *Chu Woan Chyi v Director of Immigration* [2007] 3 HKC 168 (CFI); [2009] 6 HKC 77 (Court of Appeal). The four applicants were later joined by the Hong Kong Association of Falun Dafa and its chairman, Kan Hung Cheung, who became the fifth and sixth applicants. Their argument is not relevant to the present discussion.

they did not need to go so far as to show the real reason for the denial of their entry. They would succeed if they could show that there was no rational or proper reason, or no reason at all, not to allow them in.

The case of the Director of Immigration was equally simple. He said that, in view of the sensitive nature of the security information, details could not be provided. The director denied that the decision not to let the applicants in had anything to do with their beliefs or status as Falun Gong followers and argued that no adverse inference should be drawn against him. Besides, as they were aliens who had no right to enter Hong Kong, the director was not obliged to provide them with reasons for denying their entry.

The control of immigration is of course a power that should not be exercised arbitrarily. There must be a proper or legitimate reason whenever a decision is made to deny entry. The applicants essentially said that there was no proper or legitimate reason, whereas the director claimed that there were reasons, and these were security reasons, but he could not tell them what those security reasons were.

Thus, the crux of the dispute was the reason for the denial of entry of the applicants. In order to assess the legality of the claim of the director, the court would need to know the evidential basis of his decisions. The law imposes on the government a duty of candour, which, simply put, is a duty to be full and frank to both the court and the other parties in public law litigation. It is simply an aspect of good governance and proper and transparent administration. As Lord Walker stated, the duty of candour was a duty 'to co-operate and to make candid disclosure by way of affidavit, of the relevant facts and (so far as they are not apparent from contemporaneous documents which have been disclosed), the reasoning behind the decision challenged in judicial review proceedings'.[2]

The problem with this case was that not only had the government been extremely evasive and defensive but that its technical and compartmentalized approach was, as described by the Court of Appeal, 'extremely unsatisfactory' and its evidence 'contradictory'. It is a pity that the government sometimes forgets that judicial review is an important means to ensure the accountability of the government in a civil society and should not be conducted in the same aggressive and defensive manner as hard-fought commercial litigation. The manner of the government's conduct of this case caused great concern to, and was strongly criticized by, both the Court of First Instance and the Court of Appeal. In order to understand these concerns, it is necessary to set out the procedural history in some detail. This is another long and winding road, but it's a story that has a lot to tell us about the relation between the government and the law in Hong Kong.

---

2. *Belize Alliance of Conservation Non-Governmental Organizations v The Department of the Environment and Another* [2004] UKPC 6, para 86.

The evidence: Security risks

In response to the judicial review application, three affirmations were respectively filed by two senior immigration officers and Mr Choy, the commander of the Airport Division of the Immigration Department. Their evidence was that the four applicants had been placed on a Watch List on the basis that they posed 'security risks to the HKSAR'. When a person was placed on a Watch List, only the general reason would be stated. As far as the security risks were concerned, there would be no elaboration on the reason the person might pose a security risk, and the details would be restricted to persons on a 'need-to-know' basis. The mere fact that a person was placed on a Watch List would not automatically lead to a denial of entry into Hong Kong. It was just a starting point to enable further enquiries to be made. Upon interview, it was said that two of the applicants were uncooperative and refused to provide any details of their itinerary or the nature of the meeting that they intended to have in Hong Kong, whereas the other two applicants said that they were in Hong Kong to meet with members of the Hong Kong Association of Falun Dafa. In the event, all four were denied entry.

A further affirmation was filed by Mr Timothy Tong, the then Acting Secretary for Security. His evidence was that the applicants were placed on the Watch List as a result of an assessment of the Security Bureau and other government departments. The Security Bureau had an overall responsibility in security matters, and it made the assessment based on information that came from a number of sources, both within the bureau itself and from other government departments.

These affirmations, which were filed in late 2004 and early 2005, did not disclose any details of the nature or the gravity of the security risks, and no documents were produced to support the assertion that the applicants posed security risks. The attitude of the applicants could not be a sufficient reason to deny them entry. Thus, the main reason for the denial would be the fact that they were placed on the Watch List, but it was not explained why they were placed on the Watch List. In short, these affirmations did not say anything more than that they posed 'security risks'.

The hearing of the application for judicial review was scheduled for 20 September 2005. On 29 August 2005, the applicants' solicitors, Messrs Ho, Tse, Wai and Partners (HTW) wrote to the Department of Justice requesting disclosure of all documents material to the decisions to refuse the applicants' entry to Hong Kong, and in particular, documents containing or associated with the Watch List. Although this was a late request, it was later regarded by the Court of Appeal as perfectly legitimate, relevant, and proper.

On 8 September 2005, the Department of Justice replied saying that there was no right to discovery in judicial review proceedings, and that no case had been made out for specific discovery. Faced with this unhelpful reply, HTW then took out a discovery summons on 12 September 2005 to apply for specific discovery of nine classes of documents. Class 8 and Class 1 referred respectively to documents recording reasons

why the applicants were placed on the Watch List and documents containing information that they were placed on the Watch List. (Discovery is a process of disclosure of
relevant documents by the parties to litigation before trial.)

The discovery summons was heard on 20 September 2005, the date originally
scheduled for the hearing of the judicial review application. The parties reached an
agreement on the disclosure of a narrower category of documents under Class 1 and
Class 8, and the discovery was confined to those documents that were available to the
two senior immigration officers, the decision makers in this case. The Court of Appeal
later expressed surprise at this concession by the applicants, as documents not available
to the two senior immigration officers were clearly relevant and could explain why
the applicants were considered security risks. In the course of the hearing, Mr Justice
Hartmann expressed his concern about the lack of contemporaneous documents and
made it clear that the critical issue in the case was the reason why the applicants were
denied entry.

As a result of queries raised by Mr Justice Hartmann, the respondent filed two
further affirmations, one by Mr Choy, the commander of the Airport Division, and
one by Mr Timothy Tong. The second affirmation by Mr Tong, which was dated 22
September 2005, was instructive. For the first time, some two and a half years after the
judicial review proceedings had begun, there was finally some, albeit feeble, attempt to
explain the nature of the security risks. The material part of Mr Tong's evidence said:

> As stated in paragraph 3 of my first affirmation, the Security Bureau and related
> Government departments had, in the case of the 1st to 4th Applicants, come to the
> view, based on information and intelligence obtained, that the entry into the HKSAR
> of a number of individuals including the 1st–4th Applicants would pose security
> risks to the HKSAR. The intelligence obtained included intelligence to the effect
> that, *certain persons including the 1st–4th Applicants were involved with some other
> individuals engaged in organizing disruptive activities which pose threats to the public
> order in Hong Kong.* In the view of the Security Bureau and related departments of
> the HKSARG, the admission into Hong Kong of said persons including the 1st–4th
> Applicants would, by reason of their involvement with the above-mentioned persons,
> be contrary to the public interest. *Further confidential and sensitive details such as the
> identities of the individual involved and the details of the disruptive activities concerned
> cannot be disclosed as they fall within the ambit of public interest immunity and are
> therefore privileged from disclosure.*[3]

A few points of interest emerge from this paragraph. First, it provided for the
first time some details of what was meant by 'security risks', that the applicants were
involved with some other individuals in organizing disruptive activities that posed
threats to public order in Hong Kong. However, there was still no indication of the
nature, the degree, or the gravity of such risks. Secondly, no documents to substantiate
the claim were exhibited. Thirdly, a claim for public interest immunity was made for

---

3. Reproduced in para 34 of the Judgment of the Court of Appeal; italics added.

the first time in judicial review proceedings. It was strange, to say the least, that no such claim had been made before. The claim also presupposed that some documents were available but these documents could not be disclosed on the ground that, in view of their sensitive nature, their disclosure would not be in the public interest.

Notwithstanding this claim for public interest immunity, Mr Choy filed an affirmation on the following day, in which the respondent confirmed willingness to provide documents in Class 1 and 8 as amended, that is, those documents that were made available to the two decision makers on the Watch List. No public interest immunity was claimed.

The destruction of documents

The case took another dramatic turn on 21 November 2005, when the Department of Justice, pursuant to the above agreement, provided the two categories of documents. A List of Documents was provided. In accordance with the usual practice, Schedule 1 of the list set out those documents that would be produced, and none of them provided any details of why the applicants were denied entry, apart from 'security grounds'. Schedule 2 of the list set out a number of documents relating to the applicants. A covering letter said that 'the paper files and computer records enumerated in Schedule 2 are no longer in existence as they were destroyed in accordance with standard Immigration Department practice after the names of the persons in question were removed from the Watch List. Based on the entries under the "Date of Destroy" column in the relevant pages of the Confidential Register, it can be seen that the destruction of the said files and records took place on 12th March 2003.'[4]

This revelation was astonishing. Two years and nine months after the start of the judicial review proceedings, it was said for the first time that the relevant documents had been destroyed, and they were destroyed on 12 March 2003, barely three weeks after the relevant decisions were made. As the Court of Appeal subsequently observed,

> A dramatic revelation such as this required a proper explanation from the Respondent not only as part of the duty of candour he had to fulfil but also because the very act of destruction, without explanation, necessarily gave rise to questions of motive for the destruction and as to the bona fides of the decisions challenged. It also required elaboration. Furthermore, if important documents had been destroyed, what was the basis of knowledge for the belief of the various deponents for the Respondent; a question lent more force because the reasons for refusal [were] said to be time or event specific. And reference was made to 'standard Immigration Department practice': what was this and what was the status of documents that [were] not in the possession of the Immigration Department but in other Government departments? [sic][5]

---

4. Para 54 of the Judgment of the Court of Appeal.
5. Para 56.

A narrow view taken

Another point made by the respondent was that, as the respondent was the Director of Immigration and the decisions being challenged were immigration decisions of denial of entry into Hong Kong, the duty of candour would only require the director to disclose documents within the Immigration Department in relation to these decisions, but it did not require the Director of Immigration to go beyond his department and disclose documents in other government departments. As a result, the applicants took out another summons to amend their application for judicial review to include a challenge to the decisions that placed the applicants on the Watch List. The summons was strenuously opposed, and a contested hearing took place on 6–9 February 2006.

Mr Justice Hartmann was not impressed by this highly technical and compartmentalized argument. The Court of Appeal later described it as 'extremely surprising' and said that it had no merits at all, adding that to suggest that only the Immigration Department was involved was a 'bizarre' and 'hollow' submission.[6] Indeed, it did not sit with the fact that evidence was filed on behalf of the respondent by Mr Timothy Tong, the then Acting Secretary for Security, at the very beginning of the judicial process. Mr Justice Hartmann allowed the amendment to extend the scope of challenge to the Watch List, which he considered had always been germane to the original challenge, so that the amendment was only a matter of form.[7]

> In my view, however, the Director, and those who represent him legally, must always have understood the real issue in dispute in these proceedings. If the asserted reason for refusing the first four applicants permission to enter Hong Kong was based on the fact that they posed a security risk, they must have understood that such reason would itself inevitably be subject to challenge.

At the same time, Mr Justice Hartmann expressed again his dissatisfaction in his judgment on 6 June 2006 at the piecemeal manner in which information was provided:

> Mr Harris said that, if one of the Director's senior officers was able in a recent affirmation to state that the first four applicants had been refused permission to enter Hong Kong on the basis that they posed a security threat, that information must, in all common sense, have been obtained from a written source of some sort. That source, however, has not been discovered by the Director. Mr Harris argues that, while that source material may not now be in the possession, control or power of the Director, it must surely be somewhere in the archives of Government. Mr Harris pointed to the fact that, although the Director is the cited respondent in these proceedings, he stands as a representative of the Hong Kong Government as a whole.

Paul Harris SC, who represented the applicants, was obviously right in this regard.

---

6. Para 63 of the judgment of Justice Hartmann, reproduced at para 63 of the judgment of the Court of Appeal.
7. Ibid.

Further confusion and inconsistencies

On 6 June 2006, immediately following the judgment on the discovery hearing, HTW wrote to the Department of Justice requesting the discovery of all documents within the whole of the government which were the source of information indicating that the applicants were engaged in organizing disruptive activities.

Notwithstanding the strong indication from Mr Justice Hartmann, the reply from the Department of Justice was both obscure and surprising. In its letter dated 20 June 2006, it simply said that the discovery of the requested documents had already been provided and the respondent had fully complied with his discovery obligations. This was surprising, as the request was directed to documents within *the whole of the government*. The previous stance of the respondent was that, until the amendment to the application for judicial review in June 2006, the respondent did not know that the discovery was intended to cover documents from other government departments. It would be astonishing if no other government department apart from the Immigration Department was in possession of some relevant documents at some stage. There was also no mention of any missing documents or of the destruction of documents. Nor was there any claim made for public interest immunity.

Not satisfied with the response, HTW repeated its request for documents in another letter dated 29 June 2006. It also asked the respondent to confirm that, in the preparation of their affirmations, Mr Choy and Mr Timothy Tong relied only on documents that had been disclosed and not on any other documents.

On 7 July 2006, the Department of Justice replied by repeating its assertion that full discovery had already been made. There was now a reference to the destruction of some documents. The letter ended by saying that 'it is plainly wrong for you to suggest that both Mr Choy and Mr Tong only relied on those documents which [we have already provided to you] and no other documents or materials that were in the possession of any Government department'. This suggested that either Mr Choy and Mr Tong did rely on other documents, or that the documents that they had relied upon had since been destroyed although the latter situation would have been fairly bizarre, given that they had been destroyed less than three weeks after the challenged decisions of denial of entry.

There was further correspondence between the parties. In a letter dated 2 August 2006, the Department of Justice stated that Mr Choy and Mr Tong did not rely on any documents that had not already been made the subject of discovery. This was in direct contradiction to its letter dated 7 July 2006, and no explanation was given for this change of position.

No further discovery applications were made, and the applicants hadn't asked to cross-examine Mr Choy and Mr Tong. The case was ready to go to trial and was set down, after a number of adjournments, to be heard in March 2007. Despite the numerous applications to court and the extensive correspondence between the parties, no one was any the wiser as to why the applicants were considered security risks four years after the judicial review application has been taken out.

The substantive hearing before Justice Hartmann

The substantive hearing finally took place from 5 to 8 March 2007. The respondent was represented by Daniel Fung SC, former Solicitor General, and Johnny Mok SC, who subsequently became a member of the Basic Law Committee. The applicants were represented by Paul Harris SC, a founding member and former chairman of Human Rights Monitor.

Mr Justice Hartmann was obviously troubled by the lack of contemporaneous documents that could shed any light on the reasons for the denial of entry. Throughout the hearing he frequently expressed fundamental incredulity at the respondent's case in relation to disclosure of documents and his deep frustration at the piecemeal manner in which facts were put before him. He was concerned with the lack of candour on the part of the respondent and remarked twice that it seemed possible that there had been some sort of 'hoovering' of government papers. He posed the question at the outset of the hearing: 'Is it credible that suddenly all the government files and papers have been washed clean?' The respondent's counsel was indeed asked to take further instructions to confirm the position during the lunch break of the first day of the hearing. The exchange in the afternoon between the Bench and Daniel Fung SC, who had taken instructions from 'the highest level', illuminated the unsatisfactory situation:

> Court: All right. Then if you say to me that there simply is no material or there has been no material available in the archives of government which has any relevance to this matter, and which, in fairness, should have been shown to the court, even under public interest immunity . . . in respect of 80 people being refused permission to enter Hong Kong, with proceedings taken within six weeks. Is that what you're saying?
>
> Mr Fung: My Lord, yes. Because I can only act on instructions . . . And we have checked and double-checked this point, including over the lunch hour, in response to your Lordship's question, at the very highest level of those responsible.
>
> Court: Well, I'll accept what you say. I have no reason not to.
>
> Mr Fung: We've even brought the confidential register—the actual, the original register with us in order to satisfy your Lordship that there's been no tampering, if that is the suggestion. My Lord, that's the only . . .
>
> Court: Mr Fung, don't—I did not suggest there was tampering.
>
> Mr Fung: Well, if . . .

Court: What I actually said at the end was, you should go and take instructions so that, if for example there has been destruction of material in the ordinary course of events to protect individuals, you can explain that to me this afternoon. The point I made was that on the face of it, to receive discovery of documents which are protected by public interest immunity, and to have a situation in which those documents say nothing of anything, at its face, when you're aware that government as a whole here was being held liable not just the Director, seems strange. But if you say to me that all of the documentation concerning this matter in the archives of government was removed, destroyed or done away with insofar as it may have any relevance to these proceedings . . .

Mr Fung: My Lord, absolutely not. Let me just illustrate that, just make that . . .

Court: When you say 'absolutely not', do you mean it was destroyed, removed . . .

Mr Fung: It was destroyed, but it wasn't destroyed because we didn't want to show it . . .

Court: So if somebody wanted to write a history of this in 25 years' time under the Freedom of Information Act that we don't have here, that person would be told, sorry, everything's gone.

Mr Fung: Well, I mean, he can search all the files, both electronically and on paper . . .

Court: because Mr Harris, apart from anything else, says that the real reason for these people being refused entry was simply because of their beliefs. You say that's not the case . . .

Mr Fung: That's not the case.

Court: Mr Harris says, well, his argument can be supported by lack of candour on the part of government and that lack of candour is shown in the fact that somehow or other there's not a document in existence which says anything about the reasons for the decisions.

Mr Fung: That is not the case.

Court: And that's why I specifically referred to my ruling of 26 May when I said 'as to the nature of the additional documents, it seems obvious to me they must contain the essential intelligence or a distillation of it', and when I then said 'I was wrong in drawing that inference, they don't contain anything'. But it may well be that I have—and Mr Harris— have to accept and do accept that this type of information does not have a shelf life, that in order to protect individuals it is done away with, and that's what you're saying to me, and that's where we stand with it.

Mr Fung: So it's not as if there is, as it were, a three-week magic period of shelf life only.

Court: No, obviously not. If you've got files that are current you don't destroy them . . .

Mr Fung: Less sensitive, yes.

Court: Or if they're especially sensitive you don't destroy them.

Mr Fung: And so on. Now there's no, as it were, [cookie-cutter] approach to these matters, so I understand, as to how the records or the underlying files are destroyed or not, as the case may be, and the Watch List being this computer tool to protect Hong Kong's interests—not just security interests but all sorts of other interests—it's constantly being upgraded . . .

Court: Of course.

Mr Fung: And depending on the nature of the file, is either downgraded or destroyed and if it's downgraded, it's still in existence . . .

Court: You've given me your answer now and I have it. So the matter has been clearly stated from your point of view, which is, on instructions, that the Watch List entries which I knew already—because my judgment was not concerned with the Watch List entries—are deleted in order to protect individuals within a reasonably short period of time, and that's why I mentioned it this morning, and that other documentation, either which was discovered under public interest immunity or otherwise, or which was not discovered, there are simply no documents of relevance to this case as to the reasons why these people were not allowed permission to enter Hong Kong in the archives of government.

Mr Fung: My Lord, we have taken steps directly in response to the various observations made by your Lordship at the highest level to give your Lordship, and confirm to your Lordship, that what we stated in the discovery process—and your Lordship sees that in the letter to which I've made reference and in the list of documents is entirely accurate . . .

Court: I have your undertaking, on instructions, the government does not in its archives have any material that goes to why these 80-odd people were refused permission to enter Hong Kong.

Mr Fung: My Lord, that is correct. We have not just gone to the Immigration Department, may I make that point . . .

Court:	And all I'm saying is and all I meant to say this morning, is that the ordinary man on the street, he may say—leaving aside the Watch List, which was never part of anything else, it is puzzling that there would be no documentary evidence of any kind in the archives of government anywhere going to an issue which was only six weeks old and involved the refusal to entry of 80-odd persons and the carrying of two of them against their will back to their aircraft, in respect of an organization which some would call notorious and others would say has about it considerable sensitivity.

Thus, for the first time, after almost four years, the government had made it clear that the documents underlying the reasons why the applicants were considered security risks, so that they were placed on the Watch List and were denied entry into Hong Kong on 20 and 21 February 2003, were all destroyed as a matter of standard practice. This applied to all relevant documents within the government, and the destruction took place on 12 March 2003, less than a month after the decisions on denial of entry were made. It should also be noted that the explanation came from the Bar table as a matter of instructions. It is generally not for counsel to give evidence at the Bar table.

If this were the case, why couldn't it be explained to the court much earlier? This led to the exasperation of Mr Justice Hartmann when he asked, 'Why did we have to go through all of this in the first place then? Why not simply have said: all of this material—the Watch List—works on the basis that it's destroyed within x number of days. This is what happened. It's standard procedure?'

For anyone who knows Mr Justice Hartmann, he is a most patient and courteous judge, for whom I have great respect. It was most exceptional for Mr Justice Hartmann to burst out and vent his frustration in court. Mr Justice Hartmann was prepared to accept the explanation of counsel and eventually found that the respondent was not in breach of the duty of candour. The Court of Appeal did not agree and was more sceptical of the respondent's conduct, including the conduct of the legal team advising the respondent.

The appeal

The appeal was heard by Mr Justice Geoffrey Ma, the then Chief Judge of the High Court and later the Chief Justice; Mr Justice Frank Stock, a Vice-President of the Court of Appeal who was later appointed as a non-permanent judge of the Court of Final Appeal; and Mr Justice Barma. The appeal was originally scheduled to be heard on 22 January 2008. On that date, the Court of Appeal expressed considerable concern over the lack of any details or documents on the question why the applicants were denied entry into Hong Kong. Notwithstanding the explanation of Mr Fung to Mr Justice Hartmann, the Court of Appeal asked why the destruction was never explained to the court until the hearing before Mr Justice Hartmann, when there had been plenty of occasions before the hearing when this could have been done. Mr Fung referred to the understanding of the respondent that the discovery was considered to be directed to the Director of Immigration, who did not know that the Watch List was also an issue until leave to amend the Applications for Judicial Review was allowed by Mr Justice Hartmann. Mr Justice Geoffrey Ma rejected this argument outright as 'obviously unsustainable', 'extremely surprising', and having 'no merit to it at all'.[8] The suggestion that only the Immigration Department was involved was 'bizarre' and 'hollow', especially when the respondent had seen fit to involve the Acting Secretary for Security to give affirmation evidence at the outset. He was not prepared to accept this as a reason. It was also incredible, he said, that nowhere in the whole of the government would there be a written record of the reasons why the applicants were considered security risks. Even if all the documents were destroyed, there must still be persons within the government who would be able to provide details of what was in the destroyed documents that might explain the reasons why the applicants were denied entry. Further, if all relevant documents had been destroyed on 12 March 2003, then on what basis could Mr Timothy Tong depose to the facts contained in his second affirmation in September 2005? The court also pointed out that Mr Fung had indeed given evidence at the Bar table, which was unsatisfactory, and no attempt had been made to confirm what Mr Fung had said by an affirmation from any government officials, and that no application had been made for cross-examination of the main deponents of the respondent.

As a result of these concerns, the hearing was adjourned to 29 October 2008. In the meantime, a number of applications were made by both parties to address these concerns, including a number of applications to adduce new evidence. All these applications were eventually rejected. It is unnecessary to go into the details of these applications.

At the appeal, the applicants were no longer legally represented, and instead they acted in person. The respondent continued to be represented by Daniel Fung SC and Johnny Mok SC. Paul Shieh SC, who later became the chairman of the Bar Association, was appointed as an amicus curiae which literally means 'a friend of the court'. An amicus is normally a barrister invited by the court to provide independent assistance to the court. An amicus is appointed normally when the matter involves great public interest and justice might not be served because, as in this case for example, one party was not legally represented. The amicus does not represent the unrepresented party but simply provides legal arguments, sometimes even arguments on both sides, to assist the court.

The Court of Appeal was highly critical of the way the respondent had chosen to reveal the factual basis justifying the refusal of entry on security grounds. While there were two decisions that were impugned—the decision to refuse entry and the decision to place the applicants on the Watch List—the latter was merely a corollary of the

---

8. Para 63.

decision to deny entry and arose only to test the basis of the respondent's claim of security risk. The court emphasized that it was quite wrong for crucial statements of facts to be presented as they had been to Mr Justice Hartmann by leading counsel, referring to the unsatisfactory manner of explaining the destruction of documents by counsel without an affirmation verifying these allegations. It was fundamental that statements from the Bar table did not constitute evidence, unless agreed.

The court was also frustrated by the inconsistent way in which leading counsel had addressed the court during the appeal. Before Mr Justice Hartmann, the impression given by the respondent was that all relevant documents throughout the government had been destroyed as a matter of standard practice. This naturally gave rise to the court wanting to know on what basis Mr Choy and Mr Timothy Tong made their second affirmation in September 2005. What were the sources of their statements of belief? It may be recalled that Mr Tong said in his second affirmation that the applicants were 'involved with some other individuals engaged in organizing disruptive activities that pose threats to the public order in Hong Kong', and Mr Choy confirmed the same. Had they read documents that had been destroyed on 12 March 2007? Or, were they deposing to matters within their own personal knowledge? Or, did these matters originate from other unspecified sources? At one of the hearings on 23 September 2008, when the respondent applied to adduce further evidence, the court was told that the various deponents filed their affirmation on the basis purely of their own memory, as all relevant documents had been destroyed. This point came up again on the first day of the substantive hearing on 29 October 2008.

> Stock VP: What I can't remember, because the facts have become so complicated and the papers so voluminous, what I can't remember is whether it is the government's case that it knows of the detailed reasons though the papers have been destroyed, on the one hand, or, on the other hand, whether because the papers have been destroyed, the precise reasons, in other words, precise as opposed to security reasons, are now forgotten.

> Mr Fung: It's really the latter.

Now this was the second time that the government had changed its case. Its initial position was that there were documents but, in view of their sensitive nature, the government would claim public interest immunity. Then before Mr Justice Hartmann, it was said that all relevant documents throughout the government had been destroyed. Now before the Court of Appeal, confronted with the sources of information that the various deponents relied upon in making the affirmations, the government case was that they made their claim purely on memory and the precise reasons were now forgotten! This explanation emerged for the first time in the litigation and contradicted the previous position. It was inconsistent with the second affirmation of Mr Timothy Tong as well as with what counsel told the court at the hearing referred to above on 23 September 2008. Mr Justice Stock found the answer inherently incredible, and he returned to it later in the same hearing and told Mr Fung that what Mr Fung had said was 'troubling' him.[9] As Mr Justice Stock later said in the judgment, 'according to Mr Fung, what was remembered was that the applicants posed a risk to public order but why they posed such a risk, on what basis the assertion was made, could not be remembered. Apart from the stark fact that counsel's statement did not sit at all with the evidence of Mr Tong who said that the details could not be divulged because they were covered by public interest immunity, the statement did not sit with common sense. I simply do not believe that no official is in a position, subject to the question of privilege, to say what the detailed reasons were—and indeed that is not what the officials were saying on oath. So either Mr Fung misunderstood what his client's position was or was not expressing himself felicitously.'[10]

On the second day of the hearing of the appeal (11 March 2008), Mr Fung informed the court that in fact no government department other than the Immigration Department had ever possessed any relevant documents. This was another strange submission, as Mr Tong had previously deposed that security matters and assessment of security risks were primarily the responsibility of the Security Bureau. It would defy common sense that all the relevant documents would only be with the Immigration Department. It also contradicted the statement made by leading counsel before Mr Justice Hartmann that all documents within the whole of the government had been destroyed as a result of standard practice, which suggested that other government departments did possess some relevant documents at some stage. Eventually, on the third day of the hearing (12 March 2008), Mr Fung corrected himself and said that the detailed reasons for considering the applicants as security risks were known, but if pressed, a claim for public interest immunity would be made. Finally, sensing that the court was pretty irritated, and rightly so, the respondent then offered, on the fourth day of the appeal (13 March 2008), to tender all four deponents of the respondent, including Mr Timothy Tong, for cross-examination. This was no doubt too late. As Mr Justice Ma remarked, 'this came without any real explanation as to why, when the Applicants' application for cross-examination was resisted all along and in view of the quite uncooperative way in which the litigation had been conducted by the respondent, this offer was made at all. Despite Mr Fung's submissions to the contrary, for my part, I see no reason other than this offer having been made purely for tactical purposes.'[11]

So, over six years since the applicants were denied entry, it was still unclear just what the basis for the statement that they posed security risks was, nor was it clear whether any documents existed to support it. The court criticized the conduct of the respondent and his legal advisors throughout the proceedings to be 'far from satisfactory, indeed contradictory'.[12] The Court of Appeal expressed its regret in exceptionally strong terms. Mr Justice Stock described the hearing of the appeal as 'not an attractive

9.   Para 150.
10. Para 150.
11. Para 116.
12. Para 115.

experience' and said 'the voicing of the Court's frustration resulted in much to-ing and fro-ing by counsel, taking of instructions, piecemeal revelations, some of them contradictory; culminating in an offer to present officials for cross-examination'.[13] The Chief Judge said, 'The particular coyness by which the respondent approached discovery and the inconsistent versions given as to the existence (or non-existence) of relevant documents, coupled with the way the court has been addressed on various occasions by counsel, substantially exacerbated what was already a highly unsatisfactory situation.'[14]

The Court of Appeal unanimously found that there was a breach of the duty of candour on the part of the respondent. While in the normal course of events the court would draw an adverse inference from the conduct of the respondent, and in the present case the adverse inference could be that there was no proper or legitimate reason to refuse the entry of the applicants, the court found that it was not able to do so on this occasion. This was partly because the applicants had failed to apply for cross-examination of the various deponents despite the inconsistent stances adopted by them at different stages. As Mr Justice Stock put it, it was 'not a question of balancing the conduct of an applicant who ought to but did not seek cross-examination or further discovery, and it is not a question of penalizing an applicant for not taking steps which he or she might have taken but did not. It is a question of examining what evidence there is, absent such steps, and what inferences, if any, one is entitled to draw from that evidence.'[15] The mere fact that the government was not forthcoming did not necessarily mean that the government was lying. In the absence of challenges to the untested evidence on oath or affirmation that there were sound security reasons for the refusal, the court found that it could not conclude that what the respondent said, without cross-examination, was untrue. On this narrow basis, the court found that the applicants had not shown that the decisions of denial of entry were made on unlawful grounds even though there was a breach of the duty of candour on the part of the respondent. Mr Justice Ma pointed out that the respondent could consider himself extremely fortunate, for 'if the Applicants had conducted themselves differently by, for example, making the necessary discovery applications or applying for cross-examination of various deponents, these judicial proceedings would have taken a much different course and, depending on what evidence emerged, the court may have been driven to arrive at a quite different result'.[16]

It is clear that the court was not persuaded by the argument that the relevant documents had been destroyed. Mr Justice Stock was also unhappy with the so-called standard practice of destruction of documents. He warned: 'If such a practice existed and if it persists, the result is that, whatever the motive for destruction, documentation that evidences the decision-making process is destroyed before expiry of the time for seeking leave to apply for judicial review. There would have to be compelling reasons

13. Para 154.
14. Para 119.
15. Para 151.
16. Para 131.

to justify such a policy of practice, absent which the question is begged whether the policy or practice itself is lawful.'[17]

This brings to an end a disgraceful episode that has spanned over six years. Is there anything to be learned?

The court severely criticized the government for conducting the case as if it were engaged in adversarial, tactical, and hard-fought commercial litigation, trying to be both defensive and aggressive at every stage of the litigation. It is unfortunate that this has been the attitude of the government in quite a number of judicial review cases. As an accountable government, the proper approach should be to present the government's case as fairly and frankly as possible. Just like in criminal cases where the duty of the prosecution is not to secure a conviction by all means, the duty of the respondent in judicial review should not be to seek an excuse for its conduct at all costs. Judicial review should be taken positively as a means to improve governance. In our system, the court is entrusted with the responsibility to determine the legality of administrative decisions. It can only discharge its responsibility if there is cooperation and candour by the executive government. No doubt the court will at times have to step into the arena of some sensitive information, yet there are established rules under which sensitive information can be protected. The rule of law will not be advanced if the executive government is to adopt an evasive approach to judicial review.

There is an equally important lesson for the legal advisors. A lawyer is not the mouthpiece of his or her client. While it is important to have in mind the best interest of the client, there are also times when a legal advisor has to set a limit on how the client would like to advance his or her interest. It should not be the duty of the legal team to put forward any plausible excuse, however artificial, to justify hitherto unjustifiable conduct, or to adopt an approach that is not conducive to the furtherance of the accountability and openness of the government. The stern warning of the Court of Appeal should serve as a timely reminder to all those advising the government.

Public records form a major part of the heritage of any civil society. There has been a vigorous campaign in Hong Kong for the introduction of a Public Records Ordinance, but unfortunately it has so far been ignored. It was sadly reported that, between 2012 and 2016, the government has destroyed over 1.12 billion pages of documents. Indeed, few documents from the offices of the Chief Executive, the Chief Secretary, the Financial Secretary, and the Secretary for Security have been transferred to the Hong Kong Public Records Office for archives since 1997. A proper archive system not only enhances transparency and accountability of the government, but it also fosters public confidence in decision making and preserves the memory for posterity. A most striking legacy of the British administration is the natural tendency of the civil service to put down everything in writing. One just has to look at how meticulously handwritten memos of the government are preserved at the Public Records Office in

---

17. Para 157.

the United Kingdom to get a sense of this almost sacred duty to keep records within the civil service. Sadly, this practice seems to have been lost since the changeover.

In or about September 2016, it was revealed that the government had four meetings with the major groups of the New Territories indigenous inhabitants on the development of public housing in Wang Chau. The proposal was strenuously opposed by the vested interests in the New Territories, and the number of public housing units in the original proposal was substantially reduced in the third meeting. When these meetings came to light, the government, under strong political pressure, was forced to disclose the details of these discussions. While the government was able to recall details of these talks, it was conveniently unable to find any record of the crucial third meeting! It is difficult to believe that the government kept a meticulous record of the other two discussions but then no record was kept for the most crucial meeting, at which there was a change of the original proposal. Nor was it clear whether there was only no record in the Housing and Transport Bureau, which was responsible for the negotiations, or whether there was no record at all in any government department. Did the government ever learn? It was sheer luck (or was it?) that the attention of the public was soon diverted to the disgraceful manner of oath-taking by a few members of the Legislative Council in October 2016. Had there been a duty to keep public records, some of these cases would not have happened.

26

My trip to Macau

Both Hong Kong and Macau became Special Administrative Regions of the People's Republic of China in the late 1990s. While the constitutions of both regions are fairly similar in content, the two places could not be more different. As a colony of Portugal for more than four centuries, Macau has a civil law system and most of its laws are still written in Portuguese, whereas Hong Kong, having been a British colony for about 150 years, is a common law jurisdiction where the courts play a central role in the legal system. Hong Kong is an international financial centre, a highly sophisticated metropolis with an income per capita comparable to that of most developed Western countries, a strong economy offering internationally competitive professional services at the highest level, and a fairly active civil society with an impressive diversity of views on most social and political issues. Macau, in contrast, is a small economy that relies heavily on income from casinos and related entertainment sectors. It had until recently only one university and is by and large a relatively compliant society. In Hong Kong, the government is held to account through the political process, an open society with a free press, and most notably, judicial review by an independent court. In the last two chapters, we have seen how the decisions of the government were successfully challenged in court. Both decisions were related to denial of entry of some visitors into Hong Kong. I never thought I would have to go through the same experience myself, until the following happened.

One of my former students taught at the University of Macau. He used to invite me to give an annual lecture there. On each of these occasions, I declined to stay in Macau overnight and always returned on the same day. In February 2009, I was again invited to give the annual lecture. The topic of my lecture was 'A Constitutional Right to Fair Hearing in Administrative Proceedings'. It was a public lecture, to be delivered on the evening of 27 February 2009. I took the 4 p.m. ferry to Macau, expecting to arrive at 5 p.m., which should be in time for the public lecture at 6:30 p.m. My student, Dr Perumal, was to pick me up at the ferry terminal. I planned to return to Hong Kong after the post-lecture dinner that same evening.

I arrived at the immigration desk at the Macau Ferry Terminal shortly after 5 p.m. It took quite a while for the immigration officer to check my Hong Kong Identity Card. He then left his counter, apparently to consult a more senior officer. A few minutes later, he returned with another officer and asked me to go to a small Immigration Department office there. I was told by a senior officer there that I would be denied entry to Macau, and he asked me to wait for the official document. I explained to the senior officer the purpose of my visit and that someone from the University of Macau was waiting for me in the arrival hall. The senior officer then asked another officer to accompany me to the arrival hall to explain to my student what had happened. Dr Perumal was glad to see me, but his heart soon sank when I told him that I was denied entry. The public lecture was supposed to begin within an hour. It had been well publicized, and Dr Perumal expected a good attendance if not a full house. Regrettably there was nothing I could do.

I was then taken back to the Immigration Office. I asked for the reason for the denial of my entry, but no answer was given except that I should wait. It took another 15 minutes. The same senior officer then asked me to sign a piece of paper, which said that I was denied entry because 'there are strong references that you intend to enter the Macao SAR to participate in certain activities which may jeopardize the public security or public order of the Macao SAR'. I was dumbfounded, if not amused. I asked how delivering an academic public lecture at a university could be an activity that would 'jeopardize the public security or public order of the Macao SAR'. Indeed, I produced the invitation letter and my return ticket, showing that I did intend to return to Hong Kong that very evening. (I was not asked any questions before the decision to refuse my entry was communicated to me.) The senior officer did not make any response, save to tell me that they would arrange to send me back to Hong Kong on the next available ferry.

I did not have to wait long. The captain of the next ferry was brought to the Immigration Office. He was given a brown envelope which contained my Hong Kong Identity Card and a letter from the Macau Immigration Office. The captain then accompanied me to the ferry. I was required to sit alone in the first class cabin, which, frankly, might have been considered some kind of privilege, and of course, at the courtesy of the Macau government! All along, everyone had been very polite. I was the last to leave the ferry when we arrived in Hong Kong. The captain took me ashore and handed me over to the Hong Kong immigration officers, together with the brown envelope. I then entered Hong Kong under the normal procedure, and thereupon my identity card was returned to me.

I could not figure out why I was denied entry to Macau. While I am an outspoken commentator on current affairs in Hong Kong, I have seldom written or spoken on anything about Macau, let alone anything critical of the Macau government. I have no problem with entering any country in the world, including the Mainland and Taiwan. When I told some of my friends about my experience, everyone was astonished. Mr Justice Bokhary jokingly said that I was of course not welcome as I did not spend a single cent in Macau during my visit! The media later learned about it, and it was soon blown up into an international incident and covered by major media in the West, including *New York Times*, *Washington Post*, *Guardian*, *Times (London)*,

BBC, ABC, Voice of America, *Asian Wall Street Journal*, Agence France-Presse, *International Herald Tribune*, and *The Economist*, and even media from Switzerland, the Netherlands, Australia, Singapore, and Indonesia, alongside the major press in Hong Kong, Taiwan, Macau, and the Mainland. Many friends had expressed sympathy for what I had gone through; some even volunteered to speak to someone in a position of influence and to clear me for future entry, a kind gesture for which I was grateful but which I politely declined.

The University of Macau was terribly embarrassed by the incident. They have since repeatedly invited me to visit the university and assured me that they had cleared my visit with all the relevant authorities. It was interesting that I received quite a number of invitations from various institutions to visit Macau during that period of time, including from the Prosecutorate General of Macau to join their 10th Anniversary Conference in early 2010. As a result of repeated invitations, I eventually agreed to deliver my undelivered lecture at the University of Macau on 27 April 2010. This time I had no difficulty in entering Macau. The visit received a lot of media publicity. As usual, I had dinner with the organizer after the lecture and returned to Hong Kong immediately after the dinner.

On the following day, my colleague and co-author, Professor Lim Chin Leng, knocked on my door and asked, 'Would you fancy having lunch in Macau tomorrow? I have booked a table at Robuchon Macau. If you can get into Macau, I will host the lunch.'

It was late April. Professor Lim co-taught with me on a course on Human Rights in Hong Kong, and we had just finished teaching. I said, 'Why not?'

So, on the following day (30 April 2010), we went to Macau. Professor Lim and his wife, Lyn, had no problem getting through the immigration. Then it was my turn. The immigration officer hesitated for a while. He left the counter. He returned with a senior officer and asked me to go to the same Immigration Office. I was refused entry the second time, and for the same reason! I was even more amazed, as it seemed that having lunch in Macau was considered an activity that would jeopardize the public security or public order of Macau. I told the officer that I had been allowed entry only a few days before, but this failed to move him. Apparently I was still on a stop list. I told Chin Leng and Lyn to go ahead with the lunch, but they were very kind and decided to accompany me back to Hong Kong and even agreed to treat me to a late lunch in Hong Kong.

This time I decided to write to Mr Ambrose Lee, then Secretary for Security, as I considered it a matter of principle that the Hong Kong government should do its utmost to protect the rights of Hong Kong permanent residents when there was no earthly reason for the denial of my entry. The reply was weak and disappointing. In his letter dated 4 June 2010, Mr Isaac So, on behalf of the Secretary for Security, stated:

> The Government of the Hong Kong SAR respects the jurisdictions of other immi-
> gration authorities and will not seek to interfere with their decision on the entry
> or otherwise of a visitor. Furthermore, the common international practice is that

immigration authorities will consider each entry application on a case-by-case basis, taking into account the circumstances at the relevant time.

Having said this, we attach great importance to the travel convenience of Hong Kong residents. Indeed, we have approached the Macao authority and obtained an assurance that the Macao authority had followed the common practice of considering your entry application in the light of the circumstances at the relevant time.

While it is true that all immigration authorities have the discretion to deny entry to any visitor, that power should not be exercised arbitrarily. It was very clear that the Secretary for Security had not even attempted to seek an explanation for the apparently arbitrary decisions of the Macau authority, and the so-called assurance was nothing but empty words.

In or around November the same year, I was invited to a wedding banquet by a family friend in Macau. I was very hesitant about going, but eventually, out of respect for some senior family members, was persuaded to go. The immigration counters at the Macau Ferry Terminal adopted a somewhat open design. The officers sit behind the counters, which were not covered in a booth. When a person passed through the checkpoint and looked back, he or she would be able to see the computer screen of the immigration officers. My wife noticed that, for most visitors, when the immigration officers swiped their identity document at the computer, the screen turned green, whereas in my case, the screen turned red. Again, the immigration officer hesitated. Again he left the counter, and I thought I was going to be rejected a third time, but this time he returned alone and allowed my entry. We attended the banquet and returned to Hong Kong the same evening. That was my last visit to Macau. Thus, within two years, I had been to Macau four times and been denied entry twice.

I was later told that the reason for the denial of my entry to Macau might have something to do with my stance on Article 23 legislation. In 2003, the Hong Kong government attempted to introduce local legislation on national security, pursuant to Article 23 of the Basic Law. Some parts of the proposed bill were quite draconian. As the bill was quite technical and the devil was in the details, a few of us decided that it would be useful to explain our concern to the public in a language that the public would understand. We did not object to the enactment of national security law as such. Our query was what kind of national security law Hong Kong needed, and we felt that the proposed bill had gone too far at the expense of personal liberty and freedoms. There were ten of us, including five former chairpersons of the Bar (Denis Chang SC, Ronny Tong SC, Audrey Eu SC, Gladys Li SC, and Alan Leong SC). The others were Margaret Ng, Christine Loh, Mark Daly, Professor Michael Davis, and me. It was really an honour to be in the company of such a distinguished group. It was decided that seven of us should each write on one aspect of the proposed bill in a one-page pamphlet, setting out what was wrong with the bill and what we would propose. It was Christine's idea that each pamphlet should have the same cover design and should be of different colours—red, orange, yellow, green, indigo, blue, and violet—and these pamphlets acquired the title of 'Rainbow Pamphlets'. We distributed them on the streets and went to different public forums to explain our concerns. For many of us, it was the first time that we distributed pamphlets on the streets, and I can still remember how uneasy many of us felt at that time. Nonetheless, our efforts aroused considerable public concern over the proposed bill, and our group was named 'Article 23 Concern Group'. The momentum continued to gather, and on 1 July 2003, a very hot summer day, about half a million people took to the streets to demonstrate against the introduction of the proposed bill. Despite this opposition, the government decided to push the bill through, but when the Hon Mr James Tien, a member of the Executive Council and the then chairman of the Liberal Party, decided to resign from the Executive Council, as he found himself unable to endorse a bill that was opposed by so many people, the government reluctantly withdrew it. Without the support of the Liberal Party, the government would not have a sufficient majority in the Legislative Council to secure the passage of the bill. This was heralded as a triumph of the people.

Later, the same group turned its attention to the direct election of the Chief Executive of the HKSAR, which was promised by Article 45 of the Basic Law. The Article 23 Concern Group was enlarged and renamed 'Article 45 Concern Group'. Soon after, a few of the original members of the Article 23 Concern Group decided to form a political party: the Civic Party. I was invited to join as a founding member, but I declined as I considered it inappropriate for an officer of the University (as I was then dean of the Faculty of Law) to become a member of a political party. Indeed, I have never joined any political party, but probably because of my early participation in the Article 23 Concern Group, I have always been misperceived as a member of the Civic Party. Most of the founding members of the Civic Party are my good friends whom I have known for more than 20 years and with whom I do share a belief in democracy and the rule of law. That is different from joining a political party.

Back to the Macau incident, the Macau government had just introduced their Article 23 legislation (National Security Law) in Macau at the time of my visit in February 2009. Indeed, a number of legislators and activists from Hong Kong had been denied entry for their participation in anti–Article 23 legislation activities shortly before my visit. Thus, I suspect that it was due to my association with the Article 23 Concern Group six years earlier that I was included on a stop list. I have no idea how the stop list was compiled or on what information it was based. Apart from the one-page document saying that I was denied entry pursuant to Article 17(4) of the Internal Security Law of the Macao SAR,[1] I was never told the evidential basis for placing me on a stop list or why it was believed that I was going to participate in activities that might jeopardize the public security or public order of Macau. It might be just unfortunate that I was invited to give the lecture in the same week the legislation for Article 23 of the Macau Basic Law was considered and passed by their Legislative Council. Once you are on a stop list, it is difficult to get delisted.

---

1. This section allows the security officials to 'refuse the entry of non-residents into the Macau SAR . . . who, in the terms of the law, are considered inadmissible or may pose a threat for the stability of the internal security': Internal Security Law, Law No. 9/2002.

I was also told that I was not on the most sensitive list. Apparently, I would only be denied entry on sensitive dates. These might, I suppose, include 1 May, 4 June, 1 July, etc., and might also include any date when there was to be an important official visitor in Macau, or just any date which the Macau authority considered sensitive. I would have no way of finding out in advance if a particular date was sensitive. In any event, it does not matter, as I do not intend to visit Macau again. Yet, this incident does highlight what can happen when there is a lack of transparency and public accountability of the executive government and when power could be exercised in an arbitrary manner.

Rainbow pamphlets

XI

When the Law Is Absurd

27

Could we shoot the red light?

Are there circumstances in which we can disobey the law? This question has troubled generations of jurists and philosophers and has become a question of contemporary significance in recent years in Hong Kong. Does the rule of law require just unquestioning adherence to the letters of the law, or are there higher values that the law is expected to meet, and if so, what are these higher values?

Every year, I put these questions to my first-year law students in their first tutorial of the legal system course. As most law students are eager to have a taste of the law as soon as they have begun their legal studies, I give them a case to read in their first tutorial class. It is a judgment of the English Court of Appeal in 1971. Lord Denning, with his usual clarity and eloquence, set out the issue as follows:

> For many years there has been a controversy in the Fire Service. It is this: what is the duty of the driver of a fire engine when he comes to traffic lights which are at red? The Fire Brigades Union says that he must obey the law. No matter how urgent the call, he must wait till the lights turn green. Even if it means losing precious seconds, he must wait all the same. The chief officer of the London Fire Brigade says No; he is not going to order the driver to wait. If the road is clear and the driver stops for a second and makes sure that it is safe to cross, he can shoot the lights so as to get to the fire as soon as possible. But, if he thinks it better to wait until the lights go green, he is at perfect liberty to do so. The decision is his, and his alone.[1]

It was a criminal offence to disobey the traffic lights, and a firefighter was given no exception. The driver of a fire engine who shot a red light was liable to prosecution, and if he has accumulated sufficient penalty points for traffic offences, he would have his driving licence endorsed and therefore risked losing his job. These rival views had continued for some time without a solution, and the Home Secretary declined to intervene by legislation.

In February 1967, the chief officer of the London Fire Brigade, with the support of the Greater London Council, had issued an order to all firefighters. The order stated that a brigade driver responding to an emergency call might decide to proceed against the red light if it was safe to do so. The driver should proceed only when he was

---

1. *Buckoke v Greater London Council* [1971] Ch 655.

reasonably sure that there was no risk of a collision, and the bell was to be rung vigorously and the flashing light should be in operation. The onus of avoiding an accident in such circumstances rested entirely on the brigade driver. In other words, the order left it to the discretion of the driver to decide whether to obey the law.

The Fire Brigades Union took exception to this order. They regarded it as an encouragement to the drivers to break the law. Some firefighters refused to travel with a driver unless he gave an assurance that he would observe the law and would never cross the lights when they were red. The drivers refused to give that assurance. These firefighters then refused to travel with the drivers, and the chief officer took disciplinary action against the firefighters. They then brought an application for judicial review challenging the order as unlawful. If the order was unlawful, they were not bound to travel with a driver who was under unlawful orders.

The central issue was therefore whether the order of the chief officer encouraging the drivers to disobey the law on traffic lights was a lawful order.

The statutory provision was strict. No one was exempted from obeying the red lights. Lord Denning posed this hypothetical question to counsel in the course of the hearing: 'A driver of a fire engine with ladders approaches the traffic lights. He sees 200 yards down the road a blazing house with a man at an upstairs window in extreme peril. The road is clear in all directions. At that moment the lights turn red. Is the driver to wait for 60 seconds, or more, for the lights to turn green? If the driver waits for that time, the man's life will be lost. Should the driver obey the law in these circumstances? If he decides not to obey the law, should he be prosecuted, or should he be congratulated?'

The chief officer argued that the order had already addressed the question of safety, as the driver was clearly instructed that he had to take sufficient precaution before he shot the red light. Unfortunately, just shortly before this case, there was an accident. A fire engine on an emergency call, shooting a red light, knocked down and killed a motorcyclist, who was deaf and could not hear the siren. He had not seen the flashing lights of the approaching fire engine. And to add to the tragedy, the particular call being answered by the brigade was a hoax!

The union argued that it was unfair to put the burden on the driver to decide whether he should obey the law. No one was above the law, and it was wrong to ask the driver to disobey the law even when there was an honourable cause. Obeying the law went to the very fabric of the rule of law. The chief officer said that it would be absurd to stop and wait for the change of light when human lives were endangered, and in these circumstances, no fire service and no police would prosecute the driver. It would indeed be absurd to do so. The union replied and said this simply avoided the issue. An offence had been committed irrespective of whether there was a prosecution. There was no assurance that no prosecution would be carried out. If there was such an assurance, it would be tantamount to a failure to enforce the law, which was against the rule of law. If there was no such assurance, the driver would face the risk of prosecution, and if he had accumulated sufficient penalty points for traffic offences, he would risk losing his driving licence and his job. If it was felt that the driver should be allowed not to obey the law, this should be done by legislative amendment. Yet until the law was amended, it would be wrong to leave it to an individual to decide whether to obey the law or whether to disobey it for a greater cause at his own risk.[2] The law was the law. No one should be allowed to choose whether to obey it or not.

What would you do if you were the driver in the situation described by Lord Denning? Disobey the law to save life, or obey the law and let someone die? Should the law be obeyed when this would become absurd? Yet if one can choose not to obey the law when the law is absurd, who determines how absurd the law has to be before one can justifiably disobey it? Is it true that the law must always be obeyed, whatever be the circumstances? When the Hong Kong government keeps repeating in the last few years that the rule of law requires everyone to obey the law, is that an oversimplification of what the rule of law means?

Ironically, in this case, the drivers did not object to the order. It was the crew who refused to travel with drivers who refused to undertake to obey the law.

Lord Denning would have liked to give the driver a defence of necessity, but both parties agreed that the defence was not available as a matter of law. He then changed the question. The issue was not about whether one should obey the law but what the consequences were if one were to disobey it. In everyday life, many of us may have committed a technical offence. When you try to shove your way into the compartment of a congested underground train in the morning rush hour, you may have technically committed an offence of assault against the passengers that you are pushing. Or you may have committed an offence when you cross a road without obeying the traffic light. Yet, on many occasions, the police may decide not to take out a prosecution. It is a matter of discretion, and such discretion is exercised routinely on a daily basis, no doubt on the basis of common sense. There is nothing wrong with such exercise of discretion. By parity of reason, the order of the chief officer in this case was not to tell a driver to disobey the law. Instead, its effect was that, if a driver chose to disobey the law under the circumstances as prescribed by the order, no disciplinary offence would be taken out against the driver. If the commissioner of police could give a policy direction to his officers saying that they need not prosecute a firefighter for crossing the lights at red when there was no danger, there was no reason why the chief officer of the fire brigade should not be allowed to do likewise. Accordingly, the Court of Appeal held that there was nothing unlawful about such an order.

Are you convinced? Has the court provided any answer to the question of when one is allowed not to obey the law? Could disobeying the law ever be consistent with the rule of law and justice for all? What are we going to do if the law is absurd or when higher value is at stake? Could a policy decision not to prosecute someone for disobeying the law on the ground of a high moral cause be reconciled with the rule of law? If

2.   Since then the Road Traffic Act in England has been amended to allow an exemption for fire engines, ambulance, and police vehicles to comply with speed limits and traffic lights under certain conditions. A similar exemption exists in section 77 of the Road Traffic Ordinance in Hong Kong.

one is prosecuted and convicted, could the fact that the offence was committed out of a noble cause ever be a relevant factor in mitigation? Some of these issues have been troubling Hong Kong in the last few years. These complex and multidimensional issues are not to be tackled by a simple 'yes' or 'no' answer, and to equate the rule of law as blindly obeying the law is an oversimplification, if not also misleading.

28

Let's kill all the lawyers!
When is a pigeon not a pigeon?

Every now and then, there are cases which may puzzle, if not also be amusing to the general public, as the decisions seem to be contrary to common sense. Sometimes an awkward decision of the court is the result of poor drafting of legislation, especially when ill-considered amendments were hastily introduced (or well-intended amendments were arbitrarily rejected) in the course of the legislative process.[1] Sometimes it may just be the sheer limitation of human ability to foresee the future. The pigeon case may be one such entertaining incident.[2]

Section 15 of the Waste Disposal Ordinance provides that no person shall keep 'livestock' at any premises in a 'livestock prohibition area' (which generally covers the urban area). 'Livestock' is defined to mean 'pigs or poultry', and 'poultry' is in turn defined to mean 'chickens, ducks, geese, pigeons and quails'. A contravention of section 15 is a criminal offence.

The Hong Kong Racing Pigeon Association, which had some 380 members, was a sporting association which raced pigeons. The pigeons were trained to fly long distances, sometimes over 1,000 kilometres, from Hong Kong to China and other countries. This sport, or hobby, was taken seriously by its members. The pigeons were generally kept in well-maintained lofts that were brightly lit, draught-proof, water-proof, and vermin-proof. They were expensive. A pedigree pigeon could cost up to HK$20,000 and the unhatched eggs cost about $1,000 each (at 1994 prices). As a result, they were kept in very good conditions. The lofts were large enough to allow a person to get in to do regular cleaning. Since quite a few birds inevitably got lost or were killed on the long-distance races, the members usually kept a substantial number (30 to 40) of them. The problem was that, when the members kept the pigeons in an urban area, they were in contravention of section 15 of the Waste Disposal Ordinance.

By an originating summons, the association sought a declaration that these racing pigeons were not pigeons within the meaning of poultry for the purpose of section 15 of the Waste Disposal Ordinance despite the explicit reference to pigeons in the

---

1. An example would be the amendment to the Housing Ordinance to restrict the amount of increase in rent for public housing estates at times of inflation without realizing that there could be deflation in the economy as well: *Ho Choi Wan v Housing Authority* (2005) 8 HKCFAR 628.
2. *Hong Kong Racing Pigeon Association Ltd v Attorney General* [1994] 2 HKLRD 309.

definition of poultry. The case was argued by my former chamber mate, Mr Benjamin Chain, who had placed before the court a considerable amount of materials to substantiate the point.

It was argued that, first, poultry normally means certain categories of birds which were kept either for breeding or eating. Though racing pigeons could be eaten, they were kept for the purpose of racing rather than for the purpose of food. Secondly, it was argued that racing pigeons are different from domestic pigeons. A pigeon comes from the family called *Columbidae* with some 306 species. There are domestic pigeons, ornamental or fancy pigeons, and homing or racing pigeons. The main difference between racing pigeons and domestic pigeons is that racing pigeons are much smaller in size, some 15 ounces compared to about 2.2 pounds in large domestic pigeons. Unlike fancy pigeons which have fancy tails, racing pigeons are compact. Thirdly, as revealed in the legislative debate, the intention of the legislature was clearly to restrict large farming operations from taking place in the urban areas to provide food for the people of Hong Kong. The legislature certainly did not have in mind or contemplate racing pigeons when it enacted section 15 of the Waste Disposal Ordinance. Fourthly, in 1969, the House of Lords had decided that the word poultry in the Fertilisers and Feeding Stuffs Act 1926 meant birds that were kept for supplying the table with meat or eggs and was not wide enough to cover pheasants that had never been in captivity!

Finally, from a public health point of view, these racing pigeons were carefully maintained and were kept at a high standard of hygiene, especially as they were so expensive. It would be odd if one could keep a large number of parrots in one's property but could not keep a large number of racing pigeons that were normally kept in much better and more hygienic conditions. In this regard, counsel also referred to the fact that the Urban Council had kept a large number of ornamental pigeons in its park within the urban area in contravention of the ordinance!

Mr Justice Sears was evidently highly amused by this learned and ingenious argument. He first described this hobby as a 'worthwhile pursuit' that was taken seriously. As this was 'an important pastime', and since the ordinance provided criminal penalties for its contravention, the court should examine the matter from a liberal point of view. The difficult question for him was whether or not he could limit the meaning of pigeon as poultry to only those pigeons that were kept for food, taking into account that eating pigeon was a common occurrence in Hong Kong. He first found that the English decision of the House of Lords was not helpful, as the word 'poultry' was, unlike in the Hong Kong legislation, not defined in the English Act. So he had to turn to the meaning of poultry in the Hong Kong legislation, which expressly included pigeons. The judge then noted that the word 'poultry' also appeared in the Public Health (Animals and Birds) Ordinance, which, among other things, restricts the public from importing animals and birds on the grounds of public health. Birds were defined as 'poultry and all other birds', and in this context, poultry was defined to include 'domestic fowls, turkeys, ducks, pigeons and geese'. Although this was a different category of poultry, the underlying public health concern for restricting the import and movement of birds in affected areas, especially where disease was discovered, would be equally applicable and of equal cogency. While he had considerable sympathy for the association, he could not hold that racing pigeons were not pigeons for the purpose of the Waste Disposal Ordinance. He was relieved to be informed by the Department of Justice that a relaxation of the ordinance had been made to allow association members to keep up to 20 pigeons on their premises and that the Urban Council had now been exempted from the ordinance so that it could continue to keep ornamental pigeons within the urban areas!

Accordingly, Mr Justice Sears held that racing pigeons were pigeons within the meaning of the Waste Disposal Ordinance, and those persons who kept more than 20 racing pigeons in the specified urban areas were liable to prosecution under section 15.

On appeal, the Court of Appeal found it unnecessary to refer to the legislative material or the Public Health (Animals and Birds) Ordinance, which was in a different context and of little assistance to the interpretation of the Waste Disposal Ordinance.[3] The association was represented by a different counsel, Mr Hui Ka-ho, who argued that pigeons were not poultry as a matter of ordinary English language, citing in support the meaning of poultry in the *Oxford English Dictionary*. Poultry, it was argued, referred to table birds. The court had no difficulty in rejecting this argument, noting the extent that pigeons were consumed on the table in Hong Kong! Mr Justice Nazareth held that 'pigeons' means pigeons. It was a plain and ordinary English word which must be given its plain and natural meaning. There was no ambiguity or obscurity in the statutory definition. The term 'pigeons' must be intended to cover all kinds of pigeons, be they table birds, fancy birds, show birds, or racing pigeons. The purpose of the ordinance was to address the primary mischief of pollution caused by the waste of livestock, be they pigs or poultry or pigeons. Mr Justice Liu added that the purpose for which the pigeons were kept was simply irrelevant! In contrast, Mr Justice Bokhary expressed his sympathy with the association but pointed out the weight of the word 'pigeon' in the statutory definition of poultry was too heavy for the association to overcome.

Statutory interpretation is rarely a mechanical process. More often than not, there is a choice of a range of possible meanings, and the courts are guided, not only by the language of the statute, but also its purpose and context, and not surprisingly, their own sense of justice and fairness. The decision of Mr Justice Sears was eminently sensible with a nice human touch. The judgment of the Court of Appeal was impeccable though it may convey a rather stern and literal-minded impression. Lawyers from both sides approached the case from different perspectives, and possibly with some ingenuity in this case. Those who have read the judgments might be forgiven for expressing sympathy with the cry in Shakespeare's *Henry VI*: 'The first thing we do, let's kill all the lawyers'!

---

3. Civ App No 158 of 1994 (11 April 1995).

XII

Law and Moral Choices

29

Whose life is it anyway?

Unlike doctors, lawyers are not always thought of as persons involved with making decisions of life and death. Yet for those who practise family law, this is not an uncommon occurrence, and on those occasions, lawyers are relieved that they are only advocates and not the decision makers themselves.

John asked,[1] with tears in his eyes, 'Honey, are you sure?' 'Yes, I'm sure,' Mary replied. Her tears had already dried. She turned her head away from her husband and gazed at the grey-blue sky outside the window of the hospital ward. 'This will be the best for her,' she murmured to herself.

Court No. 3 of the Royal Court of Justice

Clerk: Court.

[All rose. The judges came out and took their seats.]

Ms Ryan QC: My Lords, I appear on behalf of the Hammersmith and Fulham Local Authority. This is an urgent appeal from a judgment made by Justice Ewbank this morning when the learned judge decided that the parents' wishes should be respected and refused to make an order to authorize the hospital to carry out an operation on a newborn child ...

Mr Gray QC: My Lords, I appear for the parents. This is a very poignantly sad case. It is a case where nature has made its own arrangements to terminate a life which would not be fruitful, and nature should not be interfered with. It is a most difficult and painful decision for the parents to make. Yet it is also a case where the views of responsible and caring parents, as these are, that it is better for the child to be allowed to die, should be respected ...

---

1. This story is based on a real case in *Re B* [1981] 1 WLR 1421, but the names of all persons and institutions used here are fictitious.

Three days ago, Maternity Ward 5B, London Chelsea Hospital

Dr Osmond walked into the room. Mary looked well, though a bit pale, having just gone through a caesarean section. She had just recovered from the effects of sedation and could not wait to see her child. John followed Dr Osmond into the room. He had been having a talk with the doctor and now looked bewildered and lost.

'Mary, you look good. You're doing well. You should be able to get up tomorrow morning,' Dr Osmond said.

'How about the baby? How is she? When can I see her?' Mary asked eagerly.

'The operation was successful,' Dr Osmond replied. 'But now I'm afraid I have some bad news.' The doctor paused for a while. John went to the bedside and took his wife's hand. 'The child was born suffering from Patau syndrome. This was caused by an extra pair of chromosomes 13. It causes serious physical and mental abnormalities, including heart defects, incomplete brain development, and mental retardation. There will also be other internal and external abnormalities. She is not in the most serious condition but is still in a serious stage. At this stage we can't tell what kind of life she will be able to lead. She won't be a vegetable, that's for sure, but I'm very sorry to tell you she will have severe mental and physical disabilities. Seventy per cent of children with this syndrome do not live beyond a year, and survival to adulthood is very rare though the longest case so far is known to have survived to the age of 33.'

Mary burst into tears. 'Is there anything you can do? We'll do anything!'

Dr Osmond looked sombre. 'I'm afraid that's not all. She also suffers from intestinal blockage, and that requires an immediate operation. If she does not have this operation, she will die within a matter of days. Please discuss this between you. Take as much time as you need. I will need your consent to carry out the operation.'

Two days ago

'At least she'll have one or more years to live. Who knows, maybe her condition will be curable by then. Maybe there will be miracles. I'll do everything to give her a happy life,' John said, and tried to sound hopeful.

'And what if it's not curable by then?' Mary's voice was sad but determined. She had had no sleep since the news yesterday. 'We have to be realistic, John. Think how stressful it will be to take care of a child with severe mental and physical disabilities. You have a job, and we need you to work to support the family. I'm not sure I can cope—not for myself—but how can I bear to watch her suffer for months or even years and to witness her dying gradually with all the suffering? What kind of life will she have?'

The couple clung to one another and cried for quite a while.

'Honey, are you sure?' John asked. 'Yes, I'm sure,' Mary said. 'This will be the best for her. Take me to see our child. I want to see more of her before she's gone.'

'This is Dr Osmond.' In discharge of his duty, Dr Osmond reported the matter to the Hammersmith and Fulham Local Authority. 'I have to report to you that the parents have refused to give their consent to the operation. The parents are sober, calm, and well educated. They know what they are doing, and they think that it's in the best interest of the child to let her go peacefully. I told them that we could keep her from pain and suffering by sedation. However, as a doctor I can't recommend this course. If the operation is not carried out, the child will die within days. If we do operate, there may be heart complications, and as a result she might still die within two or three months. But even if the operation is successful, she has Patau syndrome, and the present assessment is that her life expectancy is about one to a few years. With possible medical advancement, this is not a short time. My duty is to save life, not to end it.'

An urgent conference was held at the local authority that afternoon. It was decided that the authority should intervene in the matter.

A day ago

An urgent application was made by the local authority to the court, applying to make the child a ward of the court, asking the court to give the care and control of the child to the authority and to authorize them to direct that the operation be carried out. On the strength of the evidence of Dr Osmond, the judge so directed.

The child was removed to St Thomas Hospital for the operation that afternoon. Dr Phillips, the consultant surgeon who was to perform the operation, was hesitant when she learned about the objection of the parents. She decided to speak to them, and they told her on the phone that, in view of the fact that the child had Patau syndrome, they did not wish to have the operation performed. Dr Phillips, in a later affirmation to the court, stated:

> I decided therefore to respect the wishes of the parents and not to perform the operation, a decision which would, I believe (after about 20 years in the medical profession), be taken by the great majority of surgeons faced with a similar situation.

This morning

The local authority went back to Mr Justice Ewbank, armed with a further affirmation from Dr Taylor, a surgeon of the London Chelsea Hospital, and Dr Riley, another surgeon of a neighbouring hospital. Both Dr Taylor and Dr Riley were of the view that the operation should be carried out. Mr Justice Ewbank was asked to decide whether to continue his order that the operation should be performed or whether to revoke that order in view of the conflicting medical evidence. The parents were served with the relevant documents and appeared before Mr Justice Ewbank. They maintained their view that there should be no operation. After hearing the parties, Mr Justice Ewbank decided that the parents' wishes should be respected.

The local authority lodged an urgent appeal to the Court of Appeal in the afternoon. The Official Solicitor intervened and was represented by Mr Jackson QC. Ms Ryan QC appeared on behalf of the local authority, and Mr Gray QC acted pro bono for the parents.

Court No. 3 of the Royal Court of Justice

Ms Ryan QC: My Lords, while there are conflicting medical opinions regarding the operation, there is a consensus that if it is successful, the child will live for about one to a few years, and maybe even longer, as there are reported cases of survival to adulthood. We certainly appreciate the burden on the parents and respect their wishes. However, the child is now a ward of the court, and the paramount consideration must be her best interest. Insofar as it is a matter of care, the local authority is prepared to give whatever support we can so that this unfortunate child can be provided with a happy life as far as this can be done. The local authority is also prepared, if this is considered desirable, to make good adoption arrangements so that the burden of taking care of this unfortunate child could be borne by persons other than the natural parents.

Mr Jackson QC: The duty of the Official Solicitor is to protect the best interest of the child. The question for this court is whether to allow an operation to take place which may result in her living for one to a few years, and maybe even longer, as a sufferer from Patau syndrome, or whether (and this will be the brutal result) to terminate the life of the child because she also has an intestinal complaint. My Lords, the overriding consideration is what is in the best interest of the child. No doubt your Lordships should give weight, and heavy weight indeed, to the wishes of the parents. To be sure, the shock to these caring and loving parents must be overwhelming, and no doubt they came to their decision in grief and great sorrow. They had to make this decision also under great time pressure. Under these harrowing circumstances, while their views should be accorded great weight, they should not necessarily prevail. The determination of what lies in the best interest of the child rests with the court and no longer with the parents or the doctors. It is a decision of the court that is to be made in the light of the evidence and views expressed by the parents and the doctors. But at the end of the day, it is for this court to decide whether the child should in effect be condemned to die, or whether her life is still so imponderable that it would be wrong for it to be taken from her. The life is that of a child. No prognosis as to the child's future can be made at this point. Medical advancement is progressing at tremendous speed these days. Who knows if, in a year's time, this disease would not have become curable, or her conditions could not have become improved? Should she be deprived of this opportunity? My Lords, this child is in no different a position from many other unfortunate Patau syndrome children, except that she happens to have an intestinal problem that needs an operation. Should she be put in the same position as any other child born with this condition and be given a chance to live? The life is hers, and hers alone. On this, my Lords, I rest my case.

Mr Gray QC: It is easy to argue for a right to life in the abstract, but what kind of life are we talking about? My Lords, the decision of the parents, no doubt one taken in grief and great sorrow, is also a calm and rational choice, made after the most careful consideration of what is best for this unfortunate baby. Let me make it very clear that it is not because of the difficulties which will be occasioned to them that they make this decision. As loving and caring parents, no difficulties would so great as to compel them to shed their love and responsibility to take care of their unfortunate child. It is precisely from that love and responsibility that they have made the decision that their daughter should not be made to bear all the pain and suffering for the rest of her life. It is agreed by the doctors that, even if the operation is successful, she will only have a short life expectancy. Thirty per cent of the children cannot survive beyond a few months; seventy per cent cannot survive beyond a year; and it is rare to have survival beyond adulthood. They also agree that it is certain that she will be very severely mentally and physically challenged, and there will be internal and external abnormalities. To put it brutally, her existence will be nothing but painful—painful to her and painful to people around her. Yes, there is always a theoretical possibility that medical science may advance in the years to come, but there is a limit for optimism. Would it be in the best interest of the child to condemn her to months and years of certain and foreseeable suffering, for a mere theoretical possibility, which no one can possibly say for sure will come true, in the distant future? Yes, no one can tell what kind of life is in store for a child with Patau syndrome who survives till adulthood, but one thing is certain. She will have severe mental and physical disabilities, and no one can expect that she will have anything like a normal existence. It is true that no prognosis as to the child's future can be made at this stage, and probably not for a further few months to a year, but the doctors are not optimistic. I am afraid there is no reason at all to expect that the child will be able to lead a quality life. Indeed, the odds are against that. My Lords, a right to life must imply a life of bearable quality. Not only would she not have a meaningful quality of life, but it will also put unbearable burden on those who have to take care of her for the rest of her life, who would have to spend days, weeks, and years to take care of her, only to meet the inevitable and heartbreaking destiny at the end of that journey. Are we as a community imposing an unjustifiable burden on the parents and pain and suffering on the child so that the rest of us can feel morally good? My learned friend Mr Jackson QC asked why this child should be treated differently from other children with Patau syndrome. Without meaning to sound harsh or brutal, this child has a fatal intestinal problem. God or nature has given the child a way out. Where nature has made its own arrangement to terminate a life which could not be a fruitful one, nature should not be interfered with.

The Court of Appeal adjourned for consideration of its judgment. What will the court decide? How would you decide? What would be a just decision? And justice for whom?

30

When a woman is not a woman

The transgender case

One afternoon in 1985, a charming student called Andrea Fong came to my office at the University and asked if I could be the supervisor of her graduation dissertation. She intended to write about the plight of transgender persons. I agreed and suggested that, as it involved different disciplines, she might wish to consult my colleagues at the Medical Faculty and the Psychology Department of the University of Hong Kong. I sent her to Dr Tsang Ka Tat of the Psychology Department.

A couple of months later, at the Senior Common Room of the University, I had lunch with Dr Tsang to discuss the dissertation. It happened that Dr Ng Mun Lun of the Department of Psychiatry of the Faculty of Medicine was around. In those days, the Senior Common Room was a place that colleagues from different faculties and disciplines would meet and discuss interesting issues and share research ideas. Over the years, I have visited many leading universities, and one common feature is that they all place considerable emphasis on a place where colleagues from different disciplines can meet and interact. Such encounters and discussions spark new ideas. Unfortunately, in recent years, the University of Hong Kong has treated the Senior Common Room as nothing but dining facilities for staff and is reluctant to put in resources to turn it into an integral part of the academic life.

At that lunch meeting, we found that there were indeed considerable demands for transgender operation services in Hong Kong. Dr Ng Mun Lun is a specialist in this area. He noted that there were patients who could not accept their own gender and would go to great length to relieve themselves of the acute mental and emotional distress. Some of these patients would administer self-help by injecting hormones; some may mutilate themselves in order to get rid of the gonadal organs they detest. My colleague Professor Sam Winter vividly described their plight many years later: they 'considered themselves females imprisoned in the male bodies, and vice versa'.[1] It was a well-recognized medical condition, and medical treatment in public hospitals in Hong Kong was first available in 1981. These patients did not normally respond to psychiatric or psychological treatment, and the only cure was to have a sex reassignment surgical operation. This operation was painful, complex, and irreversible, and therefore great care and assessment should be carried out before the operation.

---

1. Affidavit evidence of Professor Sam Winter in *W v Registrar of Marriage* (2013) 16 HKCFAR 112, at 127.

Unfortunately, there was no standard practice of assessment, and malpractice was not unheard of. At the end of that lunch, we decided that, since there were only a small number of professionals working in this area, we might try to work out some standard assessment procedures.

After a few months' discussion, we gathered a team composed of psychiatrists, psychologists, and plastic surgeons, in addition to Dr Ng, Dr Tsang, and me. At that time sex reassignment surgery was performed at Princess Margaret Hospital only, and later at Queen Mary Hospital (apart from private and overseas clinics), and we managed to get the plastic surgeons at the two public hospitals on our team. We devised a year-long assessment process during which patients would have to undergo various psychiatric and psychological assessments and go through a year of real-life experience living in their preferred gender, to ensure that this was a proper case for the irreversible sex reassignment surgery. My role was to meet them at the beginning of this assessment process to advise them on the legal position, and then to meet them again just shortly before the operation to advise them on any change in the legal position. The law at that time did not recognize the post-operation gender, and this would have various legal ramifications.

Since then I have met a dozen transgender patients. Most of them were already cross-dressing and living the life of a different gender. An overwhelming majority of them were 'male to female' patients. Most of them were from the lower working class; a number of them were street or dance performers. A significant number of them had a history of being abused by their cohabitees. Of the dozen patients that I have met, there was only one who came from a middle-class professional background and was my only 'female-to-male' transgender patient. While all the male-to-female patients had put on make-up, and had already administered hormones themselves or received hormonal treatment, they still had a rather coarse appearance and a hoarse voice. They invariably adopted a very low profile and appeared a bit shy in dealing with people. The secretary at the law department did ask me on a few occasions who they were, as they looked 'strange' to her. One of our difficulties at that time was that there was considerable social stigma against this group of persons, and they disappeared as soon as the surgical operation was completed, making it very difficult for us to follow up on how well they had adjusted to life in the post-operation gender.

I left the assessment team after two years when I went on sabbatical. I heard later that our assessment process was adopted and refined by the government and became a standard process at government hospitals. The assessment period has been extended to two years. Since then I have moved on to other things and had forgotten about this area, until the issue surfaced again more than two decades later.

The W case

W was a post-operation male-to-female transsexual person. She was born a male, but from an early age she perceived herself as female. She was diagnosed as suffering from gender identity disorder and underwent psychiatric assessment and hormonal treatment between 2005 and 2008. In January 2007, she went to Thailand to have genital surgery (orchiectomy) and then changed her name to a female name by deed poll. After having successfully gone through the real-life experience assessment under professional supervision, she went through the sex reassignment surgery at a public hospital in Hong Kong involving the removal of her penis and the construction of an artificial vagina to enable her to engage in sexual intercourse with a man. With a supporting letter from the Hospital Authority, she successfully changed her gender to female in her educational records, her identity card, and later her passport.

In November 2008, she wrote to the Registrar of Marriage seeking confirmation that she was able to marry her male partner. The registrar replied:

> According to our legal advice, the biological sexual constitution of an individual is fixed at birth and cannot be changed, either by the natural development of organs of the opposite sex, or by medical or surgical means. The Registrar of Marriages is not empowered to celebrate the marriage between persons of the same biological sex. For the purpose of marriage, only an individual's sex at birth counts and any operative intervention is ignored.

A challenge to this decision set in train legal proceedings in the following five years, resulting in a major change in social and legal policy.

The law was deceptively simple. Section 40 of the Marriage Ordinance said that 'every marriage under this Ordinance shall be a Christian marriage or the equivalent of a Christian marriage', meaning a 'voluntary union for life of one man and one woman to the exclusion of all others'. At the heart of the case is the meaning of 'a man' and 'a woman'.

At the outset, W's legal team was at pains to emphasize that this case was not about same-sex marriage, which was a highly controversial subject. The issue was a narrower one, whether 'a woman', for the purpose of marriage, included a post-operation male-to-female transsexual person?

The English court has given a negative answer. In the leading case of *Corbett v Corbett*,[2] which was decided in 1971, Mr Justice Ormrod held that natural heterosexual intercourse was an essential element of the institution of marriage on which the family was built, because it was the basis of procreation. This was in line with the notion of Christian marriage, marriage ordained for the procreation of children. The learned judge identified five possible criteria for determining one's gender: (1) chromosomal factors, (2) gonadal factors (the presence or absence of testes or ovaries), (3) genital factors (including internal sex organs), (4) psychological factors, and possibly (5) hormonal factors or secondary sexual characteristics. However, given the essentially heterosexual character of the relationship in marriage, the judge concluded that the criteria must be biological, for even the most extreme degree of transsexualism in a

---

2. [1971] P 83.

male could not reproduce a person who was naturally capable of performing the essential role of a woman in marriage.

As the determining factor is biological, gender is determined at birth and cannot be changed. This case was the leading authority for determining gender in the following four decades. It led to an amendment of the Nullity of Marriage Act 1971 in the United Kingdom, which in turn led to the amendment in our Matrimonial Causes Ordinance and Marriage Ordinance that reproduced the English enactment in identical term. With this drafting history, all nine judges involved in this case agreed that, as a matter of construction, the terms 'a man' and 'a woman' could only be construed as referring to a biological man and woman, the gender of which was governed by biological factors, for the purpose of marriage.

The remaining question was whether such a narrow construction should continue to be adopted 40 years after *Corbett* was decided, and if such a narrow construction were to be adopted, whether such construction would be consistent with the right to marry under the Bill of Rights and the Basic Law. The courts were divided on these issues.

The Court of First Instance and the Court of Appeal

At first instance, the Chief Judge of the High Court took 'Christian marriage or its equivalent' as the starting point and held that '[a]ccording to the doctrine of the Church of England, marriage is in its nature a union permanent and lifelong, for better or for worse, till death them do part, of one man and one woman, to the exclusion of all others on either side, for the procreation and nurture of children, for the hallowing and right direction of the natural instincts and affections, and for the mutual society, help and comfort which the one ought to have of the other, both in prosperity and adversity.'[3] Taking into account the drafting history of the Marriage Ordinance and the ordinary usage of the term 'man' and 'woman', the learned judge held that the biological definition of sex in *Corbett v Corbett* represented the current state of law. While he accepted that there were medical advances and the social changes of attitude towards the institution of marriage, the question of recognition of a change of sex raised a series of other questions which the court was not in a position to answer. The court was not to fill a gap in social policy. In this regard, the learned judge identified the difficulties that would be posed by such a fundamental change in the law. These difficulties included: the uncertainty surrounding the circumstances in which gender reassignment should be recognized for the purposes of marriage; the fact that recognizing gender reassignment for the purposes of marriage is part of a wider problem which should be considered as a whole and not dealt with piecemeal; the implications of same-sex marriage; the different tests and rationales put forward to determine when a transsexual individual should be recognized in his or her desired sex; and the question

---

3. HCAL 120/2009, para 116.

of disclosure. All these difficulties pointed to the conclusion that any change in the law should be made by the legislature and not the court. While the right to marriage should be in accord with general social consensus, 'the versatility of the constitutional right to marry does *not* give the courts a judicial licence to engineer a fundamental social and legal reform of the institution of marriage. In other words, what is constitutionally guaranteed is the right to participate in the institution of marriage as informed by the contemporary societal consensus, everything else being equal. Absent any compelling reasons, the constitutional guarantee does not mean that a Hong Kong resident can ask a court to construe the right to marry in such a way that does not enjoy contemporary societal consensual support, and, in substance, to effect a fundamental social and legal reform of the current institution of marriage to accord with the resident's idea of what it ought to be.'[4] In other words, it is not the constitutional role of the judiciary to engineer fundamental social changes with far-reaching consequences. The Court of Appeal essentially agreed with this reasoning.[5]

The Court of Final Appeal disagreed.

The Court of Final Appeal

A majority of the Court of Final Appeal held that, in the past 40 years, there were far-reaching changes to the nature of marriage as a social institution. In present-day multicultural Hong Kong, procreation was no longer regarded as essential to marriage. It was never a legal requirement for marriage that a couple should be able to or wish to procreate children together. As the Chief Justice and Mr Justice Ribeiro stated in their joint judgment, 'the importance attributed by Ormrod J to procreation as the essential constituent of a Christian marriage has much diminished. Men and women who decide to share their lives together now exercise far greater choice in deciding whether to marry at all, whether to have children, how their property should be dealt with and indeed, whether they should remain together as a couple. While many in society will still no doubt regard procreation as of great importance to a marriage, many others will take a different view. Many people now marry without having children, while many others have children without getting married, neither group attracting social opprobrium.'[6]

At the same time, with the advance of medical knowledge, transsexualism is much better understood now and has been widely recognized as a condition requiring medical treatment, with diagnostic criteria approved by the World Health Organization. The latest medical classification of sexual identity is by reference to both psychological and biological factors. The psychological aspects include gender identity (self-perception of being male or female); social sex role (living as male or female); sexual orientation (homosexual, heterosexual, asexual, or bisexual); and sex of rearing

---

4.   Para 192.
5.   CACV 266/2010.
6.   At 154.

(whether raised as male or female). Gender identity disorder refers to the condition of patients possessing the chromosomal and other biological features of one sex but profoundly and unshakeably perceive themselves to be members of the opposite sex. They may persistently experience acute emotional distress, feeling trapped in a body which does not correspond with what they firmly believe to be their 'real' sex. The aetiology of the condition is still uncertain, and the degree of psychological distress varies from mild gender dysphoria to severe transsexualism. For the latter group, sex reassignment surgery is the only cure. The operation comprises various elements. It is a painful process, and the procedures differ for male-to-female and female-to-male patients.[7] Sex reassignment surgery has been available in public hospitals in Hong Kong since 1981. Between 1 October 2007 and 30 September 2009, 86 patients were diagnosed with gender identity disorder, and from January 2006 to September 2009, 18 patients successfully underwent sex reassignment surgery in public hospitals. It is also the practice of the Immigration Department to issue a replacement identity card with a new gender to these patients, upon production of a letter from the Hospital Authority certifying the completion of sex reassignment surgery.

The court had considerable sympathy for the plight of transsexual persons. In 2003, a transsexual person, Louise Chan, was stalked and 'outed' by the local media. Her life was considerably disturbed, and she lost her job. On 21 September 2004, she committed suicide. Two days later, another transgender woman, Sasha Moon, also committed suicide. Apart from social stigma, the denial of their right to marry was total. It was argued that there was no legal restriction of their right to marry, as a male-to-female person could still marry a female person. The court rejected such an argument as unrealistic and running counter to the whole purpose of sex reassignment surgery as a form of treatment of transsexualism. Another objection was that, once the post-operation gender was recognized for the purpose of marriage, it would open the door to same-sex marriage. The court emphasized that this case was about recognition of post-operation gender only, and it expressed no view on same-sex marriage. It further rejected the lack of a social consensus in favour of recognition of reassigned gender as a ground for rejecting a right of the minority, for otherwise it would amount to an entrenchment of prejudice against a minority. As Mr Justice Bokhary forcefully stated, 'What is involved is a constitutionally guaranteed human right. One of the functions—perhaps by far the most important one—of constitutionally guaranteed human rights is to protect minorities. Why is there any need to guarantee a right to marry? After all, no society is likely to put impediments in the way of the majority entering into marriages as they like. The greatest and most urgent need for constitutional protection is apt to be found among those who form a minority, especially a misunderstood minority.'[8]

---

7. Evidence of Dr Ho Pui Tat, associate consultant in psychiatry at Kwai Chung Hospital, and Dr Albert Yuen Wai Cheung, consultant surgeon and chief of surgical service of Ruttonjee Hospital: at paras 5–14.
8. At 187, para 220.

Finally, the court also recognized the international trend towards recognition of post-operation gender, including not only Western countries such as Canada, part of the United States or most European states, but also Asian countries such as Japan, India, Singapore, South Korea, Indonesia, and Mainland China. The European Court of Human Rights has found the *Corbett* definition a violation of the right to marry under the European Convention on Human Rights, and it led to the enactment of Gender Recognition Act 2004 in the United Kingdom.

While these are powerful arguments to depart from the *Corbett v Corbett* definition of sex, the appeal raised again the question of the proper role of the court. As Mr Justice Patrick Chan powerfully put in his dissenting judgment, 'giving recognition to the reassigned gender for the purpose of marriage involves a change of social policy . . . The role of the Court is to give effect to a change in an existing social policy, not to introduce any new social policy. The former is a judicial process but the latter is a matter for the democratic process. Social policy issues should not be decided by the Court.' Mr Justice Chan was not persuaded that, for the purpose of marriage, the ordinary meanings of man and woman in Hong Kong have changed to such an extent that it is now necessary to accommodate a transsexual man and woman. At least there was no evidence before the court of any change of social attitude to the traditional concept of marriage or the degree of social acceptance of transsexualism. He accepted that the problems facing transsexuals should be recognized and a comprehensive review was required, but this should be done by the legislature and not the court. While he was the only dissenting judge on the Court of Final Appeal, there were altogether five judges who have adopted this approach if one includes the lower courts.

Nonetheless, this is how our legal system works. By a majority of four to one, the Court of Final Appeal, adopting a remedial interpretation of the Marriage Ordinance, held that the meaning of 'woman' and 'female' in the Marriage Ordinance and the Matrimonial Causes Ordinance includes a post-operation male-to-female transsexual person whose gender has been certified by an appropriate medical authority to have changed as a result of sex reassignment surgery. This was the final verdict.

At the same time, the Court of Final Appeal recognized that its judgment had far-reaching implications and could give rise to difficult issues that need to be addressed. Hence, it took the exceptional step of staying the effect of its judgment for 12 months to allow the government to introduce necessary legislation. The court took an even more unusual step of identifying some of the issues that need to be addressed by the legislature. The first issue was how to decide who qualified as 'a man' or 'a woman' for the purpose of marriage and other purposes, such as adoption, succession, tax, property, immigration, gender-specific criminal law, and social welfare. The court in this case accepted that someone who has completed the sex assignment surgery should have the reassigned gender recognized but left open whether this would be the appropriate line to be drawn. Instead of leaving the matter to the court to draw the line case by case, the court suggested that an expert panel be set up for this purpose. This issue turned out to be so controversial that it sabotaged subsequent legislative initiatives.

Another issue involved the impact of a legally recognized gender change on an existing marriage, such as, for example, the impact on one's spouse and children when a person has undergone sex reassignment surgery during marriage. There is no doubt that these are important issues that need to be addressed. While it is helpful for the court to outline these issues, it also strengthens the concern of Mr Justice Chan that the court was entering the realm of law making rather than law interpretation.

The aftermath

In any event, this case stands as a milestone in our legal development. After long and tedious litigation that lasted five years, this case was rightly hailed as the champion for the rights of the transsexual persons. Yet the battle was only half-won.

In the following 12 months, there were extensive debates on what the new legislation should look like. The government was prepared to introduce a simple scheme that was modelled on the English Gender Recognition Act. It proposed to give effect to the judgment of the Court of Final Appeal by recognizing the post-operation gender. Those who were aggrieved by the decision of the court, particularly those from the Church, continued to oppose the new legislation. Those who campaigned for the rights of transsexual persons considered the new legislation too conservative and failed to recognize that many transsexual persons who were clearly suffering from gender identity disorder might, for some good reasons, not wish to undergo the painful sex reassignment surgery. Thus, the new legislation was attacked left, right, and centre. No agreement was reached after 12 months. The judgment of the court came into effect at the expiry of 12 months. Persons like W could now marry, but sadly, a whole host of questions arising from the recognition of post-operation gender remain unanswered. With hindsight, the Court of Final Appeal was right not to leave the case to the legislature after all!

Index

About the author

Johannes Chan SC (Hon) is professor of law and former dean (2002–2014) of the Faculty of Law at the University of Hong Kong. He specializes in the areas of constitutional law, administrative law, and human rights, and has published widely in these fields. His written and edited books include *Law of the Hong Kong Constitution*, *Hong Kong's Constitutional Debates*, *Immigration Law and Policy in Hong Kong*, *Reflections on the Academia* (翰林隨筆：在公義路上的反思), *On the Road to Justice* (走在公義路上), and *Insights on Law and Politics* (法政敏言). He was also the BOK Visiting International Professor at the University of Pennsylvania Law School, Herbert Smith Freehills Visiting Professor at the University of Cambridge, and held other visiting positions at the University of New South Wales, the University of Zurich, and University College London. He is highly regarded internationally as a leading scholar as well as a transformative dean. He has appeared as a barrister in many leading human rights cases. In 2003, he was appointed Honorary Senior Counsel in Hong Kong, the first (and so far the only) academic silk in Hong Kong. He is also a well-known media commentator on current affairs and has written a weekly column in *Ming Pao* on law and politics since 2003.

Part of a thank-you card from one of my first-year legal system tutorial groups in 1998–1999. '翠河' (River Verdon) is the name of the horse that holds the record of being three-time champion in three racing seasons in Hong Kong in 1990–1994.